UNSETTLED FUTURES

Unsettled Futures

*Carceral Circuits
and Old Age in Japan*

JASON DANELY

VANDERBILT UNIVERSITY PRESS
Nashville, Tennessee

Copyright 2024 Vanderbilt University Press
All rights reserved
First printing 2024

Library of Congress Cataloging-in-Publication Data

Names: Danely, Jason, author.
Title: Unsettled futures : carceral circuits and old age in Japan / Jason Danely.
Description: Nashville, Tennessee : Vanderbilt University Press, [2024] | Includes bibliographical references and index.
Identifiers: LCCN 2024011660 (print) | LCCN 2024011661 (ebook) | ISBN 9780826507006 (paperback) | ISBN 9780826507013 (hardcover) | ISBN 9780826507020 (epub) | ISBN 9780826507037 (pdf)
Subjects: LCSH: Older prisoners--Japan. | Ex-convicts--Japan--Social conditions. | Recidivism--Japan. | Older people--Japan--Social conditions.
Classification: LCC HV9812 .D36 2024 (print) | LCC HV9812 (ebook) | DDC 365/.608460952--dc23/eng/20240430
LC record available at https://lccn.loc.gov/2024011660
LC ebook record available at https://lccn.loc.gov/2024011661

For Jī

CONTENTS

Acknowledgments   ix

INTRODUCTION   1

1. "Prison Is Easy"   11
2. The Prison Culture Festival   26
3. Mother House   41
4. Twenty Yen   52
5. Winds of *Shaba*   62
6. "We Hear the Screams of Life"   73
7. Warm Heart, Cool Hands   84
8. Wounded Kinships   97
9. Conclusion   115

Notes   123
Bibliography   145
Index   165

ACKNOWLEDGMENTS

I am incredibly privileged to have had the chance to work alongside so many individuals for whom confronting the deep injustices of the penal system and providing care and support for formerly incarcerated people is not merely a job, but a vocation. It has been immensely humbling and rewarding to have the chance to watch and learn from each of these individuals, whether they were raising their voices in spaces of institutional indifference or spending a quiet moment with someone who just needed company. Although I was only able to stay a few short months with them, they offered their time, trust, and encouragement, and this research would not have been possible without their generosity.

Most of all, I would like to thank Hiroshi Igarashi and all of the people involved in Mother House for opening their doors and welcoming me into every aspect of their community, whether that meant babysitting toddlers, attending mass, joining a cleaning crew, or folding newsletters. Mother House taught me what it means to be a family in a fragmented world, and what can be achieved when we show up for each other with love. Through my time at Mother House, I was fortunate to meet and discuss my initial ideas with an amazing group of scholars and activists, including Prof. Shinichi Ishizuka, Rev. Kaoru Fujita, Yusuke Kazama, Hiroshi Abe, and Shinnosuke Endo, each of whom deepened my understanding of carcerality and sharpened my thinking. For reasons of confidentiality, there are many individuals and organizations I cannot name in these acknowledgments, but I hope that my deep gratitude and admiration reaches each of them.

Conducting fieldwork for the first time in a place like Tokyo is daunting, and I would have been lost without the steady guidance and support that I received. During my Fellowship, I was generously hosted by the Tokyo Metropolitan Institute of Gerontology. I would like to thank the Institute's CEO, Dr. Hideki Ito, my supervisor, Yoshinori Fujiwara, and my officemates, Erika Kobayashi and Yoh Murayama, for all of their support. Shunsuke Sasaki deserves a special mention of thanks for helping me with my travel and many important visa issues. I am also deeply indebted to Yoko Hosoi (Toyo University), who not only provided invaluable introductions to individuals and organizations that formed the basis of the book but also provided constant encouragement and ideas throughout. Our long discussions on aging and criminal justice in Japan, often accompanied by a serene and surprising contemporary piano performance, were profoundly restorative in the midst of this intense fieldwork. Tom Gill (Meiji Gakuin University) offered valuable feedback and insights that helped shape my thinking around the lives of impoverished older people in San'ya and other underclass urban neighborhoods in Japan.

Seed funding for establishing preliminary collaborative partnerships in Japan was provided by the Great Britain Sasakawa Foundation. I am grateful to Hafiz Khan and Pia Joliffe for their interest and initial discussions about the possibilities of this research. Intensive long-term fieldwork was critical for this project, and this would not have been possible without the time, resources, and organization provided by the generous support of the Social Science Research Council and Japan Foundation Abe Fellowship program. Their commitment to this project and their vision of its potential to improve the lives of the most marginalized older adults in Japan has been deeply appreciated.

Not only did this project take me to new field sites, but it also took me into new areas of anthropology, gerontology, and criminology, where once again, I quickly realized that I had a lot to learn. Thankfully, there were many others who were willing to share their knowledge and experience with me as I stumbled through my notes and transcripts, writing (and rewriting) many drafts of this book. I am grateful to everyone who took the time to read and offer responses to early versions of these chapters: Lone Grøn, Lotte Meinert, Cheryl Mattingly, Janelle Taylor, Lawrence Cohen, Robert Dejarlais, Paul Brodwin, Daina Stanley, Kathryn Goldfarb, Danilyn Rutherford, Joseph Hankins, and Anne Allison. I am grateful to the Europe Japan Research

Centre at Oxford Brookes University and all of the organizations that offered me opportunities to speak about the research for this book and engage with new audiences. These include the Department of Social Anthropology, University of Manchester; the Japan Research Centre, SOAS University of London; the Department of Social Anthropology, Stockholm University; and the Care Forum of the Elizabeth D. Rockwell Center on Ethics and Leadership, University of Houston.

I thank Vanderbilt University Press for their enthusiasm for the book, and for their patience and understanding when the pandemic created longer than usual delays. All of the support and encouragement from the editorial team has made this process a genuine pleasure. I am also grateful to the anonymous reviewers of the first draft of the manuscript for their detailed and thoughtful suggestions, some of which became keys to unlocking arguments in ways that I had not anticipated but that were critical to this book. An earlier version of the section "Forgotten Items" appeared on the blog Somatosphere as "Gramps and the Gangster Visit the Memory Clinic" (March 26, 2019).

I am grateful to my research assistant, Anna Riley, who helped with interview transcriptions in the small spaces between assessments in her busy final year of undergraduate studies. Thanks also to Brenda Lipson and Manuel Bedran for the providing a quiet space for intensive writing work that was crucial for finishing this book. Paul and Jan Stoub gave their home and hospitality to our family during the months of my fieldwork, as well as several summers of writing; I cannot thank them enough for their endless kindness, love and generosity.

Writing a book, especially during the years of pandemic, takes time. I am forever grateful to my wife, Robin, for being my steady companion on this journey (again), and for everything she did to protect my writing time, keeping things running while I went away for conferences and writing retreats or just spent long hours at the office. Knowing that she believed in me and in the importance of telling this story carried me through many difficult days at the keyboard. I am incredibly privileged to have a family whose care I can always depend on, and this reminds me of my responsibility to extend care to others, a lesson at the heart of this book. Thank you.

INTRODUCTION

I was alone in the office when a face appeared, stopped, then quickly disappeared again from the sliding glass doorway left open onto the quiet side street. A moment later, the face appeared again, its owner asking timidly, "This is Mother House, right?"

No doubt, the sight of a solitary person at the desk (a foreign one at that) was not what the man was expecting, but when I assured him in my friendliest Japanese that he was in the right place, he exhaled a sigh of relief and embarrassment. "Oh, that's lucky! Someone told me you might be able to help me. I'm looking for work, mainly, but I also need a new place to stay. I'm in a temporary dormitory, but I was told I have to move out in two weeks." His pained, apologetic smile was endearing, even if there were a few missing teeth.

I welcomed the man, whom I will call Maeda, inside the office and poured two hot coffees for us as we waited for the director of Mother House to return. Maeda wore a dark blue corduroy jacket that hung loosely on his narrow shoulders as if draped on a wire hanger. His hair was shaggy and streaked with grey, and while he tended to avoid looking at me directly, I could see the gentle creases of age pulling down at the corners of his eyes, giving him a perpetually forlorn and melancholy expression. He told me he turned sixty-eight that year.

As we drank our coffees, I told Maeda more about myself and my research, taking the chance to ask if he would be comfortable sharing some of his own story with me while we waited. Although the invitation was unexpected, Maeda wondered aloud if our meeting might be "some sort of '*en*,'" or "connection" between our destinies. He agreed to the interview, even after

I repeated my disclaimer that my research would not be connected in any way to decisions related to his case. He nodded and took my business card, placing it on the table in front of him as a sign for us to begin.

The first thing that Maeda mentioned was that he had no family members who were willing to act as his guarantor on release from prison. What this meant was that rather than being granted release on parole to finish his sentence under supervision in the community, Maeda served the entirety of his sentence confined in prison. This was his fourth time leaving prison, and although his offense was a relatively minor case of theft, he was incarcerated for a little more than two years. This last sentence had been harder, he said, his expression locked in a grimace, "my health has been getting worse, and it's not easy to see a doctor [in prison]."

Maeda was given a place at an Independence Support Center (*jiritsu shien sentā*), a kind of dormitory for recently released ex-offenders, but these centers expect residents to move out within six months. In a few days, he would be back out on the streets. Even though he tried to mask the blank spots of his past incarceration when filling out job applications (divulging one's criminal history on employment applications is not mandatory in Japan), Maeda found it impossible to find anyone who would hire him. His age, his lack of employment, and absence of a guarantor all made it virtually impossible for Maeda to rent an apartment by himself. Very few landlords were willing to take the risk of a tenant who is older, alone, and living solely on public welfare assistance. But Maeda was also afraid of staying at another shelter, where older men like him were vulnerable targets for other recently released residents.

As I listened, the details filtered into the mental checklist I used each time I spoke to a formerly incarcerated older person: details about each individual's age, income, housing, health, and so on, that helped me situate them within the context of other cases that I came across. I would then be able to discern patterns or problems, systems and not just singularities. Perhaps, as anthropologists like David Graeber have argued, this sort of "simplification" has the potential to produce the kinds of intelligence and theoretical understanding that we need to challenge systems of injustice.[1] I would like to think so. At the same time, I was also keenly aware that I needed to treat my checklists critically, and carefully, to keep them from clouding my view of the person in front of me and the responsibility I took on as witness to his personal and complex story. This was not an easy line to walk—Graeber also pointed out that identical techniques of simplification and standardization are the hallmarks of the subtle, stupid, and deadly boring forms of bureaucratic structural violence.[2]

Although he framed his concerns, at first, mainly in terms of practical needs, as the conversation went on, Maeda began to express his frustrations about the less tangible, difficult to articulate barriers to resettlement:

> You know, when you've been in prison, you don't see things the same way. You see things that other people can't see. And things people see, you can't see. The things you see are just different. I'm sorry, it's just hard to explain. . . . It's here, in me—my feeling, my *kokoro*. I don't really know how to explain . . . I don't think I can face other people. And I can't tell anyone about where I was or what I did. So, it is like this wall or fence between me and the life of ordinary people.

Maeda's anxiety about things seen and unseen, things that need to be hidden from others, contained behind the wall of his heart (*kokoro*), were not the sorts of images or feelings that can be reduced to the checklist. As I accompanied him on this path, we moved on to talk about Maeda's perspective this time after release:

> I guess I always think it will be [different] at first. I think this time my feeling (*kimochi*) is different. I have more of a will (*ishi*) to change. For older guys, it can be hard to find that goal (*mokuteki*), they can't get a job and don't have a family. I feel like that too. It is complicated. But you know, you can't see the future, you don't know what is going to come next.

He pointed a finger up at the ceiling. "Only god knows [the future]."

Here, Maeda pushed me to go further than the checklist allowed, to take up questions of feeling, of will, of aging, and change. Each of these were aspects of his everyday experience that shaped the conditions of possibility for his future—a future that did not unfold in the normative patterns of production and reproduction, labor and family, but had to transcend those patterns. "Only God knows the future" hung in the air, grey and ambiguous. Its fatalism seemed to contradict his assertion that one needed "will" and a "goal," yet there was also a faint ray of hope at its edges.

Soon, the director of Mother House returned, and as Maeda got up to follow him into another office, we quickly bowed to each other, and I said thank you. This was the last time we spoke. About two weeks later, I found out that Maeda had been arrested and would be sent back to prison.

Unsettling Futures

It is an unsettling thought, growing old in prison. But equally unsettling for formerly incarcerated older individuals like Maeda, was life on the outside. Like him, more than 70 percent of the approximately six thousand incarcerated people over the age of sixty-five (13 percent of Japan's total incarcerated population) have a history of prior incarceration, accounting for the highest rate of recidivism of any age cohort.[3] One in five older adults released from prison will return within two years—twice that of ex-offenders twenty-nine and under.[4] In 2018, the year that I spoke to Maeda, more than one in five arrests (21.5 percent) were also older adults, a ten-fold increase in the last twenty years (2.1 percent in 1998).[5] While overall crime and imprisonment rates in Japan are falling, the demographic composition is changing dramatically, aging at a much faster pace than that of the general population. Beneath each of these numbers is a human story, like Maeda's, life that is unsettled yet surviving, trying to find a place in a broken world.

This book is my attempt to gather up some of the tangled threads of unsettledness that fray and fragment at the edges of the carceral condition. It looks at the complexities of lives like Maeda's, as well as our own complex responses to those lives, as reverberations of this "unsettledness," which permeates the carceral condition, both inside and outside sites of confinement. "Unsettledness" is a term which can mean both a state of being troubled or disturbed (in Japanese, *fuantei, ochitsukanai*), as well as being unresolved and open to possibility (in Japanese, *mikessai, mikaiketsu*) in a more neutral sense. Unsettledness, as I use it here, is not the opposite of 'resettlement,' but rather, the political and affective thread that ties the physical violence of incarceration to the structural violence of post-release welfare bureaucracy. In other words, *resettlement itself, as both an institutional process and a moral narrative, amplifies and reproduces unsettledness*. At times, this contradiction is so blatantly obvious that it leaves one dumbfounded by its absurdity. At other times, however, it is subtler, arising from actions meant to support or care for the individual, but which end up confining them in other ways. Even my own research became unsettled (and unsettling), mirroring other techniques of surveillance and simplification that echoed harmful carceral logics—"carcerality," writes Aisha Khan, "is capacious."[6]

To understand the ways unsettledness has become embedded in the everyday lives of older adults in particular, this book focuses on the case of Japan. Although Japan presents, in some ways, a unique set of social circumstances that have exacerbated the criminalization of older people, the underlying conditions of structural violence that have led to this situation are much more widespread, namely, a growing public anxiety about aging and an increasingly punitive penal system. The convergence of these two trends brings the punitive power of incarceration into the service of an anti-aging social welfare system, where those who do not remain contained within the narrow boundaries of acceptable aging are contained within the carceral circuit of the penal-welfare state. Old age may not be avoidable, but, in the logic of carcerality, it can be locked up.

Finding a path to liberation for criminalized older adults, then, requires confronting the debilitating effects of structural ageism, and imagining futures where men like Maeda could find and sustain meaningful connections to the world. The more we pull at the unsettled threads of the carceral condition, the wider we make the openings for ways of aging otherwise. The stories and voices of formerly incarcerated older adults not only expose the ways carceral circuits and structural violence affected their lives, but they also suggest directions toward decarcerated alternatives to anti-aging. Some groups, like Mother House are already working toward realizing these alternatives. This book will look at some of the efforts of these third-sector organizations and their efforts to create places of belonging (*ibasho*) and connection (*en*) that re-envision kinship and generations. If the vulnerability of old age sharpens our ability to sense the absurdity and cruelty made possible by the structural violence, then these new "families" assembled in the wake of the carceral offer glimpses of ways to rethink communities to include and value a more expansive range of aging futures.

Care and the Carceral in an Aging World

It is currently estimated that the world's population will peak at around ten billion people by 2070—within my lifetime if I am lucky to reach the age of ninety-two (and, I imagine, also within the lifetime of many of you reading this book)—before gradually falling to less than nine billion by the end of the century.[7] Globally, the proportion of older people is growing faster than that of younger age cohorts, and by 2050, the WHO estimates that 22 percent of the world's population will be over the age of sixty.[8]

Japan has been considering issues of population aging for arguably longer than any other country in the world. In 1970, Japan fit the United Nations classification of an "aging society," when 7 percent of the population was over sixty-five. Fifty years later, the proportion of the population over sixty-five had more than quadrupled to 29 percent. By 2040, it is estimated that this number will grow to more than 35 percent, more than half of whom will be over seventy-five.[9] Average life expectancy at sixty for women stands at around twenty-nine additional years, while Japanese men can expect to live another twenty-four years. What these numbers indicate is a degree of longevity and population aging that is completely unprecedented in the history of human life on earth, but it is an uncharted territory that much of the world will soon be following, in Japan's footsteps.

Rapid social change is almost sure to be unsettling, particularly when it touches on fundamental existential fears around old age, illness, and death. The sense of insecurity around the aging society has intensified in Japan over the last half of the twentieth century, as modernization and mobility appeared to destabilize traditional relationships of mutual care within the household and community. As the Japanese government pushed for a major overhaul of the long-term social care system at the end of the twentieth century, this public insecurity around aging was leveraged to support investments in the science of "antiaging," an ideological construct that brings together medical and cosmetic industries to promote a range of "active" or "successful aging" interventions presented as the solution to the problem of longevity and care.[10] The successful aging paradigm has been widely critiqued within social gerontology, but its basic tenet remains intact in social policy and public consciousness: it is up to individuals to prevent or delay aging for as long as possible.[11] Aging, in this model, is not chronological, but pathological: the loss of physiological functioning and independence due to illness, frailty and disability. But anti-aging is not merely about promoting health; it is about constructing a particular kind of subject, one that is rational and calculating, who sees risks and seeks to minimize or prevent losses by becoming an informed consumer of goods and services in the anti-aging marketplace and by adopting healthy lifestyle habits and values.[12]

Japan's long-term care insurance system (LTCI), promoted as a hybrid between a universal socialized welfare model and a market-based system, embraces the paradigm of successful and "independent"(*jiritsu*) aging. While some advanced welfare states, most notably the Nordic countries, provide the security of government-supported professional care services for all frail and disabled older people who require them, Japan's system relies on unpaid family care alongside a government regulated third-sector service market.[13] Labor analysts have noted that while one of the primary initial aims of LTCI was the gradual "de-familialization" of elder care, more recent trends indicate a "re-familialization," as paid care becomes harder to access and older people are encouraged to remain in the community. Despite the rhetoric of providing relief for family carers, no evidence has been found that LTCI has had a significant effect on the time family members spend on care-related activities. Instead, growing demand for extra-familial (paid) services has risen *alongside* increased family involvement in care, with family still needed to help manage the services and provide care to fill the gaps.[14] Home care has been adopted as the preferred mode of care service delivery, saving on costs of residential care homes. With fewer places in residential homes, the LTCI care needs assessment threshold to meet eligibility for more advanced care was raised, making it accessible only to those with very serious needs.[15] Meanwhile, Japan's paid care sector faces a deepening labor shortage crisis, with an estimated worker shortfall of 690,000 by 2040.[16] Some volunteers and neighborhood welfare groups may provide supplemental informal support, especially for older people living alone or without family living nearby, but this is widely variable depending on local or municipal circumstances.[17]

If the current LTCI system in Japan presents challenges for frail and disabled older people who remain dependent on unpaid family care, the situation is even more difficult for older people without good relationships with their families. Whereas in the past, extended family relationships might have provided a network of support for older people facing difficulties in later life, today, more and more older people are living on their own. In 1986, 55.9 percent of older people resided in multigenerational households, while only 31.3 percent lived alone or with a spouse only. Thirty years later, in 2016, the proportions had reversed: only 31.7 percent lived in multigenerational households, while 58.3 percent lived alone (27.2 percent) or with a spouse only (31.1 percent).[18] Poverty is a growing problem among these elder-only households and is one of the main factors contributing to Japan's high overall poverty rate (15.4 percent according to the most recent OECD estimates). More than one in four adults in their seventies continue to work (more than any other country in the world) in order to avoid poverty, despite the high risks of occupational injury. A 2018 report by the Japan Industrial Safety and Health Association noted that while the overall number of occupational injuries have steadily declined over the two decades preceding the survey (1989–2017), the number of incidents involving workers aged 60 and older had doubled (from 12 percent to 23 percent), including the highest rates of work-related deaths of any age cohort.[19] Those who cannot or do not work subsist on a small pension allowance or must resort to Protection of Livelihood Assistance (*seikatsu hogo*), a social welfare provision that provides a minimum living allowance for individuals living in abject poverty. About 45.5 percent of those receiving seikatsu hogo, are over the age of sixty-five.

Poverty in old age, particularly when it overlaps with "care poverty" or the "poverty of social networks," may explain why older people are committing crimes, more than half of which are relatively minor incidents of theft (*settō*) and shoplifting (*manbiki*), but we should also be cautious about reducing crime to merely an economic issue.[20] The narratives of formerly incarcerated older adults like Maeda point to much more unsettling existential concerns, about seeing and being seen, about grief and uncertainty about the future, and about the pain of aging alone. In a sense, Maeda had been lucky. Tens of thousands of isolated older people in Japan die each year without being discovered for weeks or even months, having fallen through the widening gaps of the unsettled care system's social safety net.[21]

One term often used to describe both the isolation of individuals that leads to these lonely deaths, or, in other cases, to chronic recidivism, is *muen*, translated by Anne Allison as "dis-belonging."[22] *Muen* is the shadow side of a social and cultural system where relations are based on *en*, or an "ineffable connection" to others, whether by blood (*ketsuen*), work (*shaen*), or, as Maeda alluded to when we first met, a serendipitous encounter where the underlying significance may only manifest later. *En* is so important in Japan that it extends past death, honored and cultivated through practices of memorialization.[23] This makes being *muen* at the end of life even more painful, as there is a strong consciousness that one's spirit will be left abandoned and unsettled in the other world, haunting the living.

ARRESTING AGING

The antiaging ideology has not significantly reduced aging, let alone the public anxiety around growing older. In Japan, the average person who has reached the age of sixty will still spend around six years living with chronic conditions, frailty, or disability that increase their dependence on care.[24] Anti-aging has, however, supported the political project of the neoliberal retrenchment of the welfare state, and the consequent exclusion and further stigmatization of older people who age "unsuccessfully." Anti-aging and carcerality both hinge on a logic of individual culpability and moral responsibility, clearing the state of accountability for inequalities and vulnerabilities of disadvantaged people.[25] By taking responsibility for the prevention of aging, by continuing to work, exercise, or participate in social activities, for example, some older individuals may feel a sense of agency and empowerment, even as they willingly submit to the control over their everyday lives.[26] Those whose lives fall outside of this restrictive normative model of anti-aging, on the other hand, not only suffer additional social stigma and blame, but are also further disadvantaged by the tightening of restrictions on welfare and social care that it justifies. A common theme running across the stories of formerly incarcerated older people described in this book is the experience of everyday forms of exclusion and alienation that make leaving prison more unsettling than entering prison.[27]

Part of David Graeber's argument about the inner workings of everyday structural violence is that it allows those in power to remain ignorant about those they have power over, and it renders the powerless "stupid" as they expend their efforts trying to understand, interpret and anticipate the perspectives of those in power.[28] Suzuki and Otani, evaluating the treatment of incarcerated older adults in Japan have adopted Elaine Crawley's term "institutional thoughtlessness" to describe the ways the ideology and design of penal institutions perpetuates practices of ignorance about the particular vulnerabilities of older people.[29] These practices render older adults more susceptible to coercive violence, both within and after release from prison, since, like Maeda, the penalty for re-offending is likely to carry a harsher punishment. The case of Japan's "thoughtless" criminalization of older adults demonstrates the dangerous intertwining of structural and coercive violence, as well as the unsettledness that disempowers those caught within the churn of its circuitry. In the next chapter I will look more closely at the carceral, and the ways it perpetuates ignorance through techniques of separation and disbelonging. While anti-aging has been the neoliberal response to public anxieties and uncertainties around longevity and the aging population, similar public concerns about crime have resulted in increasingly punitive carceral landscapes of containment.

The stories of formerly incarcerated older adults in this book must be understood within the context of anti-aging and punitivity, neither of which originated in or are unique to Japan. Therefore, many of the lessons we learn from these stories will be relevant in other cultural contexts where older people are similarly confined in unsettledness. The ethnographic perspective I take can help us critically dismantle popular representations of Japan as a country free from both ageism and crime; it can also show how community-based efforts to support formerly incarcerated older adults utilize and expand local cultural frameworks in ways that offer glimpses of the possibilities for care and transformation.

CHAPTER 1

"Prison Is Easy"

As I stepped out of the train station and down a narrow, open-air shopping arcade, the sun was casting the last of its warm glow across the tops of the buildings, while just below, the globe-shaped streetlamps came to life, as if eager for the gloom of night. The buildings lining the arcade were all four or five stories tall, packed tightly together. Several storefronts had already pulled their corrugated metal shutters down for the night, while others were just opening up. A kōban, or police outpost, was situated just at the end of the arcade. This one made itself especially conspicuous with red emergency lights built into the concrete facade. The oversized windows across the front of the kōban revealed a brightly lit room, but the only faces inside as I passed were those of fugitives glaring with unblinking eyes from the "wanted" posters covering the back wall.[1]

My destination was a small Catholic church just a few blocks past the kōban, and by the time I reached it, the streets were dark. The door was open, and as I removed my shoes in the entryway, I could smell food cooking and hear the din of metal pans. I followed the sounds and smells down a corridor to the kitchen, where Endo, dressed as usual in jeans and a blue long-sleeved shirt, was busily directing several other men, chopping onions and carrots and dropping them into large steaming pots.

"Ah, glad you made it!" He gave me a quick nod and motioned for me to follow him to a room at the end of the hall. As we walked, he pushed up his shirtsleeves to his elbows, revealing a tattoo on his forearm of a skull pierced through with a dagger. I couldn't help but notice again the unsettling sight of a finger on his right hand, severed at the knuckle. The first time I met Endo was a few weeks prior, when, like other people I had met either working or volunteering in nonprofit organizations (NPOs) supporting formerly incarcerated older adults, our conversation reached a point where words seemed to fail us. Helping older people coming out of prison, many of whom are frail, poor, and alone, meant contending with a world of pain and uncertainty that almost repels the comforting simplicity of ordinary narration. Our language couldn't provide the tools to convey the intricate ways incarceration affected people, and it only just skimmed the surface of why people returned to prison over and again throughout their lives. Then again, our conversation may have stopped because of my clumsy Japanese, or because I was asking the wrong questions. I hoped that maybe there was something else that couldn't be said, something that came from being together with people, listening to them directly. "Better if you came and saw for yourself sometime" he said, as if reading my mind. So I did.

I made a plan to meet Endo at the church that night for dinner, followed by a walk around the neighborhood to take food to people living on the streets nearby. Endo also wanted me to meet Chiba, a formerly homeless eighty-year-old man whom he had recently helped to find an apartment in the area. Despite his age, Chiba had only been out of prison for six years, and when Endo met him, he was living on the streets and drinking heavily. Chances were good that this would have led him back to prison, or worse.

Recidivism rates for formerly incarcerated older adults like Chiba are now higher than any other age cohort in Japan. While recidivism rates are also high in several other countries, it has largely been accepted as fact among criminologists that rates decline gradually with age.[2] The aging prison population of the US, Australia, and Europe, for example, is mainly a result of people growing old in prison for offences committed when they were still young.[3] Aday and Krabill have noted that although it is predicted that one-third of the US prison population will be over fifty by 2030, the same group has the lowest overall crime rate.[4] In other words, the aging trend in the US (and other countries that have adopted similar sentencing guidelines) is driven less by the increase in older offenders than by harsher sentencing laws and mandatory prison terms.[5] As a result, much of what we know about older people in prison and after reentry concerns individuals who have served very long or indefinite sentences, or who have been incarcerated for historical (mainly sexual) offenses.[6] In contrast to this picture, not only do older adults account for more than 22 percent of all annual arrests in Japan, but formerly incarcerated older adults in Japan are reoffending *as* older adults. Among currently incarcerated older people in Japan, 70 percent have had five or more past convictions resulting in a prison sentence.[7] Statistically speaking, Chiba was lucky; around half of all formerly incarcerated older people in Japan will return to prison within five years, and many of them will have been living in situations similar to Chiba.[8]

"Chiba! I've brought Professor Jason to talk with you, is that okay?" I reflexively winced at being called "Professor," and awkwardly tried to laugh it off. I would have to learn to carry the label with as much humility as I could. The old man who was sitting alone on a folding chair in the corner of the room looked up, a little dazed, as if just waking from a nap. His clothes were a strange fit for his thin, frail body: baggy black jeans, a black bomber jacket, two chains dangling at his hip, one attached to his wallet, another to a silver flip phone. Next to him was a little black zipper bag with his prescriptions, ID cards, various proof of his disability and welfare benefits.

Endo stopped beside Chiba and leaned in close, raising his voice and speaking each word clearly, pointing up at me, "He wants to know about older guys who have been in prison— how many times have you been to prison again?" Chiba nodded, looked down, then looked up at me again silently, unsure if he ought to smile. Endo repeated the question, and Chiba looked down at his hands, counting slowly on his fingers. After a moment, he held up both hands, all ten fingers raised. He gave me a slightly sheepish, unsure look from behind his thick glasses. "There you go!" Endo smiled, giving me a quick glance that said he had to return to the kitchen, "I'll see you later!"

Stories in Fragments

I had been sitting as close as I could get, almost leaning on Chiba's shoulder as we talked. He held my gaze through the distortion of thick glasses. His bottom lip hung down, heavy and slack, his dentures stiffened his jaw, and his tongue lay heavy in his mouth as if numb. He would only manage a few words at a time, his voice, quivering and sonorous like a muted trumpet, would suddenly linger on some syllable while the next word was slowing getting ready. Every now and then, a detail would come out clearly, emerging from the murky fog of sounds then dipping back. The conversation progressed slowly:

> JASON: When was the last time you left prison? You said you were in your seventies?

[14] UNSETTLED FUTURES

CHIBA: It was ... um ...
JASON: Do you remember, the last time you were released?
CHIBA: It was, after I finished my sentence (*manki*)
JASON: I see, a full sentence. And you came to this city?
CHIBA: I, uh, I was in _____ [a part of the city]. A daily rent.
JASON: And what were you doing?
CHIBA: Well, it ... I uh, it, I forget sometimes
JASON: Did you do anything for work?
CHIBA: I, uh, races.
JASON: Gambling then? And that's how you got by? Gambling?
CHIBA: Uh, I got a room, and, I have it written in a notebook somewhere.

I felt like I was fishing around in the dark and not getting very far. I wasn't sure if he understood my questions, and I was starting to realize Chiba was living with some symptoms of cognitive impairment, which Endo never mentioned. Most of all I wondered, why I was asking these questions in the first place? What was the answer that I was hoping to draw out? As much as I hoped for a clean, steady narrative where causes and effects linked his precarious life on the outside to his time in prison, Chiba was only able to give me an account that was fragmented, hesitant, disjointed. It was as if aging was no longer legible as a linear flow of experiences and memories, but was more like a deck of shuffled cards. There was no way to tell how much of this was due to age-related cognitive impairment or his years of heavy drinking, and how much was shaped by a life moving in a jagged line between two worlds, each bound within its own routines of day-to-day survival, its own embodied rules about what could be said and what was best kept quiet.

Chiba began shuffling around in the pocket of his jacket. He brought out a small yellow pamphlet, holding it up close to his glasses, then pointing to a passage for me to read. The pamphlet was from an Alcoholics Anonymous meeting he attended, and the words were the Serenity Prayer. I start to read it aloud, "Grant me the serenity (*ochitsuki*), to accept the things I cannot change ..."

"This was something I could never get!" Chiba interjected, "I thought that I was the only person that mattered!"

For a moment, my worries about the interview calmed, as I thought about what this "serenity" meant to Chiba, and why he seemed so intent on showing me the pamphlet. It wasn't quite coherence that it offered, but a relinquishing of control. Things did not have to make perfect sense to him, as long as he was able to depend on others. Giving up on the idea that life outside of prison meant relying solely on himself allowed him to shift toward being more open to connecting with others. Was this what it meant to be settled (*ochitsuita*)?

Unlike younger people, most formerly incarcerated older people are unable to find work or count on family support after prison, consequently serving the entirety of their sentence in prison (*manki-shussho*), rather than receiving parole and community-based probation and resettlement support (*kari-shakuho*).[9] As a result, like Chiba's narrative, life after prison usually feels disjointed. The prison and probation system; the disability, health, and long-term care systems; the housing sector, NPOs and charity assistance organizations; police and courts—all working separately and with few points of communication or cooperation, were easily overwhelming to an older person who had spent years removed from any ordinary public social interaction, let alone navigating complex institutional bureaucracies.

But Chiba reminded me that this was not the entire story. The reason I was sitting in a church on a Friday evening was not simply to indulge in the harrowing stories of prison or life on the streets, but to listen and be present to Chiba and the way he experienced life in that moment, as a fellow human, and not just an ex-offender. What Chiba felt was serenity and settlement, a sense of rebuilding a life from the inside out, letting go of a stubborn will to go it alone, and letting others, like Endo and his support group, connect and care for him. "Release" from the prison gate was not the same as letting go. For Chiba, this started much later, and after several failures, when he encountered others who were like himself. These encounters, not the social welfare system, were what allowed him to settle and to develop a new orientation to the world and to himself in old age.

This book approaches the problem of older people affected by the criminal justice system not by taking the view from behind the prison walls, but by situating our attention at the edges of the carceral, where those leaving prison are soon pulled back into custody as they are churned through welfare institutions and zones of exclusion and abandonment.[10] "Carceral 'churn'" writes Moran, is "the repeated release, reoffending, re-sentencing and re-imprisonment of former prisoners, argued to operate to deliver the high rates of re-offending and re-imprisonment amongst prisoner populations in a variety of contexts."[11] Yet, however strong this churning twister is, a few manage to grab hold of someone or something else at its edges and break free from its force. It is along these edges that we might be able to best see both the limits of institutional control and the possibilities for resistance and liberation.

It is tempting to fall into binary thinking in the boundary zone of the carceral: on one side, there is the successfully rehabilitated and reformed ex-offender, and on the other, the chronic recidivist. The voices of formerly incarcerated older individuals tell a different, more complex story, one that is told less often. Formerly incarcerated older people still bear the embodied traces and stigma of criminality long after they paid their debts, and older people in custody may feel more ease and belonging while in custody. When we take seriously these experiences, the black and white world turns into shades of gray. Part of this complexity is due to the fact that not only have penal techniques entered the social welfare and care system, but also that due to the growing number of older people churning through the carceral continuum, prison has become a place where older people access health and social care. Prison has become a place where they have a dim sense of belonging, a home. In other words, the often disjointed and disrupted life stories of formerly incarcerated older adults reveals the chaos and violence enacted by linking care to punishment, the ambivalence and repetition that keeps them always marginalized, contained, and invisible.

Prison? That's easy!

When I asked Chiba if he'd ever thought about returning to prison, his response came out clearly.

"Anything's better than prison" he told me, still holding the yellow pamphlet in his lap, "I don't want to ever go back. But still, life in the outside world (*shaba*) is hard. Prison, that's easy!"

He made the slightest of laughs after he said this, or maybe he was just clearing his throat. I leaned in closer.

While it is crucial to understand the way powerful social institutions operate to construct, perpetuate, and normalize violence, exclusion, and inequality, even prisons have limits in their capacity to determine a person's ideas and feelings. While it was hard for him to recall sequences of past events as if filed in a row of neatly labeled folders, he was able to hold onto the AA pamphlet, a sign, perhaps, of being grounded in a new life path, an alternative space to imagine another possible self.

These spaces of opening and possibility cannot be fully captured in terms like "resistance." They are emergent self-orientations that present us with alternatives to the logics of the carceral that operate through techniques of enclosure and repetition. In other words, it is from the perspectives of formerly incarcerated older adults, like Chiba, who have escaped the cycle of recidivism, that we are able to stand back and critique the full scope of what Michel Foucault terms the "carceral continuum," in which disciplinary power and penal tactics are embedded throughout everyday social institutions, from schools and barracks to welfare assistance and hospitals.[12]

While the majority of the older people in Japanese prisons serve short sentences for relatively minor property-related crimes, some, like Chiba, had been involved in more serious illegal activity from a younger age. Chiba told me that his first prison sentence was a ten-year stretch, after he was convicted of murdering a man in a drunken fight at a bar. At the time, Chiba had been working as an informal labor broker (*tehaishi*), or as he put it, "I bought people." This was a lucrative but often dangerous job that involved securing day-laborers for subcontractors, whose compliance with the brokerage system almost always depended on enforcement from organized crime syndicates (*yakuza*).[13] The incident occurred during a night of heavy drinking, when Chiba confronted a laborer who had repeatedly received payment but did not show up for jobs that Chiba had arranged. As a former member of the Japanese Self-Defense Forces, Chiba told me he "knew how to use his fists," and unfortunately this had fatal consequences.

"He had training in all these hand-to-hand combat techniques, you see," Endo told me when I was confirming the details later. "A lot of the day-laborers are really a mess already, like, you're always hearing stories about someone just falling over dying, so it wouldn't take much [to kill them], and [Chiba] had strength. It's just happened like that."

This tragic backstory and the subsequent decade Chiba spent in prison as a result was not the end, but only the entry point of his journey through the churn of the carceral system. Like others I'd met who had spent long stretches of their lives moving in and out of prisons, Chiba struggled to locate realistic prospects for rebuilding another life in the community after release, time and again. He had no family nor legal work to return to, and like many other formerly incarcerated older people, he found it frustrating to try and navigate the administrative bureaucracies of social welfare system alone. Each time he came out of prison, he would drift back into the same low-income enclaves and underground economies and addictions that he had inhabited before, and from there, back to prison. This cyclical chronicity of recidivism is not unique to Japan, but it is a feature of impoverished and criminalized communities around the world. What does appear unique to Japan, however, is the way older people like Chiba are increasingly caught up in it as well. As they circulate back and forth from prison to community and back to prison again, older people are remaking penal institutions and social welfare, drawing them closer together under a shared logic.

Gill et al. refer to this as "carceral circuitry," a spatial and temporal zone characterized by both its enclosure and its mobility.[14] The first and most prominent aspect of carceral circuitry is the principle of *return*, which, they argue, "captures a key duality":

> For investors, return refers to the profits made on investments, whereas for those "released" to impoverished communities with prospects and liberties equal to or worse than when and where they left, return captures the cyclical wastefulness of contemporary carceral systems.[15]

To return individuals to the conditions that directly or indirectly led to their incarceration, or to return them to a prison environment that brings further and faster decline for older people living with frailty or disability, is both wasteful in the sense that it diverts public resources to institutions that fail to ensure public safety and, more insidiously, it makes the carceral subject a *waste*—something beyond even a future exploitable surplus.[16] The circulation of older people through the carceral "waste processing" system makes people feel like shit—like something dirty and shameful that should be hidden from public view.[17] It is little surprise that the rapid increase in the number of older offenders has coincided with the rise in public discourses promoting of independent, responsible, active aging, and even "anti-aging"; the imperative to fight aging is backed up by the threat of abandonment and imprisonment.[18]

Carceral circuits, like waste disposal systems, operate through returns and enclosures. The repetition of recidivism is not bound by the moment of reoffending, but subsumes the entire thread of events leading up to that moment, the carceral enclosures that keep the loop intact. Repeat offending closes off possible futures, keeping one stuck in the well-worn rut of the circuit, lined with ghosts of the past, incessantly returning.[19] *Re*entry, *re*settlement, *re*habilitating, *re*covery. Each word places the future in the return to the past, a past that with each subsequent imprisonment sinks deeper into shadow and unsettledness. What past could Chiba resettle in, but the past that sent him to prison?[20]

Chiba finished his last prison sentence in his seventies, for an offence committed not far from where he was first arrested (again, related to his drinking). Chiba had slowed down with age and frailty, his feeble movements making him easier to catch. Yet, because of his history of past incarceration, even the most minor of offences, like leaving a restaurant without paying a bill (*musen inshoku*), could put him back in a cell for what very well might be the rest of his life. With age, the carceral circuit becomes even more certain, its value even more diminishing, its risks even more serious.

Chiba was not the only formerly incarcerated older person I spoke with who felt that life outside of prison was harder than life inside. In fact, this was one of the most frequent ways formerly incarcerated older people would describe the difference between life before and after prison. But saying that prison was "easy" should not be mistaken for claiming it was desirable. First of all, for Chiba and others I spoke to, prison takes away one's freedom. Life in prison meant being unable to decide when one would wake-up, how one could walk, when one could speak, what one could eat. It meant living under constant surveillance and threats of corporal punishment. This is a hard price to pay for the convenience of basic daily provisions, work, and health care.

Life after prison was "free," but the kind of freedom that formerly incarcerated people talked about was not the kind of rights-based freedom that most of us associate with life in liberal democracy (although it was that as well). Instead, they spoke about the freedom of a "normal life," one that was free from stigma and discrimination and from the indignities and uncertainties of life without work, getting by on a basic pension. The normal life was one where the crippling anxiety of carceral enclosure no longer haunted day-to-day life.

But a "normal life" was elusive for many formerly incarcerated older people. Physical health, mental health, disability, and elder care assistance, all operating through separate schemes, made the so-called safety net of social support a tangle of confusion that most wanted to leave well alone. The winter Endo met Chiba, for example, he was in his late seventies, drinking heavily and living on the streets. After seeing that Chiba was earnest about getting sober and off the streets, Endo took him to the Prefectural Hospital, where he knew a doctor who had seen other formerly incarcerated patients and could be trusted. Formerly incarcerated people fear discrimination from doctors and may avoid them as a result. Japanese healthcare facilities and care homes frequently turn away patients like Chiba, who would not be able to provide the name of a "guarantor" (*hoshōnin*), usually a family member, upon admission. Like many formerly incarcerated older adults who have experienced homelessness and chronic alcohol use, Chiba had numerous physical and cognitive impairments, conditions that complicated his access and management of care.

Age, disability, and cognitive impairments do not automatically exempt offenders from prison sentences. It is estimated that more than one in ten older prisoners in Japan is living with some form of dementia.[21] An estimated two-thirds of prisoners have some kind of chronic health condition, and the proportion even higher among older prisoners.[22] Within the prison, older adults' health issues may go unnoticed and untreated for longer, meaning a greater risk that these conditions become worse. Japan does not currently have a policy similar to other countries and some US states, of medical, geriatric or compassionate release, wherein prisoners can be released if they are seriously ill, infirm, or near the end of life.[23] People living with cognitive and intellectual disabilities are also much more likely to reoffend, given the lack of rehabilitative support pre- or post-release.[24]

Another area where formerly incarcerated men find it difficult to establish a "normal life" is finding work and maintaining an income. Unable to gain legitimate employment and estranged from family, Chiba told me that his main line of work after release was gambling at the motorboat races. Various sorts of gambling were often mentioned as popular leisure activities among lower income older men, often leading to further impoverishment and debt. Without other avenues for generating income, Chiba saw the races as his only option for getting by. Lawson has argued that the stigma of a criminal history is not only prohibitive for finding employment, but also carries stigma that stains their ability to establish new social relationships or participate in community life.[25]

Formerly incarcerated older adults with more advanced care needs may be turned away from long-term care facilities not only for lack of a guarantor, but because of the type of offence they were convicted of. Minor convictions for theft or shoplifting might warrant a probationary period, but arson or violent offences could be grounds for exclusion. The increased privatization of all levels of the care service sector has made it easier for these facilities to deny patient care, as became evident when thousands were turned away at the height of the COVID-19 pandemic.[26]

Housing was also a common issue for older people leaving custody. Landlords, afraid of individuals "dying alone" (*kodokushi*) in their rental units, frequently denied applications from anyone in their late sixties.[27] Again, a guarantor was typically required to secure a rental agreement. According to his long-term care assessment (*yōkaigo nintei*), Chiba, who was living with mild Alzheimer's disease and had mobility limitations that meant he was unable to climb stairs, was still considered too fit and independent to be eligible for residential care. With some help from Endo, however, Chiba was able to find a first-floor rental unit in an older persons apartment complex (*kōreisha jūtaku*, what might be called "sheltered housing" in the UK). While Chiba did not tick the boxes for residential nursing home care, his disability, chronic illness, addiction, poverty, history of incarceration, and estrangement from family all meant that living alone would only deepen his precariousness as he aged. In-home community-based care might allow him to stay alive until he eventually qualifies for transfer to a care home, but given the serious nature of his past offenses, few facilities would agree to accept him.

Working with Older Offenders

I did my best to keep the conversation with Chiba moving, but he seemed to lose interest in talking about the "bad things" he had done or the times he spent in prison, and even with Endo's help, I still struggled to make sense of how the pieces of the story fit into a timeline. My default narrative scaffolding kept getting in the way of what Chiba was saying. The noise in the room got louder as more and more guests arrived. I tried to keep asking questions for a little longer, unsure if I'd get the chance again, but Chiba's responses dwindled to a few mumbled words. Finally we sat together as bowls of soup were set around the table.

This situation was not unusual. Most of the formerly incarcerated older people I spoke with for this research were reticent when it came to talking about their arrests or imprisonment, but they also were unsure about what to say about life after prison, their health, their concerns, or hopes about the future. Having conducted ethnographic research with older Japanese people on various topics for many years, this reticence came as a surprise, since I had been used to listening to story after story with only minimal amount of prompting. Instead I had to find ways to adjust my conversation style to find a topic they had some interest in and to sense when I could shift into particular topics or avoid the conversation from running dry. If they were strong enough, I would suggest a walk outside or just around the block while we talked. The stiflingly drawn out pauses and silences were a struggle to sit with, and there were times where I doubted my abilities as a researcher, my place in even trying to do this research at all. I felt increasingly like an unwelcome intruder on the lives of strangers, even while I was encouraged by individuals who worked with older marginalized people to amplify their voices. My attitude began to change as I got to know a few formerly incarcerated older individuals better over the course of the research, not because they spoke more, but because we were able to share moments of silence together. This was an invitation to rethink my own assumptions about the ethnographic emphasis on oral testimonies and, instead, appreciate the shape of these silences and what they might express about settledness and unsettledness that could not be put into words alone.

The preponderance of silent gaps in my interviews was not completely unexpected. If many of the men I spoke to were solitary or anti-social prior to their incarceration, the silence and stress of prison deepened their reticence. In other cases, like Chiba, the formerly incarcerated older adults I spoke with were living with cognitive or learning disabilities and may have only achieved a minimal education.[28] Prior experiences of abuse, bullying, or other traumatic life events created other invisible barriers to communication, even before involvement with the criminal justice system, making the flow of interviews twist away from our grasp. And so, the fragments of their stories pieced together in this book are still only fragments of fragments, like reflections in a broken mirror.

Ethnography on the Edges of the Carceral

The stories of formerly incarcerated older adults, however incomplete or ambiguous, were crucial for stripping away the layers of abstraction presented in demographic reports and policy analyses on the aging prison population. While the masses of data gathered on arrests, indictments, imprisonment, and recidivism are all relevant for situating individual stories within a wider comparative context, the theory—that thread that connects particular, singular experiences to more general experiences of being human—that would have to be built up from stories of the formerly incarcerated older men themselves.[29]

Rather than starting my fieldwork with the Ministry of Justice, the Probation Office, or any of the other governmental institutions officially engaged with those affected by crime, policing and incarceration, I took a ground up approach, beginning with nonprofit organizations, groups that worked one-on-one with formerly incarcerated older adults on a daily basis and who were more aware than anyone else about the gaps and inadequacies in the official system. Although various small-scale local interventions aimed at older ex-offender rehabilitation have been piloted across Japan, there are no organizations that work exclusively with older adult ex-offenders. Instead, I ended up working with three different nonprofit organizations (NPOs) that together provided introductions to individuals with experiences of incarceration (*tōjisha*), some of whom became research participants. These organizations included Mother House, an organization assisting in the resettlement of ex-offenders; Safe House (pseudonym), an organization assisting people who have become homeless; and Grace (pseudonym) a faith-based organization offering various assistance to impoverished people.[30] Each of these sites offered opportunities to volunteer alongside and spend down time socializing with staff and service users on a regular basis.

All of these organizations operated primarily in the Greater Tokyo Metropolitan Area, which extends well beyond the twenty-three wards that make up the City of Tokyo to include parts of the neighboring prefectures of Saitama, Ibaraki, Gunma, Yokohama, Kanagawa and Chiba. This comprises the largest and the most populated metropolitan area in the world. More than thirty-eight million people live in this area, and it continues to grow even as the population in every other region in Japan steadily declines.

Between 2009 and 2012, the Japanese government, in an unusual cooperative initiative between the Ministry of Justice and the Ministry of Health Labor and Welfare, established a new national system of Community Resettlement Promotion Corporations (*chiiki teichaku sokushin jigyō*). While each of Japan's forty-eight prefectures would be able to decide how to administer this system, many set up Community Resettlement Support Centers, which, unlike the previous system of temporary "rehabilitation" (*kōsei*) or "independence" (*jiritsu*) centers, worked exclusively with formerly incarcerated people living with disabilities and/or over the age of sixty-five, and would arrange individual housing and support plans that would be ready on the day of release. In the final weeks of my fieldwork, I made several visits to one of these centers and was permitted to shadow the staff on "follow-up" visits with some of their older clients. While the NPOs and charities I worked with all felt that independence from the government was essential for the integrity of their interactions with those whom they assisted, the Community Resettlement Support Centers cooperated closely with local governments and the prisons and probation services, and most could be classified as "quangos," or semi-autonomous, quasi-public nonprofit organizations.[31]

As a result of depending on introductions from third-sector organizations, the sample of participants is not only small, but selective. All of those who I interviewed were individuals who were actively seeking help, if only temporarily, from support organizations. But for those released after serving a full sentence, receiving assistance, whether from a Community Resettlement Support Centre, an NPO, or on one's own, was voluntary, and many of the most marginalized and isolated could simply disappear. Too often, these were the individuals who would reappear in prison soon after release. While a more sustained, long-term approach would have been ideal to gather stories from these individuals as well, even the snapshots of individuals I've collected here have value in a field where so often the stories are either crushed under the weight of tables of data, or confined to the genres of journalism or memoir.

The most important lesson I quickly learned when I started this research was that behind anyone with a criminal record, was a story, even if fragmented. These stories inscribe the borders of the carceral in ways that extend them past the prison walls and into welfare offices, shelters, and streets. They also allowed others to accompany the formerly incarcerated across these borders of indifference and otherness and to disrupt the carceral circuit. Stories were more than simply ways of humanizing individuals who had been labeled as criminal (or worse), or a means of critiquing the violence of the criminal justice system. They were also bridges to imagining alternatives to incarceration that held the potential to transform the ways we think about aging and later life.

A Mirror

After dinner, Endo and I walked Chiba to the bus stop, making sure he remembered where to get off. We walk backed to the church, Endo lighting a cigarette.

"Are you coming out with us?"

"Yes, if that's ok?"

"That'll be nice. You can see what we do. Not a lot of places take meals out to guys like this. In other places, they all line up for food, right? (Right.) If you do it that way, there are a lot of guys who just live in flophouses (*doya*) and stuff, and they come out for meals but maybe not the people who really need it. The people who are sleeping out on the streets. I see those guys, and I know that they have been through a lot. *They are my mirror.* I see myself. When I talk to them, I learn something about myself, I think about why I do this."

He finished his cigarette and turned once more to me. "We'd better help the others."

A few minutes later, Endo has managed to secure a pot of hot soup to the wire rack on the back of his bicycle and we carefully walked back to the train station. The station was still busy and well-lit, but the last buses had just left and a few men had started busily moving large pieces of cardboard into place against the wide pillars next to bus stops. Trains rumbled overhead, and car engines growled down the streets, a crowd was gathered around a jazz band busking nearby, and small groups of businessmen in disheveled shirts stumbled past us to the lights of the bars. Over the next hour, we walked from the station to the parking garage, through covered arcades and eventually to a community center, where several men were setting out their sleeping mats beneath a printed sign reading "Please refrain from sleeping, eating or drinking here." When we arrived, some of the other volunteers were tending to a man who had just collapsed on the sidewalk from a seizure, blood smearing his face. When the ambulance arrived, one of the volunteers jumped in the back to go with him. None of the other rough sleepers showed any interest. We handed out the rest of the rice balls and headed back.

Charitable acts like food distribution can be one way of following religious or moral principles, a performance of the gift that cannot be reciprocated, or is reciprocated through a relationship with the divine.[32] But Endo's resonance with the homeless and suffering introduced another dynamic, that of the mirror. Endo had been through gang life, prison, addiction, and recovery. The pain of the streets was familiar, and each time we poured a bowl of soup, passing it to a hand reaching out of a makeshift cardboard shelter, he would make a little conversation, casually moving across some unseen border that most people chose to ignore. He knew what it was like to be on the other side of the mirror. Seeing oneself reflected in the suffering of others means seeing more than what is presently visible. It means reflecting on what was and imagining what could be for oneself and others.

Through mirroring, third-sector organizations and individuals like Endo also benefit from formerly incarcerated older people, cultivating a sense of mutual connection (*en*) and belonging (*ibasho*). In contrast, prisons and other carceral institutions are sites where invisibility and indifference are normalized. I turn to these sites next, in part to provide a context for the stories of formerly incarcerated people that follow, but also to sketch out a few notable differences between prison life in Japan and elsewhere in the world.

CHAPTER 2

The Prison Culture Festival

My first visit to the grounds of a Japanese prison was on a crisp, sunny day in early November, 2018. I boarded a train traveling west on the Musashino Line from Shinjuku Station, where the iconic skyscrapers of Tokyo's Metropolitan Government buildings rise up like steely monuments to dreams of progress, while on the ground, the noise and neon dazzle of the Kabuki-cho red-light-district tickles other fantasies. It is hard to ignore the dramatic contrast of the vertical landscape symbolizing and celebrating the dizzying disparity between the social classes, even as the capillary maze of narrow side streets abound with places of more horizontal community, as well as sites of refuge or anonymity. As I watched through the window of the train, the dense urban landscape gave way to a flat, repetitive, suburban sprawl, of bland gray buildings. It felt like I had crossed over some border already, faced with another Tokyo, one that seemed to be watching that great city from the outside. The suburban sprawl where the ordinary reproductive labor of families had settled and sustained the thrum of Tokyo's heart, stretched endlessly across the horizon.

The train station at Kita-Fuchu was pleasantly quaint compared to the sprawling labyrinthine of tunnels of stations in the center of the city. The sunlight warmed the platform, and the sky was no longer filtered through the forest of tall buildings. I walked across the street and soon found myself following a long concrete wall. Just beyond the wall, row after row of identical blocks of apartments for prison staff, all in a drab cream color, were brightened by occasional flutters of colorful futon blankets and laundry hanging up on the balconies. There were no guard towers or menacing barbed wire fences that have become iconic of prison architecture in the US and elsewhere. Instead, the gate was shaded by cypress, maple, and ash trees, while just across the street, one could hear the sounds of children at the local elementary school and high school.

As I approached the gate, I began to see more and more people, some with cameras, or holding folded picnic mats and blankets. Families, some pushing strollers, walked alongside older couples, bent over canes. The closer I came to the gate, the more I was joined by others, all of us happily crossing into the prison grounds below a bright yellow inflatable archway welcoming us to "The 43rd Fuchu Prison Culture Festival." Despite the looming prison buildings around us, the atmosphere was similar to the typical Japanese neighborhood festival one might visit on the grounds of a local school or Shinto shrine, where families would meet and socialize while queuing up at food stalls for small plates of fried noodles, frankfurters, or spun candy floss. But the Fuchu Culture Festival was more than simply a transposition of an event from "outside the fence" (*hei no soto*) to the inside. It was also a way for the prison as an institution to shape its own image in the eyes of the public, revealing select aesthetic traces of the prison while keeping actual prison life hidden and separate from view. In this way, the festival both dramatized and hid the separation between inside and outside, containment and release, policing borders in ways that can seem unremarkable (even fun). In the end, it is not the imposing fortress-like structure of the prison that sustains the carceral, but the reproduction of a public that accepts and supports the confinement and punishment of its fellows. Maintaining this feeling involves the production of a popular fiction of prison (e.g. that sentences are just, that it is only for the most dangerous offenders, that treatment is humane and rehabilitative, etc.), while shielding the details of individual human lives.

If the idea of a culture festival at a prison is an example of bringing the outside in, the notion of "the carceral" tends to imply a movement from the "inside out." This movement was articulated most notably by Michel Foucault, in what is probably his most famous work, *Discipline and Punish: The Birth of the Prison*.[1] Foucault described how the development of modern penal systems introduced and normalized a new and more extensive form of power and control over not only offenders, but the broader national citizenry as well. Taking the genealogy of the French penal system in the seventeenth to nineteenth centuries as his principal case study, Foucault described how prior to the use of prisons as punishment, power was displayed through the public spectacle of corporal punishment, torture, and execution. Paradoxically, prisons, which developed in the context of new Enlightenment discourses regarding social welfare, humanism, rights and liberty, also formed a new way of exercising punitive power through techniques of confinement, discipline and surveillance, in which, crucially, violence becomes both "visible and unverifiable."[2] The iconic image of this form of power is the panopticon, an architectural design devised by English philosopher Jeremy Bentham, wherein a guard tower stood at the center of radiating spokes of cells. Foucault argued that this design revealed the structure of this new form of punishment, which functioned by producing a consciousness of surveillance and self-discipline among inmates, even if the guards were not looking.[3] Foucault is asking us to critically reflect on the ways "the carceral circles widen and the form of the prison slowly diminishes until it finally disappears altogether."[4] How do we impose the guard's gaze on our thoughts and actions, the ways we might even come to depend upon or desire this gaze and its enclosure.

The last chapter of *Discipline and Punish* is titled "The Carceral." In this chapter, the "carceral" refers not only to the various techniques of control, but also to the *configuration* of power-knowledge and subjectivity. Foucault argued that the new configurations of power that were refined in the design of the modern prison were gradually adopted by other extra-penal institutions, constituting a "carceral archipelago" that included orphanages, convents, and moral improvement associations, "organizations that handed out assistance but also practiced surveillance."[5] If we are to understand the life worlds of formerly incarcerated older adults, then, we cannot limit ourselves to boundaries of the prison and be content with the colorful displays of community and prosperity of the festival outside. In order to understand the ways the carceral is pressed and molded into other rehabilitative and public welfare institutions, we must first look at the experience of life inside Japanese prisons.

Inhabiting and Embodying the Prison

Were the visitors to the Culture Festival able to visit the other prisoners, they would have experienced an atmosphere that could not be more different from the festival that was happening out on the grounds. Japan's forty-seven thousand incarcerated men and women are distributed across seventy-five prisons, including six juvenile detention centers, and four medical prisons. While there are some differences across prisons, I will concentrate here on the experiences as they were related to me by the formerly incarcerated older men that I met. These accounts recall the stress of the relentless panoptic gaze and the eyes of other inmates, the daily repetition and routine and bodily training and meaningless work, and the disorienting feelings of separation not only from particular people, but from any kind of ordinary sociality.

Access to Japanese prisons for research is tightly controlled by the Ministry of Justice, but reports by journalists and human rights organizations, and first-hand accounts of formerly incarcerated individuals confirm that older and disabled adults face dehumanizing conditions that damage their chances of future reintegration into mainstream social life after release. Andrew Coyle, founding director of the International Centre for Prison Studies (Kings College London), toured Fuchu prison in 1996 and found the physical conditions "relatively good," but he also noted a "complete lack of any human rapport between staff and prisoners." He continues, "The level of regimentation both for individuals and for the population as a whole was intense. . . . The penalties for any breach of discipline were severe and on the day of our visit, there were over forty prisoners in the solitary confinement unit."[6]

While most older prisoners endure this regimen alongside younger ones, some special prisons, such as Onomichi prison in Hiroshima, have developed special wards for older prisoners living with additional care needs due to impairment or disability. More than half of the older inmates at Onomichi are living with dementia.[7]

Japan is not the only country to experience a rapid increase in the proportion of older adults in prisons and other secure detention facilities, and despite the large body of evidence concerning the inadequacy of current accommodations to insure the health, safety, and human rights of this population, changes have been slow and piecemeal. In Europe, ethnographic research with older people in prisons has provided rich, full, and compassionate descriptions of daily life, where the violence of imprisonment is punctuated by experiences of kindness from prison officers or personal growth and sense of community.[8] Qualitative research in the UK and Australia, has tended to focus on the overall unsuitability of prisons for older people due to their frailty and tendency to be more "compliant" and thus more vulnerable to victimization and neglect.[9] They have also found that incarcerated older people often experience heightened fear and anxiety around the prospect of re-entry and resettlement, a sentiment that appears largely justified by the lack of offender rehabilitation in prison and support after release.[10] While the treatment of older prisoners in Japan might be comparable to that in other countries, there can be no doubt that the interrelated factors of high rates of arrest, recidivism, and short-term sentences among older offenders in Japan indicates a level of continuity between the conditions inside prison and unsettledness on the outside that has not been as prominent an issue for older offenders elsewhere.

Entering prison for the first time, I was told by one Japanese former prisoner, feels like having the "color drained out of the world." Everything, from the uniforms to the walls is the same shade of washed out khaki or gray-green. "It's nothing like the bright orange clothes you see in American movies," he added, "it's the same drab color for *everything*." His description resonates with Alison Young's description of the atmosphere in the Japanese prison as one of "withdrawal, reduction and diminishment."[11]

The lack of color creates a sensory field of uniformity and anonymity. The use of a prisoner's number, rather than their name and the strict enforcement of the uniform and bodily posture and movement have a similar effect. Prisoners could not move about freely, but whenever they were out of their cells, they were marched, swinging their arms and keeping pace (this is modified for older people using walking frames or wheelchairs). Exercise was thirty minutes each day and consisted of uniform synchronized drills, such as quick marching in circles. All of this was done in silence, and eye-to-eye contact with other prisoners is forbidden. When Coyle visited a Japanese prison, he noted that "prisoners were obliged to face the wall when any staff or visitors walked by."[12] This was also the case when two lines of prisoners approached each other, marching in opposite directions. The prison officer would instruct one group to face the wall while the other passed in order to maintain the ban on eye contact. One formerly incarcerated man told me that after release, meeting the eyes of others made him so anxious that he hesitated when using a busy crosswalk. When the walk light turned green, he felt frozen as a group of people started walking toward him.

Personal items, such as books, letters, or writing paper are highly restricted so that coded messages cannot be sent back and forth to people on the outside, and the contents of rooms are checked regularly during the day to make sure prisoners are compliant. Each room had a television that was centrally controlled to broadcast approved programming and a table for meals, which were taken in the cell rather than a cafeteria. Prisoners slept on futon mattresses laid on the floor and folded up during the day.

"Our room was supposed to be for six people," one man told me, "but sometimes there might be seven people, but that was really hard, when you are sleeping, it is like the person next to you is overlapping with your futon, and you knock into them if you roll over."

Silence was also enforced when prisoners were eating meals with cell mates or were in their cells, except between the evening hours (around 6 p.m. to 9 p.m. lights out). The first line of the Human Rights Watch Asia report from 1995 reads: "From an outside observer familiar with different prison systems throughout the world, perhaps the most striking feature of Japanese prisons is the silence."[13] Alison Young, who conducted rare ethnographic observations in Kyoto Prison described the silence of the Japanese prison as "a fundamental element of the carceral atmosphere," an extension of both the control over the bodies of the carceral subject, as well a form of invisibility and identity erasure.

None of the formerly incarcerated men I spoke with formed friendships with cell mates, and most spoke of the constant tension and stress from the lack of privacy. "You get into a sort of pattern of doing things, just a way of thinking or something," one formerly incarcerated man in his fifties told me, "When you are in a room shared with six other guys, you have no time to think about yourself. You are out with the guys all day, and then go back to your room and still have to deal with them. So when I came out, [my emotions] were probably even worse."

The lack of privacy even included the toilet, which was located in the room separated only by a glass wall. "Yeah, it's hard to take a shit," one man explained, "and in the morning, it's really hard, everyone trying to use it and if you're last, you might not have time."

"Can you get up and use the toilet while you are at work?"

"Yeah, but you have to raise your hand like this, 'Please can I have permission to use the toilet?!' and then you march up to the front and you have to do it really loud and perfect and sometimes even then they don't let you!"

Washing and bathing are also silent and monitored. Prisoners must finish within a set time (around twelve minutes according to one man). If a frail or disabled older prisoner requires assistance bathing, the staff will select another prisoner to take on the task, but they would have to work quickly, since there would be no adjustment to the strict time frame. It is common to appoint carers from among the other prisoners at prisons with a large proportion of physically or cognitively impaired inmates. This is especially challenging at times because the carers themselves might be old (*rōrō kaigo*), or because an individual is living with dementia and unable to understand and comply with all of the rules.[14]

Prisoners were fed three meals each day meant to provide adequate nutritional balance. Older prisoners with health-related dietary restrictions or who require soft food would be provided with special meals. While the Fuchu

Prison Culture Festival visitors were able to sample the 'typical' prison meal of curry and rice mixed with millet or a 'prison roll' (*choeki koppepan*), they were not subjected to the daily hunger and sensory deprivation of bland food day after day. One result of this was that when better food was served, the stress of eating with cell mates became worse. "I hated being the one who had to portion out the food for everyone!" a younger ex-offender told me, "if someone got just a little more, people get angry, and then if you're having something good, like beef rice, other people will try to steal someone's portion (*shari-age*)." Another formerly incarcerated man added "We hardly got any meat in prison."

> JASON: No meat?
> FUJITA: No, just rice mainly, and some little vegetable dishes and stuff. So the beef bowl was the best.
> JASON: Did you get fish?
> FUJITA: [grimacing] Yeah, but it wasn't anything like the fish you get in stores here, it was so rank, and some guys wouldn't even eat it. It was disgusting. [Others at the table nod] . . . But the good thing is that when you are out of prison, everything tastes amazing! (patting his stomach)

The prison world that formerly incarcerated individuals described, the place they inhabited and that reshaped their subjectivities, was simultaneously a world that lacked feeling and at the same time, overwhelming in its sensory penetration of every minute.

The Virtue of Industry

The most popular area at the festival was the marketplace for goods manufactured by incarcerated people in prisons across Japan. The goods included everything from decorative hand-bound notebooks to hand-carved wooden toys, chopsticks, lacquer handicrafts, leather goods, and even furniture. Browsing the stalls, shoulder to shoulder with the other visitors, I was struck by the juxtaposition of the incredible variety of objects piled up on the tables, as one might find at a flea market, and the impressive craftsmanship and beauty like at a handicraft emporium. The crush of products and people made it hard to linger or talk to people, so I decided to step back, letting the waves of people pass.

The shoppers were no doubt aware that the "bargain" prices were the result of the labor of incarcerated men and women, but nowhere was it indicated that this work was compulsory for all Japanese prisoners, forming the central pillar of the institution's project of disciplining bodies and minds to associate rehabilitation with authority and factory work. Yet, prisoners in Japan have been expected to work four days a week, eight hours a day in the prison factory as "moral rehabilitation" (*kaizen kōsei*) for more than a century.[15] The product labels at the market did not disclose the fact that these incarcerated workers were paid as little as 100 yen ($0.80 approximately) per month, hardly enough to buy some snacks at the commissary (with hard work, after three years, they may be making as much as 5000 yen, or roughly $40, per month). Even when they are able to save, it takes years to put together enough money for a single month of living allowance in a city like Tokyo after release.[16]

Abolitionist scholars and activists like Angela Davis and Ruth Wilson Gilmore use the term "prison industrial complex" to describe the ways carceral institutions, private corporations, and the state are deeply enmeshed with one another, not only to produce profit from the labor of incarcerated bodies, but also through the capture of land and construction of prison facilities, and through redevelopment projects outside of prison in areas where criminalized people have been concentrated.[17] While similar forces, and their underlying historical links to imperialism, are no doubt part of the story of Japan's prison industry, what I found most jarring about the prison festival market was the ways it separated and sanitized the products, making them both legitimate objects of consumer desire, and even morally virtuous. Had the shoppers heard the stories of older prisoners who made the items, would this fantasy be interrupted?

"You're not allowed to talk when you're working," one formerly incarcerated older man I spoke to told me, "one time, someone came into the factory, and it sort of surprised me, so I just looked up, and I got reprimanded for it!" Another man told me that he got in trouble for trying to use a towel to protect his hand from the sharp wires of the clothespins that he was assembling in the prison factory. "I got yelled at by the officer," he said, "Because they said it was unauthorized use of the towel—I thought, so what? My fingers were getting torn up!"

The festive atmosphere of the market stalls at Fuchu not only obscures the violent conditions involved in the production of the goods on sale, but it generates another kind of social imaginary, one where hard work and service to the community underpins a romantic story of redemption. The vast majority of products manufactured in prison factories, however, end up in ordinary shops, from high-end department stores to bargain discount stores. These ordinary, everyday items are so ubiquitous that virtually everyone in Japan has come into contact with the products of prison labor.

Frail and disabled older prisoners unable to work in the usual factory may be put to work in a separate facility (sometimes called a *ryōnai kōjō* or *yōgo kōjō*). Formerly incarcerated writer Jōji Yamamoto wrote about his shock the first time that he visited the ryōnai kōjō:

> "Oof, it stinks in here . . ." I thought, turning around to see someone there who was soiled with urine and feces. Others were mumbling nonsense to themselves the whole time, or were on so many psycho-pharmaceuticals that they stared off into space drooling, or would suddenly get up and dance as if possessed. This was the typical scene in the ryōnai kōjō.[18]

Despite these disruptions, staff still required these inmates to "work" for six hours a day, but given the chaos, Yamamoto described it as more like "baby-sitting" (*sewa-kei*) or "wasting time" rather than rehabilitative or educational.[19] Some older people appreciated having work to keep them busy, but complained that it was usually mechanical and repetitive, with the lighter jobs given to older people being particularly tedious. One older ex-offender, for example, told me that he once had the task of attaching paper handles onto shopping bags for a well-known department store. "You couldn't even take pride in the work," he said, "It was just making stuff that someone else is going to throw away."

Some have argued that older adults in prison can "thrive," discovering a new "sense of purpose."[20] This was, however, never the case among the individuals I spoke to, all of whom agreed that it was simply wasting time. While the *ryōnai kōjō* may have been conceived as an alternative form of care for incarcerated older people, in practice it is a site of structural violence where time and labor are converted into waste. The work was not generative or rehabilitative, and the products themselves were easily disposed of.

Debates and Contradictions

While there is a growing literature on the use of former prisons as museums, hotels, and other tourist attractions that echo "the spectacle of punishment in new guises," it is much less usual to have the public spectacle on the grounds of a functioning high-security prison.[21] The Fuchu Prison Culture Festival was not a site where historical narratives or artifacts were being performed or contested or where visitors immersed themselves in the macabre stories of crime and punishment. Strolling the grounds as dance music echoed from the loudspeakers, the festival did not have a whiff of "dark tourism," but rather, in the words of the Ministry of Justice, it exuded a "movement for a brighter society" (*shakai wo akaruku sure undo*), bringing awareness of the "correctional system" and its role in safeguarding the public, and expressing [the prison's] "feeling of gratitude" to the community.[22] For some attendees, however, the "bright society" cast a darker shadow as well, one which held its own sense of allure.[23] Some visitors, for example, lined up for over an hour to join a short "adventure tour" of some of the prison facilities where no prisoners were present or visible. But even these limited engagements with the prison building provided ways to sense it only from a distance, reassuring the curious that the prison was not a good place to be, but it was also not such a terrible place either.

The Culture Festival began in 1975 and had been a regular annual event for more than four decades since. When I attended in 2018, organizers estimated that there were at least sixteen thousand visitors. Fuchu Prison is currently Japan's largest prison, with a capacity for 2,842 inmates, mostly "Category B" (repeat offenders, violent offenders, and organized crime members) and "Category F" (foreign nationals). Incarcerated people with psychological, physical, or behavioral conditions that make it difficult for them to be held elsewhere are also incarcerated at Fuchu.

Fuchu was moved to its current location, some distance from the city center, in 1935, after the Sugamo Prison was destroyed in the Tokyo Earthquake of 1923. In 2018, there were about 1,800 individuals held at Fuchu, around 340 (18.8 percent) of whom were over the age of sixty-five.[24] This number has doubled over the last two decades and is well above the proportion of people over sixty-five found across the total Japanese prison population (about 12 percent) and quadruple the proportion found in most other advanced economies (3–5 percent is considered usual, while estimates in the US are closer to 2 percent).

Japan has long been considered exceptional for having one of the lowest crime rates of any developed country in the world.[25] When one considers the exceptionally high clearance rates (42 percent in 2022, or more than double the total index clearance rate of the United States), and a near perfect (99.9 percent) conviction rate, it is easy to get the impression that the Japanese criminal justice system is uniquely and enviably effective and efficient.[26] Western proponents looking at these statistics alongside other data on the way crime is managed without arrest or imprisonment in Japan have held it up as the only industrialized and urbanized nation to have avoided the problems of increased crime and incarceration seen everywhere else in the world.[27] Some Japanese commentators have gladly echoed these claims as evidence of Japan's unique and superior cultural values, such as the ethical principles of collective harmony, equality, and informal conflict resolution.[28]

The details of these arguments and their critical responses would require a much lengthier book than this one, and as crime rates continue to fall and the Ministry of Justice continues to tinker with reforms,[29] the debates on the virtues and vices of Japan's criminal justice system in comparison with other countries will no doubt continue. Organizations like Amnesty International have issued scathing condemnation of the harsh conditions and punishments for prisoners in Japan, which have changed very little since the establishment of the 1908 Penal Code.[30] At the same time, Japanese prisons are often praised by outside observers for their lack of inmate violence or suicides when compared to prisons in the US or Europe.[31]

What is most relevant here are the ways carceral systems persist in spite of what appears to be fundamental contradictions at their heart. It is these contradictions — protection and punishment, care and violence, compassion and control, totalization and fragmentation— like opposite polarities in an electrical circuit, that complete the enclosure of carceral subjects. Nowhere is this clearer than in the case of incarcerated older adults. Yet to understand why older adults have become disproportionately affected by carceral institutions since the turn of the twenty-first century, it is worth providing a brief historical overview of the relationship between prison and the welfare state over the last century.

HISTORY OF JAPAN'S PRISON-WELFARE NEXUS

The contradictions of the carceral are at first, difficult to perceive—the same way the prison building itself seems to dissolve into the background of the cheerful Culture Festival. We are content to draw a dark and immutable line between the institutions that support the welfare of the world we live in, and those that enclose the world of others in prison. Historically, however, both are more closely linked than we might at first assume. This has particularly been the case when we look at the treatment of impoverished and destitute older people. As Foucault's notion of the extending array of the carceral archipelago suggests, carcerality arises not only within forms of punishment, but also in measures enacted to provide relief to the poor and marginalized. In Japan, we might begin, for example, with the expansion of the Relief Regulations in 1875, which took the issue of poverty relief out of the hands of civic and charity organizations and incorporated it into the administrative apparatus of the state.[32] This was only three years after the opening of Japan's first modern prison facilities, themselves fashioned as a more modern and humane means of dealing with crime.[33] Just as Japan's welfare and poor relief programs were modelled after European welfare states and influenced by Christian moral doctrines, Japanese Penal Code of 1908 was modelled closely after the French *Code Pénal* (1810), architecturally inspired by the panoptic designs of British colonial prisons, and ideologically premised on a model of sin and redemption.[34]

Much has been written about construction of the Japanese household system (*ie*) in the late nineteenth and early twentieth centuries, which incorporated the family into the new model of national citizenship through bureaucratic systems and population census data.[35] In aligning kinship and the state, families became extensions of carceral logics of surveillance, control and containment. Older people (over age sixty-five), whose care, by law, was considered the responsibility of the household, were rarely imprisoned in early twentieth century Japan. At the time, the nascent social welfare state was highly reliant on unpaid family and community volunteers for the care of older and disabled people, providing limited and highly restricted formal social welfare assistance.[36] For example, despite the Japanese government's expansion of poverty assistance through the Relief and Protection Law of 1929, support still remained out of reach for many who could not prove ineligibility for employment or unavailability of family or community assistance.[37] This strategy of limited public assistance based on the inability to work and the absence of family support has remained a difficult hurdle for older people dependent on public assistance through the Public Assistance for Livelihood Protection (*seikatsu hogo*) system today.

Modern hospitals, orphanages, psychiatric institutions, and even elderly care facilities first emerged in Japan prior to World War II (owed in large part to the work of Christian organizations), and quickly expanded during the period of Japan's post-war economic growth (1960s–1980s), alongside other rapid and profound social changes, such as urbanization and rural depopulation, the nuclearization of the family, a resurgence of neo-eugenic policies and discourses, and the low-fertility aging society (*shoshi kōreika shakai*).[38] Although institutionalization in nursing homes or, in the cases of many older people, long-term hospitalization, had become more prevalent during this period, the poor conditions of these institutions and the increasingly difficult to uphold expectations that remained on overburdened family members propelled activist movements at the end of the twentieth century to demand more social support to enable independent lives for disabled and older people to reside in the community.[39] One unintended consequence of the deinstitutionalization of disabled and older adults, and the failure to replace it with a substantial and integrated system of community care, has been the increase of isolated and vulnerable people, some of whom end up in prison.

The rapid rise in the numbers of older people in Japanese prisons began in the early 2000s. This was also the period marking the shift toward deinstitutionalization of psychiatric care, disability care and elderly care, and the promotion of more community-based independent living models. Didier Fassin notes the same historical trend in France, where incarceration within asylums declined starting in the last half of the twentieth century as the numbers of people in prisons rose just as rapidly.[40] Although these groups remain differentiated in an administrative sense, there is significant overlap— as individuals get older, their chances of acquiring a disability or psychiatric condition like dementia increases, but other people living with disability will, depending on their condition and treatment, become older adults themselves. While it is tempting to draw a close causal connection between the deinstitutionalization of care in the welfare system and the rise of incarceration of groups most affected by these changes, for the moment, I leave it as a suggestive correlation that echoes the anecdotal evidence from those I spoke with.[41]

The purpose of this very brief history of what Garland terms the "prison-welfare nexus," was to illustrate how welfare policies and prisons are so closely intertwined, that it is impossible to grasp one without the other. The separation and confinement of older and disabled people, whether in almshouses, nursing homes, psychiatric hospitals or prisons, has always been part of the national strategy of control, and it has always targeted those who were destitute and disconnected from normative forms of belonging (i.e., family and work). Throughout Japan's history, we can see how techniques of control, exclusion, and surveillance stitch together the prison-welfare fabric into the cloth of the carceral continuum.[42]

The last piece of the argument touches briefly on the carceral production of the public and the role of public perceptions of criminalized older people in perpetuating their exclusion.

Captive Audience

A stage had been set up on the largest patch of grass, facing the prison, and as the sun rose directly overhead, a local amateur group dressed in bright red costumes performed traditional Okinawan folk songs and dances. Other performers and music groups would take their turns throughout the afternoon, until the headline performer, a famous former professional wrestler, would make his appearance. These celebrations of multicultural diversity and the arts (two things that were largely absent from the prison facing the performers) kept our backs literally and figuratively turned away from the prison, while the familiar sights, sounds, smells, and tastes of wholesome community life filled the air. Even the sight of children playing freely around the prison grounds or taking turns climbing into police cars and fire trucks looked scarcely different than community events I had visited at schools, where first responders would perform puppet shows about traffic safety, rewarding listeners with shiny gold badge stickers.

The mascots of Japan's National Probation Services (*hogo kansatsujo*), a black and white male penguin named Hogo and a pink female one wearing a yellow bow named Sara, waddled around the grounds in plump soft costumes greeting children and posing for selfies, their beaks frozen in a perpetual duckface grin.[43] There was even a petting zoo with baby goats and rabbits—the very cutest of captives. The atmosphere of the festival was so saturated that the prison itself seemed to dissolve into a fantasy of playful innocence. At the center of the noise of community and cultural life, was an empty space suspended and emptied of its history, its violence, and solitude.

Just as the panopticon shaped the subjectivity of the prisoner, public discourses of crime and safety shape subjectivities of neoliberal individuals in Japan's post-welfare society. In a fascinating study of everyday residential security, Misha Bykowski notes the connection between widespread perceptions that crime in Japan is getting worse (it is not) and the impulse to take personal responsibility for one's safety by purchasing and installing locks, alarms, sensors, and other personal security systems to keep this imaginary assailant at bay.[44] In this case, Bykowski argues, "locking out the other" becomes a means of self-enclosure, furthering division, suspicion, and moral panic, rather than reaching across forms of social difference."[45] Both the panopticon and personal residential security logics have a materiality, an architecture, an aesthetic feel; their power is not merely in their rational functions, but in their symbolic and affective dimensions as well.[46]

What is interesting is the ways techno-mediated forms of security are increasingly being used to monitor the bodies of older people, sensing and sending real-time data about their movements in the house or their water usage to a family member or carer's mobile phone.[47] From the point of view of the adult child, these technologies, while somewhat questionable on the grounds of privacy, are justified since they could be life-saving if the older person were to have a fall, or go missing, for example. This attitude might be compared to Foote's description of Japanese criminal justice system as of "benevolent paternalism."[48]

It is telling that these theories of discipline, enclosure and surveillance have also been applied to long term care institutions for older people as well.[49] The poor conditions and commonplace abuse, such as the routine use of constraints for those living with dementia, continued to reinforce the view of nursing homes as "obasuteyama," or places where the old are abandoned.[50] Though not a prison, they were the very definition of a 'total institution' that had become a zone of abandonment.[51] It is a tempting fantasy to lock out, or lock away what one fears— not just the stranger, but the future self as well.

Walking away from the spectacle of the festival, its songs and mascots, its markets and games, I was left with the feeling that I had spent the day in the tacky glitter of a grand distraction. Everything about it was telling me to look away. Rolling out a picnic blanket on the lawn of a prison lifted the fears of crime and disorder, as long as we did not have to see those inside. The power of the carceral, as Foucault observes, depends on this distraction from power, just as sovereign power depended on the spectacle of violence prior to prisons. This separation and invisibility has lasting traces on the lives of formerly incarcerated older people, and the creative work of repairing a sense of self deserving of recognition is at the center of the work of third-sector nonprofit and civil society organizations focused on resettlement. In the next chapter, I turn to one of these organizations and the important role that older ex-offenders have played in its mission.

CHAPTER 3

Mother House

The popular images of Tokyo are drawn mainly from the dense urban landscapes packed within the perimeter of the Japan Railways' ring-like Yamanote Line, which encircles the centers of government, tourism, culture, and shopping as well as the grounds of the Imperial Palace. Like rays of sunlight, train lines radiate outward from this central hub, taking commuters back and forth, to and from the quiet suburbs. But to the East, this expansion is interrupted by the Sumida, Arakawa, and Edo Rivers flowing into Tokyo Bay. Once major arteries of commerce and transportation for the residents of Tokyo, the Sumida River, located closest to the Yamanote line, has been particularly celebrated in poetry, dramas, and woodblock prints, as a place on the edge of the great city, full of the lively activity of ordinary commoners, of comings and goings, of aspiration and losses. While it rarely features in tourist brochures, it still captures the strong feeling many have about Tokyo, as a city composed of many worlds held together tenuously, not by bridges and train-tracks, but by histories and futures in the making.[1]

Despite the many bridges that traverse the Sumida River, it still represents a political border between several city wards, and the change in atmosphere as one gets closer to the river is tangible. Since the medieval period, the low marshlands around the river, or "shitamachi" (lit. "low-town"), were also predominantly occupied by people of a lower economic status, whose urban culture and way of life developed separately from the elites who first settled in the hills to the west (*yama no te*). While many areas on the west bank of the river have become more gentrified in the last century, the neighborhoods on the east side of the Sumida still retain strong traces of this commercial, working-class history, with hundreds of small, family operated factories, machine shops, printers, and leather tanneries mixed in with modest apartments. Walking through the back streets, the jarring metallic noise of an industrial drill press bounces off the buildings, then gives way to the sounds of children playing on their way home from school. No neon skyscrapers or animated billboards here.

Located in one of these East Tokyo shitamachi neighborhoods is Mother House, a nonprofit organization that, since 2012, has assisted and advocated on behalf of current and formerly incarcerated individuals across Japan.[2] When I first arrived, there was no sign in front of the building, nor a nameplate or business listing on the call buttons. A small, laminated label with the Mother House logo (a drawing of a round-faced cherub with soft blue wings) affixed to the heavy brown metal door inside the building was the only clue of its existence. Inside, the office shelves covering two walls reached from floor to ceiling, packed with thick blue and black ring binders (some on lower shelves bearing the tell-tale colorful scribbled marks of a child). A newly purchased slate-gray copier-printer dominated one wall of the room, on one side of a large desk. Behind the desk, two other work stations were set up so closely to one another that the backs of the chairs touched. Plastic drawer units towered like skyscrapers next to the computers, almost completely blocking the single privacy-glass window at the back. On top of one of these towers sat a bright blue plush doll of the children's cartoon character Doraemon, arms raised in frozen excitement. Next to him sat a framed portrait of Mother Teresa dressed in her iconic white cowl with blue trim, her weathered face and gentle smile glowing with beneficence.

Mother House's humble office gave little indication of the grandness of its mission and the power of its challenge to standard systems of ex-offender resettlement. Like the other nonprofit and charity organizations I spent time with in Tokyo, staying in the lowlands of shitamachi lent Mother House a kind of gritty street credibility that made it approachable for ex-offenders in ways that contrasted sharply with the antiseptic atmosphere of the probation or ward administrative offices. The chaotic aesthetic of the office fit in with the messy lives of the men struggling with life after discharge, who were coming for help. It reminded you that in shitamachi, the normal signs of institutional authority and trustworthiness were turned on their heads.

The founder and director of Mother House, Igarashi Hiroshi, was rarely at his desk for long. Energetic and animated, Igarashi-san was perpetually on the move, bursting into the office, a phone pressed to his ear, his heavy silver crucifix bobbing against his chest on a long chain, grabbing files and rushing out again. When he didn't have to appear in court or visit prisons, it wasn't unusual to see him in a T-shirt printed with the Japanese children's cartoon character An-Pan Man, or the pudgy yellow Minions, both of which he bore more than a slight resemblance to. Although short in stature, and generally good-humored and charismatic, Igarashi could become surprising forceful and intimidating when he wanted to be. His highest volume level was specially reserved for officials at the Ministry of Justice.

For Igarashi, the work of supporting formerly incarcerated individuals was his vocation, and he pursued it with an intensity of commitment that was both inspiring and exhausting to behold. Igarashi's dedication is rooted in his autobiographical narrative. He first entered prison in 1990 at the age of twenty-six. His last discharge, at the age of forty-seven, was on December 30, 2011. Altogether he had spent a total of twenty-years in custody, by which time he had become almost completely estranged from his family and felt as if he had lost the ability to interact with ordinary people. Igarashi credits his Catholic faith as the reason he was able to stay out of prison since his last release, and it was this faith that gave him his calling to help other ex-offenders.

Igarashi converted to Catholicism while serving his last sentence in prison, after being gifted a Bible by a Nikkei Brazilian man jailed in the same detention facility prior to his transfer to Gifu Prison. Igarashi's faith deepened as he read the Bible and he later began to exchange letters with Catholic volunteers outside of prison, including some nuns based in Tokyo. After his release, he made his way to Tokyo to meet the nuns and express his gratitude. A member of another church helped him with the paperwork to sign up for public assistance and find a small apartment.

Even after he had started settling back in, Igarashi felt haunted. One day, he met a formerly incarcerated older man who had become homeless soon after leaving prison and was sleeping on the streets. "I don't have a place to return home to," the man told him, and Igarashi recognized this feeling. The impossibility of returning "home" was often a prelude to the return to prison. In his memoir, Igarashi recalled what older repeat offenders told him in prison. They said,

> If I went back, I'd only be getting in the way of my siblings, my children, my grandchildren, so no one would have anything to do with me. If I stay here [in prison], I have acquaintances. I have a place to stay, if I'm in the prison, I won't be all alone, I can eat with others. So, it's better to stay here [in prison][3]

The repetition of this same sense of homelessness, inside and outside of the prison gave Igarashi the idea to set up an organization to help formerly incarcerated people. According to Igarashi, Mother Teresa herself was said to have remarked on the indifference of Japanese people toward the poor and suffering in their own country. He would not be so indifferent—"This was to be my cross to bear" he wrote in his memoir.[4] Igarashi decided to name his organization Mother House, after Mother Teresa's refuge for the destitute in Kolkata, India.[5] Spurred on by this new sense of vocation, he set out to create a place where other formerly incarcerated people could find respite from their loneliness and where they might build a network of support, a feeling of kinship and solidarity, and a spiritual community to break the cycle of incarceration.

Igarashi's passion for helping others has kept Mother House going over the years. What he lacked in formal education in social work or criminology he made up for in lived experience, faith, and hard work. His personal narrative of sin and redemption was powerful, and he never seemed more at home than when he was telling his story. Throughout my short time at Mother House, he appeared in at least three televised segments, three radio broadcasts, and half a dozen news articles. He was also a regular guest speaker for university students studying criminology, telling them about his experiences of incarceration and its effects on the offender that last long after they have served their sentence. He has a direct and dynamic way of speaking, catching the crowd and squeezing it slowly, until you're utterly convinced of his tale of suffering and salvation. For Igarashi, crafting a story of his life and retelling again and again was as much a matter of personal awakening as it was a political strategy, challenging the state's monopoly on narratives of incarceration and justice. Mother House was not simply about securing income, housing, ID cards and other necessities to begin life after prison, but it was about enabling new politics of unsettled narratives to build and to find its voice and its liberation.

A PLACE FOR STORIES TO CONNECT

After establishing Mother House, Igarashi was soon joined by other formerly incarcerated staff and volunteers. They organized more volunteers to write letters to incarcerated individuals, and Igarashi traveled to different prisons around the country to meet with individuals if they expressed interest in connecting. After release, Igarashi helped them to find housing or work, and offered assistance in registering for health and disability or welfare benefits.

But most importantly, Igarashi's goal was to foster what he called "encounters" (*deai*) by creating a place (*ba*) where fellow ex-offenders and other community members could meet, and where emotional and spiritual recovery could begin. Igarashi took risks, followed his gut, and demanded a lot from the men who were given support.

Like many other mutual peer support and advocacy groups for those who identify with a particular affliction or experience (*tōjisha*), Mother House was held together by stories, like Igarashi's, that established trust and inspired hope.[6] The stories gave shape and force to the work of relationship building. The stories of individuals who had made a life for themselves after prison were collected and assembled in monthly newsletters that were printed at the office and sent out to around 800 incarcerated Mother House members. Igarashi would also organize regular public speaking events at a Catholic church where formerly incarcerated members could tell their stories in greater depth. Mother House also held monthly tōjisha meetings, attended by both formerly incarcerated Mother House members and others who identified as their allies or supporters (lawyers, social workers, students, academics, e.g.). These meetings acted as a safe space for tōjisha to check in about their immediate situation and to speak openly about their hopes and fears. Outside of these venues, however, individuals tended to keep the details of their pasts brief. Instead, the focus of the recently incarcerated Mother House members was on spending time together, participating in volunteer activities (newsletter production, packaging and selling coffee for fundraising, landscaping and removal services, etc.), meetings, and church activities. For Igarashi, all of these activities shared the common purpose of encountering others and coming to face oneself (*jibun ni mukiau*) through those encounters.

Another one of Igarashi's often repeated phrases was "prisons are nurseries for criminals."[7] In his view, there was no rehabilitation, education, or reformation in prison, and more often than not, the released ex-offender is less socially capable than they were before entering. "In prison, everything they teach you, everything you do is the *opposite* of what people are supposed to do outside" he told me. "So, in prison you don't do anything unless you're ordered, you don't think for yourself. How is someone supposed to make it outside prison if that habit becomes part of them? So, what we have to do is try to lower the wall as much as we can."

In its first four years, Mother House had become a busy meeting place. Through its newsletter, it linked current and formerly incarcerated men and women from across Japan to a network of volunteers, Christian supporters, researchers, and media outlets. Through its fundraising, these connections became global. One of its biggest entrepreneurial ventures involved sales of "Maria Coffee" produced by Christian coffee growers in Rwanda. During my fieldwork, Mother House volunteers (all ex-offenders) sold coffee at various church events and had a kind of makeshift café space set up in the building next to the office. The connections that linked the local and global, the mundane and the spiritual, were not lost on those who came to Mother House, even if they did not profess any personal religious faith. There was a sense of being part of something bigger, of growing something still in the process of being built.

Igarashi's autobiographical narrative of transformation was also a story about moving from the narrow confines of a prison cell to a global, universal, and transcendent world, and from the loneliness of the ego to selfless virtues of love, charity, and forgiveness. Like Mother Teresa, he identified with those who the world seemed to have stopped noticing, and his story was a means of gaining a voice and reaching out to take others with him. The cost of maintaining his moral narrative, however, was that Mother House frequently found itself in conflict with the same bureaucratic systems that it relied on to help ex-offenders to obtain housing, social security benefits, health and social care, and other basic means of survival. As a tōjisha himself, he did not suffer bureaucrats and civil servants telling him what was best for current and formerly incarcerated people. Yet even this opposition to bureaucratic institutions and procedures positioned him more firmly on the side of the oppressed and victimized. The more Igarashi raised his voice, the more he could reveal the workings of structural violence that were, in the case of offenders, very directly linked to a threat of force. Igarashi was intent on writing a different story, and he was skilled at finding others to listen.

Not only did Mother House have trouble getting along with government officials, but there were also frictions with other NPOs and third-sector groups. Some members of faith-based groups thought he was too reckless and risked hurting the reputation of their organizations. Some groups voiced concerns about Igarashi's religious zeal or what they perceived as his lack of professionalism and expert training. Igarashi was also vocally critical of some of these organizations, which he saw as merely acting like charities on the outside, while being complicit with the justice system in practice, either because of corruption or because they lacked the courage or imagination to go beyond their conventional version of resettlement. The world of social justice organizations and the rumors that circulate within them, however, are a topic for elsewhere. For now, it is enough to note that any organization that depends on stories, whether Mother House or any other, runs the risk of bumping up against other stories, or telling one story too loudly. In a world where your story is too often ignored, it can be a challenge to remember to listen to others.

Poetics and Politics of Encounter

Igarashi believed that just like in his own case, other formerly incarcerated people struggling to exit the cycle of recidivism required spiritual transformation, and that this came through encounters with others. "It's doesn't matter if they have a home or a job," he quipped, "People still commit crimes when they have those things. But if they don't change their *heart*, they'll be right back in [prison]."[8]

The notion of transformational "encounters" (*deai*) was at the core of Igarashi's critique of Japan's punitive prison system and what he saw as the violent paternalism by the welfare system in the treatment of ex-offenders.[9] These institutions were "never going to do anything to change anyone's heart," Igarashi scoffed, "they just give you as little as they can and say get out! They might as well just send you [prison]." While most people would assume that services like the welfare benefit service would be received with gratitude (even if they were admittedly imperfect), Igarashi was not so naive. From his perspective, the welfare office was just as cold, anonymous, and heartless as the prison— an ugly and unsettling feeling of distance and condescension reverberated across the carceral continuum.

In contrast, Igarashi's conception of encounter recognized the close relational nature of transformation, the notion that none of us can reflect on ourselves or change all on our own apart from others. This thinking is built on a foundation of basic human commensurability (that no matter what crimes/sins we've committed, we remain children of god), yet in order to realize this, we had to be able to see ourselves in each other, and to love each other as we love our selves. Igarashi explained:

> IGARASHI: If you have good encounters, you'll follow the good path. If you have a bad encounter, you'll go down the wrong path, that's what I think first of all. For me, the most essential encounter was meeting Jesus Christ.
> JASON: That's what you feel personally.
> IGARASHI: Yes, for me. Of course, Christ is goodness, love, righteousness (*gi*), and won't ever lead you into evil. So, with that teaching in mind, when I look at people, I try to be like Christ and look at them in a more spiritual

point of view (*reiteki na me*). I've met a lot of people, and through those encounters I started to become more conscious of myself. Like, this or that point is no good. My negative characteristics. I have to look at myself and face all those things that I don't like after interacting with other people. From there I was taught deeper things. (Jason: Deeper?) Like how to practice acceptance towards people, how to forgive people (*mitsumenaoshi*), then well, you'll know this, but there are a lot of words in the Bible. There are a lot of words, but humans also have freedoms. The way I see it, it's just like Jesus said: "Words without deeds are dead." You see the real person through their deeds. *The deeds are freedom.*

Encounters with others, good or bad, were equally opportunities to reflect on and engage in ethical work of the self. In encountering the "bad," one is able to see one's own "negative" qualities and understand how they affect others. In encountering 'good' people, one learns how to love others with true compassion. In order to discern who is bad and who is good, Igarashi slightly alters the biblical reference of "faith without works" into "words without deeds are dead." It is no wonder, then, that Igarashi himself works so hard not only to keep his organization running, but as an act of faith, a practice of self-cultivation, and a way of honoring the encounter.

Igarashi believes that it is the tireless practice and work of opening up to the encounter and helping others that accounts for his sense of discernment. After learning from one Mother House volunteer that three of the men that Mother House had been supporting had suddenly left their apartment and disappeared without a word, I expected Igrashi to fly into a rage. Instead, he shrugged. The financial loss stung, but most of all, Igarashi felt disheartened that he could only do so much. "Those guys just haven't encountered themselves yet. I wonder if they ever will," he said softly as the two of us sat in the empty office.

"I've been screwed over by so many people, time and again. That's because they haven't encountered *themselves* yet. If you meet yourself, you'll take care of yourself and you'll try not to hurt others. But if you don't have that experience, it's impossible. Like love. If you don't have that experience, how can you love? People who have never experienced being loved by others don't know how to love. I don't mean the kind of love between a man and woman, but the love, the love that is about caring for others, attending to them, treating them with compassion (*omoiyari*).

"To be honest," he explained, leaning over the desk, "people ask for help and I just say 'sure, of course,' and I take in anyone who asks." His voice dropped, lower and quieter as he closed his eyes as if in pain, "But honestly, in my stomach I sometimes feel—'Oh, this one's hopeless.'"

Before I could respond, Igarashi leaned back and raised his voice again: "So that means inside of me, *I haven't met myself.* If I say, 'you have to do this, you have to do that,' they'll just resist everything I say. If you give them the reality straight—if you go right for their weak spot, right away and straight in, people naturally will pull away. Even if I feel [doubts] in my gut, I'll say 'Oh, you need help? Well, try to do your best.'"

"What happens then?" I asked.

"After that, you can tell by the person's face," he replied.

"What can you tell?"

"They're going to run away. Those who want to run away will run away."

Igarashi's own lived experience, his empathic understanding of both the desire for change and the deep resistance formerly incarcerated people feel toward being told how to change, becomes a guide for engaging with those who come to him for help. Even when he is conscious of his own doubts about the motivations or character of the person in front of him, he described the moral decision to "meet himself," facing his own fears and acting compassionately despite his concerns. The capacity to meet oneself and make better moral decisions depends on an encounter with another person. In Igarashi's autobiographical narrative, incarceration was the end result of a series of attempts to "run away" or escape from himself and his painful relationships with others. The impulse to run away was not contained by confinement, but amplified—escape and capture were two sides of the same coin, neither leading to liberation. In the same way, Igarashi felt that successful rehabilitation depended on overcoming this impulse to run and instead, becoming open to the encounter with others and consequently to oneself.

AGING AND BELONGING

Although Mother House was inspired by the tragic sentiments of older prisoners who felt that they had no place left to go, only a handful of older people came to Igarashi asking for help. Yet, having been tasked with caring for older prisoners after he converted to Catholicism in prison, Igarashi was well aware of the problems they faced and the need to do more to prevent older people from reoffending. "Elderly care in the prisons is hell," he stated unequivocally when I asked him about it after a long day in the office. As usual, however, Igarashi was able to use his experience to reflect on and strengthen his own faith:

Nobody teaches you a thing. There's no one who knows anything about it. You know, just things like do this this way and do that that way, no one teaches you. So, they just throw you in deep end and you gotta do the real thing with no prep. All of a sudden, it's change that persons diaper, take that person to the bath, change that guys clothes, all just get in and do it right away.

So, for me the biggest thing was what Mother Teresa said about helping the person in front of you. Love that person right in front of you. Really attend to their suffering. I was able to learn that through doing elder care.

I would pray.

"God."

And it's because of those prayers, that I was saved.

So through that, there was a woman who used to be carer, Sister Y**, I met her, and she taught me a lot of things, so when I had questions, I'd put them in a letter and she'd write back and tell me what to do. That's how I did it.

It's really hard, because you want to do the right thing, but you don't know how. And there are a lot of grumpy old guys in prison too!

Igarashi was interested in helping to support more formerly incarcerated older adults not only because of the particular challenges they faced, but because incorporating them into the Mother House network provided opportunities for different kinds of encounters with younger members. The encounter with the other-as-self was a way to transcend age and generation.

Over the course of my fieldwork, Mother House became instructive in other ways. As a relatively recently established organization led by people with no formal professional training, Mother House was actively seeking to establish an identity, and grappling with what it meant to provide a place of belonging (*ibasho*), a program of emotional and spiritual rehabilitation, and a means of preventing recidivism that resisted the hegemony of government authority. It was in many ways a moral experiment in progress, fighting to maintain its independent spirit, but facing an uncertain future. Despite the frictions with other groups providing similar assistance, Igarashi and Mother House remained firmly dedicated to their approach, which differed from most other organizations in one key way: their claims of legitimacy hinged on the authority of the lived experience of tōjisha over the claims of public welfare institutions.

The close intimate support that Igarashi could give to individuals in the confines of the prison did not translate as well to the outside, where a hectic life of work, family, and church activities made it impossible to make visits more than once a month. While Igarashi and the others at Mother House would try to adapt as much as possible within these limits, it was not a clear fit for older people with complex needs. For formerly incarcerated older adults, Igarashi's openness and commitment to accept and look after anyone who needs help, regardless of age or disability, was comforting. There were, naturally, also real challenges to inclusion. Older ex-offenders were less willing to go along with the others to mass or bible study, or to do the kind of soul-searching work that Igarashi demanded of the younger members. Participating in the larger network, such as attending events and volunteer activities, was also challenging for older people with disabilities. Providing day to day company or help was also difficult at times. Adapting to the challenges of an aging ex-offender demographic would be a test of Mother House's model of fostering encounters and creating new spaces of mutual care.

CHAPTER 4

Twenty Yen

One of the reasons Igarashi was interested in my research was because there were more and more older people needing help resettling, and they were some of the most difficult cases for his NPO to deal with. Efforts to re-humanize the treatment of older offenders, as illustrated by charitable NPOs like Mother House, looked for alternatives to the current system not in idealized notions of Japan's culture and history, nor in more radical calls for prison abolition, but rather, in progressive reformist models like restorative or community-based transformative justice.[1] These were particularly appealing to Igarashi as they resonated with his religious values of grace and forgiveness found in the encounter with others. At the same time, even reformist models were still strongly critical of the trends of the increasingly punitive criminal justice system, where alternative restorative approaches have been more myth than reality.[2] Still, Igarashi worried about the capacity for Mother House to accommodate older ex-offenders, and one case proved to be a particularly tricky test for his experiment in tōjisha mutual rehabilitative support.

One afternoon, as I was about to leave the office, I suddenly stopped, as the gentle ringtone melody of "Some Say Love, it is a River" began drifting from a nearby desk. Igarashi answered with a quick tap of his finger, "moshi moshi!"

As he pressed his ear to the phone Igarashi stiffened his posture and become uncharacteristically concise in his responses. After hanging up, he sank into his seat looking deflated. He shook his head and sighed.

"He's done it again. Seventy-three years old and this 'ojīsan' has gone and got arrested."

The *ojīsan*, or grandfather that Igarashi was referring to was usually just "Jī," or "Gramps," to the younger men at Mother House. This truncation of the nickname would typically be considered impolite (both *o-* and *-san* indicate respect), but in this context, it had an easy feeling of close kinship. Igarashi told me that Mother House had been assisting Jī for a little while, helping to provide him with a place to stay and helping him manage his money by giving him a regular allowance for food and daily needs. This was not unusual practice at other NPOs or care facilities, since mismanaging or quickly spending all of one's money was a major risk factor in reoffending. Igarashi hadn't heard from Jī recently, so although it was not unexpected, the specific details of the call still came as a shock.

The police officer on the phone told Igarashi that Jī had been caught stealing money from the donation box of a Shinto shrine. He only managed to steal ¥20 (about $0.20), telling the arresting officer that he had run out of money and had nothing to eat. Jī had been wandering around the neighborhood all afternoon, moving slowly as a result of a past injury to his left knee. After he stole the money, he didn't get very far before he was caught and arrested. Jī was to be kept in detention until his appearance before a judge in the coming weeks, and because of his prior convictions, was facing the possibly of going back to prison for up to one year.

"What's the point in putting him prison? He's got a speech disability, he's got a bad leg!" Igarashi was exasperated, "Of course breaking the law is bad. That ojī-chan was acting badly. I'm not arguing with that, but for society to just abandon him — I mean, if someone were to just try and *connect* with him, as a person, I'm sure they could figure out something better!"

Igarashi buried his head in his hands and started speaking to himself: "Turn it over to God! This person just has to change, and all I can do is pray and try to keep moving forward."

Jī's sudden arrest brought the full force of the carceral condition of older people in Japan into stark relief. Here was the case of an older person with chronic disability, living alone on inadequate public assistance, who receives no additional support despite his history of past incarceration. Nobody in his neighborhood knew him, and he had no contact with any family. Yet, rather than resolving this incident by assessing Jī's unmet needs, the immediate and strict enforcement of the law took absolute authority. Jī's actions were witnessed, and he admitted his crime, triggering the legal machinery that would land him, again, in prison. The "institutional thoughtlessness" that characterizes life for older people in prisons, carried over to the world outside.[3]

Carceral Returns

Already, carceral mechanisms of surveillance, capture, and removal had destabilized Jī's life. Clearly the cost of arresting, detaining, and trying Jī would be thousands of times more than the negligible amount that Jī stole, and the added cost of a prison sentence would, from a strictly economic perspective, seem completely absurd. What does society gain from this cost? The retribution for the crime seemed completely out of line with the harm done. The notion that Jī would need to be incapacitated because he was a danger to others is similarly farfetched. The only way to see a logic in this incident is to see it as but one brick in a much grander wall, an edifice that is so imposing that it seems impossible to question. As Graeber noted concerning the blind spots of structural violence, "interpretive labor no longer works," but at the same time, "if we ignore them completely, we risk becoming complicit in the very violence that creates them."[4] From this vantage point, Jī's arrest, in its own small way, was not about him or protection of the shrine, but about upholding a system of moral control over older people and punishing those who deviated.

Had this incident occurred two centuries ago, prior to the establishment of national institutions of policing and prisons in Japan, someone like Jī, who was destitute and lacking family ties, may have been subject to reprimand appropriate for his hereditary caste, perhaps facing punishment from the head of the local beggars guild, whose role it was to manage the collection and distribution of alms to professional beggars.[5] Even a century ago, before the development of the national social care system and still early in the history of the prison, Jī more than likely would have been placed in the responsibility of local welfare associations, with the matter resolved informally.[6] While Jī may have avoided a prison sentence, we should be cautious not to over-romanticize these historical alternatives, even though it seems to resemble the kinds of community-based conciliation advocated by decarceration reformers and abolitionists. The mobilization of local citizens groups in early twentieth-century Japan, mentioned previously, was closely aligned with state hegemony, the promotion and enforcement of a patriarchal and hierarchical family system, and the construction of surveillance and suppression of deviance. A century earlier, Jī still may have found himself abandoned to the unlivable poor house and the dehumanizing carceral conditions. But just as I would advise caution when digging through the archives for a mythical time when poor, disabled, and isolated older people were treated with dignity and care, I would be just as cautious when using various historical accounts to build a narrative that overstates continuity.[7]

While the carceral condition is always concerned with the control of deviance, the social categories and institutional structures through which carceral power could be mobilized have changed dramatically. Since the post-bubble era, the rapid neoliberal shift toward the deinstitutionalization, marketization, and individualization of long-term care has coincided with a rise in the number of impoverished and solitary older people. As the examples of Jī and Chiba (Chapter 1) illustrate, even older people living with significant impairment are routinely assessed as capable of living independently and ineligible for care services under the long-term care insurance (LTCI) scheme. Not only are solitary individuals marginalized for their lack of family or close community ties (typically cultivated through long-term household involvement in neighborhood affairs), but also for their failure to meet ideals of self-managed, "independent" aging in place. The sharp end of the carceral comes down at the point where these forms of marginalization converge, but behind this point lies a much more expansive (and expensive) set of norms, fears, and fantasies that animate and bring affective power to bear on older people.

JI'S STORY

After his release, Igarashi moved Jī to a residence in a small town outside of Tokyo where a younger formerly incarcerated person had been housed. Jī had spread out a pink futon mattress on the tatami floor of the only room of the house with a working air conditioning unit. Despite the fan being turned up to the highest setting, it hardly seemed to ease the stifling heat inside the house. Jī sat cross-legged on the futon in a white t-shirt and bottle green shorts. He appeared healthy, with a full head of thick gray hair and remarkably smooth unblemished skin, but when as he moved to make space for me, his movements were awkward and difficult, as if trying to carry a large fragile dish without breaking it. A bottle of green tea sat on the low table next to a box of cigarettes, lighters, medicines, a hairbrush and various other personal items. Several clear plastic garbage bags filled with clothes and other belongings were pushed to the wall.

As Igarashi had mentioned, Jī had difficulty speaking clearly as a result of his stroke, and he tended to answer in short sentences, repeating words or phrases several times in an effort to get them to come out right. He would get easily frustrated after saying something over and over, only to have me ask him to repeat it. Gradually, our conversations found a stuttered rhythm, and bit by bit, Jī's life story began to emerge.

When Jī first came to Mother House, he had been housed in a small apartment in northeast Tokyo. He had been out of prison for about a year. Like other single men who settled in that area and worked in the casual labor market, Jī was not originally from Tokyo. He came from a farming family, and after graduating high school, he attended a year of agricultural college before dropping out. Jī got married at the age of twenty-two, and soon after, his daughter was born. For the next twenty years, Jī worked as a mushroom farmer, but when he was forty-three, he and his wife divorced and his daughter left with her mother.

When Jī spoke about this time, his tongue seemed stuck to his teeth, and he labored to shape each word. The responses came out in bursts of three or four words at a time, and it was difficult to press him repeatedly on details of some of the more painful parts of his life story. I was never sure why the first wife left or why his daughter also left at that time. It did appear that the divorce was costly. Jī had to get rid of his farm and instead moved to the mountains, where he became a professional hunter. His income from hunting deer, wild boar, and other wild game animals for inns and restaurants in the area was sometimes very generous, and he enjoyed the freedom and lifestyle. He got married again, but there were continued frictions with his ex-wife and, according to Jī, more demands for payments for money, ostensibly for their daughter. At some point Jī had come on hard times, lost all of his money and ran into debt. That was the first time he stole and also his first time in prison. At forty-seven, he was sent to prison for eighteen months and his wife left him. After his release, he moved to Tokyo, hoping to get away from life where he grew up. He had almost no money and had been cut off from contact with his ex-partner's daughter and most of his other family members.

His second arrest was less than five years after his release, at age of fifty-three, again for theft. Then, at around the age of sixty, he had a stroke that partially paralyzed his right side and badly impaired his speech. Not long after, his mother, whom he had been close to, died, and his health worsened. He began stealing again, and was caught at age sixty-seven, after not paying for a meal. Even though the price of the meal only amounted to a few hundred yen, Jī's criminal record and isolation from support meant that he would return to custody. This time he spent about three months in custody, where he was sentenced to work (*rōeki*) to pay back his debt. "It was hell," was all he would tell me about it.

Jī couldn't explain very clearly what had happened with this last incident. He was hungry. He had no money. He did not know that he could ask for help, and while panhandling is not uncommon among the poor elsewhere in the world, it is virtually unheard of in Japan, where it can be prosecuted as a criminal offense (classified as a form of fraud). In Jī's mind, the only option was to find 100 or 200 yen, barely enough to buy himself a little food. Instead, the shrine staff saw him fishing around in the donation box and alerted the police.

> JASON: What did you think when you were caught?
> JĪ: Well, I only took 20 yen, only 20 yen. I thought that it wouldn't be a problem if it was only 20 yen. But the police, the police, the police told me, even if it's 20 yen, it's still a crime. So then they locked me up for twenty days in all. I couldn't understand why I was put in detention. Then I just thought, guess that's the way it is (*sho ga nai*)

Jī sounded as if he became resigned to whatever the judge decided. Igarashi was worried. "I just thought what is the point of all of this? but the judge just has to do what is in the law. In the end, I couldn't do anything [to change the law] but I just thought that I have to let it go!" Igarashi went to the judge to plead to have Jī's sentence was suspended. Igarashi tried to explain to the judge that Jī had a stroke that left his speech hardly comprehensible, that he has a physical disability and couldn't walk far without severe pain in his knees, that he was suffering from cognitive impairment, maybe dementia. When the judge began to question Jī, he was confused, mixing up the judge and lawyer and others, unable to answer questions clearly. All he could do was hang his head and repeat that he'd done a bad thing and felt sorry for it. Igarashi had seen this behavior before. It was a natural response when being reprimanded, but in the context of the court, it was counterproductive. We were relieved when the decision of a suspended sentence was announced, but this was far from the end of Jī's ordeal.

ETHICS OF DESERVINGNESS

During the twenty days that Jī was in detention, he lost his public assistance benefits and his apartment. The landlord found the apartment in terrible shape, with holes in the wall and garbage everywhere. Igarashi not only had to find a new place for Jī to live, but he had to pay back rent and damages for the old apartment. He also had to arrange for an LTCI care assessment and health care, since he wasn't able to the get all of the medicines and other care he needs.

>   IGARASHI: So we've got to start all over again from zero. For now, I've got to take him to ___ and register him for *seikatsu hogo* there. But the country doesn't do anything for that old man. He'll be living together with one of the other guys, sharing a place. He's disabled, so without some help, there's no way he can make it. That's why he's come to us. [The state] is just letting him die without helping (*migoroshinjau*). When I talked to the head of the welfare department they just said, "we sent out a notice and we don't have to explain anything." They don't understand that this old man's been ejected from the assistance program. They don't get it. And they don't give any explanation. This is outrageous! They say all this stuff about the new Recidivism Reduction Promotion Act! but what does that Recidivism Reduction Promotion Act amount to? They just kick him out to the street and say "Bye-bye, have a nice life!" If that's the Recidivism Reduction Promotion Act, I think they got it wrong. (J: It is likely to have the opposite effect) Right! It's the opposite. That's why people need more than just state care. He didn't have food- he was going to die! My wife made a lunchbox and took it over to him and said "eat." I made some phone calls to the ward office and some other places and arranged a place for him. That's what it's like. It's just awful.
>   JASON: What about Jī? What did he think?
>   IGARASHI: He doesn't understand a thing! Since he doesn't understand anything, I got to explain everything simply. (chuckling) From his perspective, he was getting out and he was getting fed, so he felt relieved. But he doesn't really understand anything. I just wonder why the social welfare case workers don't do a thing for him. It's fine to just explain to him what's happened— "you've been arrested, you're being indicted, we are cutting off your public assistance benefits"—but they don't do anything. Just throw him out. Well, I got nothing to say to that.

Unfortunately, Jī's case was not unique. I heard similar stories time and again from older men who were denied or cut off from their Livelihood Assistance as a result of insecure living arrangements, confusing administrative processes, and lack of support. The ethical impulse to help those who you see suffer, to attend to the person "in front of your eyes," as Igarashi puts it, had been displaced by the bureaucratic apparatus of the welfare state, which wields care and its threat of withdrawal as a mechanism of social control. Jī's abandonment by the state demonstrated not only the "institutional thoughtlessness" of the criminal justice system, but an indifference to issues of old age, poverty, and disability.[8] This is the exercise of power that Carolyn Sufrin identifies as "deservingness," in which support becomes an extension of the carceral.[9] If the state can decide who is and isn't deserving of support and when or under what circumstances that support will be offered or denied, who is included or excluded from the means to participate in the community, it is exercising control over the lives of those who have the least.

In addition to the standard procedures of registering for seikatsu hogo, most older adults needed more extensive attention to their health and sometimes even long-term care services that Mother House was not used to negotiating with local authorities. Navigating the administrative procedures of finding the right services through the long-term care insurance scheme, or managing doctor appointments and medicines could be difficult for older people living on their own normally, but it was even more difficult for people who need to go through additional procedures to apply for fee waivers processed through the ward office. Igarashi found that age discrimination was also a problem when finding housing for formerly incarcerated older people, not only from landlords, but from local community welfare organizations:

"When you are over 68, no one wants to rent to you," Igarashi told me later, "They won't do it because if you die, who's going to take care of the mess? It costs money for that and for everything else, and if you're on seikatsu hogo, the country won't pay for it. Once you're dead, the money is stopped. It would be nice if after an old person dies, the ward office would give a little money so the landlord could have someone clean out the apartment, but they don't do that. I think that's where the problem is."

"What about the local self-governing society or neighborhood groups?" I asked, "Couldn't they help?"

He waved off the idea and choked out a laugh, "They won't, because they don't want to have anything to do with it. That person is not related to us! So it is pretty hard with old people. I've had two, three, four—four, in here, but one got caught again."

"If there are no encounters nothing will start. Tōjisha and tōjisha will have encounters amongst themselves, and then within those relationships, they'll help each other out, and as they walk that path, they make encounters with others [non-tōjisha]. That's a link to rehabilitation (*kaifuku*)."

From Igarashi's perspective, housing a formerly incarcerated older person in the community was another way of creating an opportunity for encounters. Encounters with others in the neighborhood would not only facilitate the resocialization of the ex-offender, but also produce possibilities for de-stigmatization and a natural process of community integration. Igarashi's approach was disruptive, throwing everyone into a situation where they would have to dig deep and find a common sense of humanity.

Mother House itself was beginning to make changes to build its presence in the community to model the kind of "third-space" where encounters could happen.[10] Not long before I arrived, Igarashi had rented a large ground floor unit adjacent to the office, around the size of a two-car garage. They painted the ceiling blue and the walls white, a nod to Mother Teresa, and the bare concrete floor was soon covered with cardboard and plastic boxes filled with materials, various pieces of furniture, books, and kitchen items. The entryway consisted of a large set of sliding glass doors that were opened wide on to the street.

When Igarashi first showed me the *ibasho* space on a sweltering day in mid-August, a large blue inflatable paddling pool was sitting in the open door, hanging half out onto the pavement, and two of Igarashi's children splashed and squealed in the water. A middle-aged man in sandals, his grey sweatpants pushed up to his knees and t-shirt soaked across the front played along. "This guy's been out for about four weeks," Igarashi explained, giving me a nudge that told me I ought to talk to him.

It was not until much later that I realized the reason Igarashi encouraged me to talk with the man I will call Kei. It was Kei who would end up making the most difference in Jī's life, his link, as Igarashi put it, to rehabilitation. When the kids ran off to look for their mother, I went over and introduced myself.

"Igarashi tells me you were just recently released?"

Kei's expression became serious. He took a wide stance, holding his hands behind his back, and relaxed. I could see the tattoos edging from his sleeves, just above his elbows. "Yeah, from [___ prison]. I was there for two and half years. You know, this isn't my first time either."

"How many times has it been?"

He showed me six fingers on his hands.

"Mostly for drugs, but I've done most other things too. Everything except rape or homicide."

Kei had heard about Mother House from other men he was incarcerated with and although he admitted that he had never thought too much about spirituality personally, he did pick up the Bible when he was in prison previously, and thought he might look at it again. "When I started reading it again, I still didn't understand it," he told me, "so I asked if I could join [Mother

House's] prison pen pal service to discuss it with other people." The pen pal service, which Mother House ran mostly with the help of Catholic volunteers, was a window in the high walls of prison through which Kei could start to envision forgiveness and love in ways that he'd never thought possible. "My heart changed completely," he explained, "I'd never seen anyone whose heart (*kokoro*) really changed with Buddhism, but I think it's easier with Christianity."

When he was due to be released, Mother House arranged to pick him up at the gate and take him to a small studio apartment just for him. It was still unfurnished except for a futon mattress on the floor. "But even to have that," Ito continued, "I'll never forget it. Just to know that someone on the outside was thinking of me—I was totally overwhelmed. To me it was like the most luxurious room I'd ever stayed in, really!"

Kei was in his early fifties, and despite his estrangement from family and his history of incarceration, he still held a hope that Mother House might give him a place to get back on his feet: an *ibasho* where hope and home connected him to a world with others.[11] Praying at a Catholic mass or playing in a children's pool were ways the Kei tried to rewrite his narrative, "change his heart," and build something new.

Rebuilding Jī's life was going to be no easy task. Although out of custody, in many ways, he was even more unsettled than when he took the twenty yen. The incident marked the persistence of formerly incarcerated older people's vulnerability to future incarceration and the punitive power wielded by the criminal justice system on people living with disabilities. Igarashi tried to counteract the "institutional thoughtlessness" of the system with feeling, care, and concern. For Jī, whose life, despite some family hardships, had been manageable for most of his middle age, getting older left him poor, alone, and disabled. But in this regard, he was not alone. The Japanese response to the men growing old alone and poor, has been exclusion and containment. In the following chapter, I examine how this has concentrated carceral structures around urban zones for older men.

CHAPTER 5

Winds of *Shaba*

The experiences of formerly incarcerated older and disabled people like Jī raise questions about the prison-welfare nexus and the commonsense assumption that social welfare assistance is the solution to recidivism. Even if we accept that prisons no longer function as rehabilitative institutions, surely welfare support offers a safety-net that cares for and protects individuals who might otherwise resort to crime. But not only was Jī living on public assistance benefits when he re-offended, but his arrest instantly broke off all support. And this is not just about money. While mechanisms like the Public Assistance for Livelihood Protection (*seikatsu hogo*) provide just enough income for older adults to survive (sometimes triple what they would receive from the basic pension), it also reproduces an isolated, precarious, and marginalized life world.[1] Welfare, in other words, is an extension of the carceral circuit, insofar as it is based on structural violence, or as Graeber puts it, "the allocation of resources within a system of property rights and guaranteed by governments in a system that ultimately rests on the threat of force."[2]

In Tokyo, the effects of this institutional violence are particularly pronounced in areas of the city that have historically housed high concentrations of low-income casual laborers, mostly single men who migrated to the city from elsewhere and had few, if any, links to family members. Given the frequency of formerly incarcerated individuals living in these areas, it is not surprising that these areas are also seeing the same demographic change that is occurring in prisons. This chapter looks at the lives of older individuals living on public assistance in one of these areas, as well as some of the various efforts of third-sector and charity organizations to provide an alternative to the violence of welfare or prison.

About one month after my first visit to Mother House, I met a man who volunteered at a charity soup kitchen in an area known as San'ya, Tokyo's main yoseba, or day-labor district.[3] Perhaps calling it a district is a little misleading; you will not find the name San'ya on any official map. The informality of its borders makes it invisible and ambiguous to those who do not know. But it is not a very large area, only a few square blocks between Taito Ward and Arakawa Ward in the northeast corner of Tokyo city. The man invited me to come along with him after I told him about the research. "You'll meet a lot of older men who know something about prison," he said.

On my first day volunteering, we distributed more than three hundred hot meals. Each was boxed in simple, clear plastic trays of white rice and vegetable curry made fresh by volunteers that morning. Most men took a seat under the concrete canopy of the highway as soon as they received their meal and ate quickly in silence before walking away unhurriedly. They're dressed in baggy layers of brown and navy, tufts of grey poking out under baseball caps. The volunteers and NPO workers simply refer to them as ojisan (old men). All but a few of the men appear at least sixty, and only once in ten weeks of volunteering did I meet someone getting a meal who was as young as in their twenties. I also never met a woman, although I had been told by other volunteers that occasionally one or two will show up, typically because they are together with one of the men. The volunteers, mostly Japanese Christians who have been doing this service for years, move slowly past the ojisan, tidying the used trays and plastic cutlery and thanking the men politely.

The only volunteer who was making small talk with the ojisan was Yoji, a middle-aged man who worked as a carer for clients with disabilities. He had been volunteering regularly for several years and carried himself with a calm kindness. As the weeks went by, Yoji and I would sit next to the ojisan as they ate, and sometimes he would introduce me to some of the men he knew, even taking a couple of meals around to men who had missed the distribution, sleeping off a rough night. In the moments between finishing their curry and moving on, the ojisan would exchange a few scraps of their everyday life with me and Yoji, usually concerns about not finding work or dealing with poor health. "I'd like to work, but nobody wants to hire a seventy-one-year-old guy!" one man complained. Another explained that he is living on seikatsu hogo but has got in trouble with debts. "I got debts about ¥98,000!" he told me frowning, "I'm about to get thrown out of the place I'm staying, but I figure I'll just rough it on the streets." The same man had been to prison a few years back, and occasional spoke to me about considering suicide. When I asked if he'd ever go back, just to get some stability again, he shook his head. "If I go back now, I'll be leaving out the back gate [where deceased prisoners are removed]."

Another man, tall and bald with small wrinkles around the corners of his eyes smiled as I came over and told me that I should join him for karaoke when the next seikatsu hogo payment comes through. I asked if he was working but he just shrugged,

> I'm only sixty-one, but I still can't find a job, so I'm living on seikatsu hogo. Yeah, there's nothing to do. You feel like you're getting old, I honestly feel right now that I could die at any time and I wouldn't care.
>
> (Really? But sixty is still young!)
>
> A lot of guys around here have the same feeling. Just jump in the water here [looking at the river]. There was a woman the other day, eighty-five, jumped into the river. Someone got her out and they tried to save her, but it was too late. She died.
>
> I don't want to live too long, but I just can't manage to die!

"Most of the guys who come for the free meals are living on seikatsu hogo," Yoji explained as we made our way toward the food distribution point, a strip of concrete sheltered by a highway overpass, where thick support columns rose up like an urban cathedral. "Some don't sign up and just live on the streets."

"Why don't they register?" I wondered aloud.

> Well, sometimes people say they'd rather work, or maybe they move around or don't have an address. But probably the hardest thing is that you have some family member, someone who can confirm who you are and your details. It could be a lawyer or something I guess. (Jason: Like a guarantor?) Right. But sometimes people get jerked around with the procedure, they just give up and say it isn't worth it. There are rumors around that if you are in the system, there will be all sorts of restrictions on you, a kind of surveillance that men don't like. Some guys with criminal records think that they won't get it because of that. You think about these guys who've been living on the street or even been to prison and they're real strong, right? But they're really not. Someone at the public assistance office window says something wrong and they just give up. They're scared.

As the last of the ojisan wandered off down the banks of the Sumida River or back across the bridge, I walked along with a man who I'd often seen talking to guys who were newer to the area. He had a long white beard and a face that didn't project the sense of boredom and discomfort that was so common among the other men. He pointed to one of the concrete pillars, "Here's where I sleep." I asked him about work or assistance and he explained that he had a bank account from a couple of years ago and he just lives off his small pension payments: "Only thing is that if you don't have an address, sometimes they check, and then you get your pension cut off. So I am worried about that. it has happened before." He went on,

> Sure people get money with seikatsu hogo, but you see them— they have too much! They spend it on things like drink and gambling. They aren't really living well. Better for me to live out here. I heard there are places where you could live like a shelter, but don't want to live there because then they handle all your money and stuff. Some of those places are "poverty businesses" (*hinkon bijinesu*). You can get by out here, but it can be hard, you know, you can get sick or something, a lot of people do.

Talking to others confirmed this man's concerns about the ways seikatsu hogo leads to precariousness: a monthly rhythm of spending freely at the start of the month, then scraping by until the next payment. Getting a job could risk losing one's benefit, only to lose work again and have to go through the process of reapplying.

Recipients of seikatsu hogo allowances were subject to checks by state-employed case workers, who continuously re-evaluate individuals' status and eligibility. In 2017, a group of Public Assistance case workers in the city of Odawara were disciplined after creating jackets emblazoned with the words (in broken English):

> "TEAM HOGO" We are "the justice" and must be justice, so we have to work for Odawara, finding injustice of them, we chase them and punish injustice to accomplish the proper execution. If they try to deceive us for gaining a profit by injustice, "WE DARE TO SAY, THEY ARE DREGS."

The front of each jacket featured a crest, lifted directly from the Liverpool Football Club logo, but ironically replacing Liverpool's slogan, "You'll never walk alone," with the words "HOGO NAMENNA" (Don't cheat [Livelihood] Protection). In the center of the crest, the acronym SHAT (*Seikatsu Hogo Akuobokumetsu suru* Team; team to eradicate evil-doers on public assistance for livelihood protection), and the Japanese character for "evil" (*aku*) is crossed out. Twenty-eight employees purchased jackets and some would wear them on case visits to people's homes.

Although the Mayor of Odawara commented that these jackets were "inappropriate," for case workers, their strong rhetoric reveals the ethos of a system charged with administering the just use of public funds and disciplining those who violate the rules. The jackets gave symbolic meaning to the otherwise administrative task, elevating it to the noble work of protecting national moral values. It was the public display of this symbolic role, rather than the content of statements themselves that was ultimately found "inappropriate," as the discipline of a small number of individuals did not result in their dismissal, let alone changes in the ethical standards and procedures of the welfare institution.

As this incident illustrates, state assistance remains tied to violent carceral logics of surveillance and suspicion, and it is the responsibility of recipients to demonstrate their deservingness, even as the support they receive perpetuates their marginalized and precarious position. In other words, it falls on the welfare recipient to imagine what the system expects of them, while the administrators demonstrate a lack of empathetic imagination, literally wearing this as a badge of professionalism. For impoverished older adults, however, there are few alternatives to seikatsu hogo: life on the streets, or prison.

CONTAINING OLD AGE

The experiences of life on Public Assistance for Livelihood Protection reveals the carceral grip of control through responsibilization, bureaucracy, and surveillance outside the site of the prison.[4] The state keeps its hold not only on the purse strings, but on the spatial and temporal circuits and enclosures that confine the possibilities of life.[5] In doing so, the carceral techniques of welfare weaken the trust, interdependence, and community connections that might lead to other possibilities for dwelling and the good life.[6]

Tom Gill describes Japan's approach to poverty and precarious labor as one of "containment," or producing geographic zones where marginalized people and non-mainstream life is tolerated through an attitude of "benign neglect."[7] The yoseba, like the one where I volunteered doing meal distribution, have become emblematic of this approach to marginalization, tracing this history of containment back for centuries. The history of the area was a frequently repeated narrative that the nonprofit organizations in San'ya all thought that I should know, a story that took on an almost mythic flavor that I needed to step into if I was going to get the feel of the place. Once upon a time . . .

> The San'ya region began in the Edo period [17th c]. The Yoshiwara [the 'red-light' entertainment district] was the same. San'ya was a place for [what were called] "mushuku-mono"—those without homes. People without a place to stay. You see, In the Edo period, there were castes (*mibun*)—samurai, commoners, and so on—what was called *ninbetsucho* [writes out] other words, what today you call an official register (*koseki*), There was a record of this or that person was from this or that place, their name was whatever, and so on. If you were a farmer, say, and your life was hard, and you try to escape, go to a place like San'ya and take on a new identity.

The notion that one could adopt a new identity and seek one's fortune in San'ya was possible because the area had largely been zoned as an outcaste district, a place of confinement where criminals, travelers, prostitutes, and other marginalized people could settle.[8] While outcaste groups (*hinin*) had limited choices about their occupations, they also performed valuable jobs such as butchery and leather tanning. Some also worked at the Kotsukappara execution grounds, which was located there for two centuries (1667–1867) until modern prisons were first established.[9] The "bridge of tears" that led to the execution grounds became a nationally famous landmark after celebrated Japanese manga artist Tetsuya Chiba and Asao Takamori set their boxing story "Tomorrow's Joe" (published serially between 1968–1973) in San'ya.[10] In the story, "Joe," a poor ex-offender, becomes a hero of the underclass by taking on the more professionally trained fighters. His spirit allows him to take a beating and to persevere, eventually dying as a champion in the ring. Today the canal that the bridge once crossed has been paved over, but the name is still seen on street signs. Also remaining is the temple where the remains of executed prisoners were interred in a collective grave. Today the site is looked after by an imposing stone statue of the Beheading Bodhisattva Jizo.

The NPO staff positioned themselves as responding not only to the immediate needs of homeless older people in today's San'ya, but to centuries of marginalized and criminalized communities. If Mother House's approach was rooted in the ideas of self-reflection and spiritual transformation, San'ya-based groups tended to emphasize their connection to a sense of place and history.

The day-labor market grew rapidly as Japan rebuilt after World War II, and at its peak around the time Tokyo hosted the Olympics in 1964, there were around 15,000 day-laborers living in San'ya. Men, many of them the younger sons of farming households who would not inherit the family estate, had migrated to Tokyo for work, but those who stayed and started families moved out of the area, which had been the site of clashes between police, militant labor union groups, and organized crime syndicates. As Japan entered the economic decline of the 1990s, the day labor market had already dwindled and those who were left in San'ya were mainly older, single men. As similar pattern emerged in yoseba across Japan, including Kamagasaki (Airin chiku) in Osaka, Kotobuki in Yokohama, and Sasajima in Nagoya.[11]

Charity and NPO groups expanded their work feeding and housing local men, and by the time I arrived, San'ya had become what one care worker called a "welfare town" (*fukushi no machi*).[12] One NPO staff member even claimed that "Sanya has the most highly developed comprehensive community care system in all of Japan," because of all of the charities and NPOs that were based there. But what frustrated local organizers was the way welfare support ignored the history of the place and its people. "When the Ministry of Health Labor and Welfare makes up their policies," one NPO staff member told me "they don't understand this point— that San'ya is a totally different kind of place. People here are not the kind of older people that are able to live in their own homes and use the senior welfare the way everyone else does."

If San'ya's ojisan are "totally different" than the image of the mainstream welfare model of old age in Japan, it is because they have incorporated the pain, dislocations, pride, and aspiration that kept labor cheap and flowing into the building of Japan's economic growth.[13] Though they played a critical role in the national economy, the ojisan were the antithesis of the model national citizen. As unmarried migrants, they lacked the strong family and community bonds that were expected to form a basis for care and support over the life course. As Jieun Kim puts it, the men in the yoseba are "*muen*" or disconnected from normative relations of care, making them both socially "invisibilized" and contained.[14] The effects of their marginalization would not be felt so acutely within the boundaries of the yoseba community, especially when work was still available. But in old age, they not only became dependent on the state for basic income, but also for health and welfare support as well.

One ojisan I met at the soup kitchen explained,

> [Ojisan] don't go along with society, they leave institutions because there are too many rules or they treat you like a child. But then they lose their livelihood assistance benefits or they spend it all on alcohol or gambling. Then it's gone. Sometimes they don't care. They're people that like solitude though.

JASON: Would you call this independence or self-reliance (*jiritsu*)—?

[cutting me off] It's not independence! but [searching for the word] they think, "I exist when I do what I want, and that's who I am."—It is like that phrase, "I think therefore I am," you know?

While none of the men that I spoke with in San'ya admitted to considering a return to prison, several NPO staff suspected that they might. It wasn't the sort of thing that they were likely to tell the people giving them assistance. But considering the isolation and invisibility of being *muen*, it wouldn't be surprising.

The average age of residents in San'ya is 64.7, and around 90 percent receive seikatsu hogo, which is distributed on the first of the month.[15] The jovial warmth and free-spirited charm that marked the day of benefit disbursements was always short-lived. One reformed yakuza member I met described places like San'ya as "a world where trusted relationships, friendships, don't exist," or where "people are [friends only] in particular situations (*sono ba*), only when there is money or drink around. It is a world without affection, love, connection. It's a world of loneliness and solitude."

SHABA

Shaba is slang for the world outside of prison, the world where your fate rests in your own hands. The term originates in the moral cosmology promulgated by Buddhist prison chaplains since the nineteenth century, where it refers to the mundane world of illusion (*Sahālokadhātu* in Sanskrit), a world where actions have consequences, and transgressions bear karmic punishment. D. T. Suzuki described shaba as the antithesis of the "Pure Land": it was the "world of defilement" over "purity" and "relativity" over the "absolute."[16] Shaba, in other words, implies a state of things bound in a cycle of karmic suffering, that is only overcome through a change in moral consciousness.

The use of the word *shaba* among formerly incarcerated individuals, implies a freedom that remains contingent on and colored by the experience of prison. It is not the same "free" world that "ordinary" people inhabit, the one that most of us take for granted as we go about our daily lives. Shaba implies a trace of the carceral that mediates life between the person and their environment, something that shapes attentions and affects. Shaba is freedom, but it is not easy. For those who have lost touch with family and who struggle to gain independence, there is a saying, "It's colder in the wind of shaba than it is the behind the walls" (*shaba no kaze wa hei no naka yori tsumetai*).[17]

The offender's past is always impinging on the labor of survival in the present— repetition of the past makes more sense than constructing hopes for a future. Shaba is a cycle of action and consequence, not a sequence that can be plotted on a straight line; moving away always leads back again.

In this sense, shaba reflects the ways incarceration reshapes prisoner subjectivity, the ways they respond to and inhabit their world(s), as they move from life in one sort of confinement to another. But shaba was viewed with ambivalence. Social workers and NPO staff would sometimes use the word "shaba" to encourage formerly incarcerated older men to stay out of prison, leaning in close and taking a low, serious tone: "I know things are hard, but shaba is best, right?"

On release, ex-offenders typically have no place of residence, no family ties to rely on, and very little money. For those who return to San'ya, shaba means a single-occupancy room in a flophouse (*doya*) with a shared toilet and bathroom down the hall. The rooms I visited were little bigger than closets. A single bed or futon occupied almost the entire floor space, leaving just enough room to squeeze around one side and place a shelf or TV table at one end. Because of a lack of a veranda, clothes would hang to dry from the ceiling. The carceral circuit repeats the architecture of enclosure and confinement, just as the world of shaba encloses one in the karmic consequences of past deeds. Ghassan Hage might call life in shaba "bearable life," hovering between viable and non-viable, an "abject version of Michael Jackson's 'life within limits.'"[18]

I accompanied a care worker one afternoon as he made visits to several older clients in a rooming house in San'ya. In one room we visited, a man in his eighties, invited me in to join him watching old samurai movies. A stack of adult diapers were piled in a corner, near the door. He pointed to the small plastic container of Yakult yogurt drinks on the table, motioning for me to take one. I could see he didn't have much, and declined as politely as I could, but he kept insisting, and I relented, feeling guilty. There was no space to sit down, so I drank the small bottle while awkwardly standing in the doorway. I struggled to make out most of his words, but I managed to catch the phrase "my body is wrecked (*gata gata*)." I wondered how long he would stay in that room, where he could go as shaba closed in around him.

The *doya* like the one where this man lived thrives off of convenience and anonymity. If a formerly incarcerated older person wanted a room, they would not need a guarantor or ID. If you're escaping something and needed a place to be invisible, you could do worse than a room in San'ya.

Confinement and escape. It seemed that the welfare system and old men of San'ya were locked in contradictions. While the liberal ideology of elderly welfare programs promoted self-sufficiency and independent living, for many ex-offenders, independence was unaffordable and dependence left them back in prison. Spending a night at one of the shelters in San'ya, I asked the attendant what he thought about this problem.

> ARAKI: It's more like living in shaba is harder than life in prison. Among the people we support there are several who have gone back to prison because they wanted to. They wanted to return so that's why they went back. I think there've been a lot.
>
> JASON: Because they feel more secure there?
>
> ARAKI: That's what it seems like. If that's the case, we can't stop them. They want to go so they get caught shoplifting, there are people like that. [in prison] you don't have to think about anything. In the world (*seken*) you have things to worry about. Renting an apartment, what should I do for food today, what will happen if my livelihood assistance runs out—you have to think about so much. In prison there's none of that.
>
> JASON: When you come out, you're free but not really independent. These days the long-term care policy is all about "independence."
>
> ARAKI: It's really hard isn't it? Think about it, if you're in your seventies or eighties and you've just left prison and they say "go ahead be independent," it's impossible! You don't have any job, you can't even rent an apartment. You are alone, anyway.

Araki discussed several cases of formerly incarcerated older people who have rented beds in the shelter, at one point, retrieving a file of a client who recently died from a nearby shelf, showing me that he had been arrested eighteen times, starting around the age of sixty.

As I walked back to the bus stop, I passed through a shopping arcade that ran through the center of San'ya across three blocks. The bright awnings and billboards of the shops and restaurants were stained or torn, but I was relieved that even these weathered establishments had not been replaced with spotless facades of convenience stores or fast food chains. I looked up to the brightening sky beyond the cage-like metal supports that once held a tarpaulin, providing shade from the summer heat and a dry place in the rainy season. It too had weathered badly and there was not enough money in the neighborhood to replace it. In front of most shops were dozens of bicycles, some in pieces or with flat tires, which had been lined up to keep unhoused people from setting up a makeshift shelter. Between the metal bars overhead and the bicycles below, the arcade felt both empty and unkind. I could almost feel the frigid winds of shaba, gusting down the street, and I found no place to hide.

CHAPTER 6

"We Hear the Screams of Life"

Not long after Jī was released, I rode along with Igarashi and Kei to visit Jī and discuss his new living arrangements. Kei had spent the night on a cot in the Mother House café and greeted me when I arrived just after 8 a.m.

"Professor! Time to go visit Jī, sounds like a pretty rough situation." He looked out of the big glass sliding doors facing the street and up to the darkening sky. "Oh, looks like the storm is coming too."

The rain heard its cue, and a moment later, heavy droplets were falling fast, bursting on the windows and streaking down. A moment later, Igarashi drove up to the doors in a black SUV and Kei and I rushed in. Kei took the front passenger seat. I went to the back, hanging out the door as I unbuckled one of the child seats and brushed away the dusting of crumbs and snack wrappers onto the toy-strewn floor before jumping in.

As we started moving, the radio announced that Typhoon 21 was approaching and drivers should take caution.[1] The morning sky was getting darker and as we sped down the highway, congested with traffic, a steady sheet of rain washed across the windshield. Igarashi picked up his phone with his left hand and dialed. Someone answered and Igarashi asked by name for one of the administrators who was responsible for matters related to the Recidivism Prevention Promotion Act (*Saihan Bōshi Suishin Hō*). Despite the weather and traffic, Igarashi didn't slow down, and held the phone's microphone up to his mouth, even though it was connected to the hands-free system. When a man's voice answered, Igarashi began recounting Jī's story: "I have a seventy-three-year-old man I am looking after. He has speech problems, he has emotional problems, he seems to have a few cognitive problems too. He has no money, no family."

As Igarashi drove, he explained to the person on the phone how Jī's Public Assistance for Livelihood Protection (*seikatsu hogo*) had been cut off when he was arrested and that Jī only realized this after he was released on a suspended sentence twenty days later. Since he had no savings and lost his apartment, Igarashi was requesting emergency assistance until he could enroll for benefits again in a new city. The case was complex, but it was clear enough what Igarashi was asking for. The voice on the other end seemed to hesitate, explaining politely that it was going to be difficult to give Jī a payment in such a circumstance. From what I could hear, it sounded like an application would have to be made before any kind of assistance would be considered. More paperwork. Igarashi seemed to expect this answer, but nonetheless became gradually more aggressive in his tone as the man on the other end did his best to deflect the demands. This made Igarashi even bolder, but he kept calm. I thought I could feel the SUV speed up.

> They have eight different people [at the ward office] that are all Public Assistance officers (*hogoshi*). Eight! Not one knew about this. I had to go myself over to the ward office and explain to them what had happened! What the hell is that about?

His voice was getting louder and his language coarser. I started to feel sorry for the man on the other end, who finally tried to cut things off by saying that he would have to speak to his supervisor. "Don't give me excuses like that!" Igarashi shot back.

> I'm not asking for that, did I ask for that? You are hearing this, right? You say all this about reducing recidivism and you don't know shit about the lives of these people. This guy had nowhere to live, nothing to eat, my wife had to make some lunch for him and bring it over! He couldn't eat! Is that fine with you? One day, two days without eating? That's no different from you just saying "Please die!"

As the tension rose, I did my best to keep up with the conversation, my pen flying across the notebook, catching fragments as quickly as I could, but Igarashi was racing ahead.

You in Tokyo, it is *your* fault if this guy dies, this is what you are doing to people. You are so worried about your relationship with your boss that you can't get anything done.

Don't fucking give me your bullshit about how all this is up to the [Ministry of Health Labor and Welfare], you are supposed to be in charge of these emergency aid payments, so you can see if there is something that you can do now. I'm sorry to say this because—([voice on the phone]: Just because you are telling us we can't—) I am not telling you anything! I am not telling you what to do, did you ever hear me once giving you an order? The problem is that you aren't doing your job. If you were, there wouldn't be cases like this, right?

I've never heard anyone swear to a city official like this before, let alone with such outrage. I kept taking notes, even faster as my own heart was racing, trying not to think about the highway disappearing in the heavy rain and the rising pitch of Igarashi's voice. Perhaps sensing that he wasn't going to get anywhere with this person on the phone, Igarashi, eventually changed his tone again, this time with a firm, controlled, and much quieter tone.

Maybe it is a funny way to say it, but a man had got balls and he has to use them. You can't just have empty words. That shit doesn't make a difference! You have to come up with real solutions. I'm sorry I have to say it like this, but you are a human being. When I see another person suffering, I have to help them. I don't just talk. You can say that too if you do something helpful. We can say this because we are helping. We hear the screams of life and we are not just civil servants.

I was amazed that the man on the other end was still there, even though he was clearly unable to give any firm commitments. Eventually Igarashi let him go and pulled the SUV into the parking lot of a highway rest stop. The worst of the storm had just past, and as we got out of the car, the sky had relaxed into a low wooly gray.

Igarashi was clearly passionate about justice, especially when it involved older or disabled ex-offenders. For him, recidivism prevention was not a theory— it was in the living breathing body of another person for whom he felt personal responsibility. This feeling was the core humanist moral principle of Igarashi's sense of vocation, the reason that he could feel deserving of grace, the simple insistence that being a person (*ningen*) meant coming to the aid of those who were suffering, refusing to let others die from hunger while you live in comfort. Igarashi's confrontation with the official at the city office was an attempt to appeal to this principle, to awaken the man's body and emotions to the urgency of this fundamental moral demand. Igarashi implored the man on the phone to transcend the rules of administrative order and be a body that can transcend ("use his balls" rather than his mouth): "We hear the screams of life and we are not just civil servants."

Formerly incarcerated older people not only fall through the gaps in the social welfare safety net, but they can become caught again between the interests and ideologies of both the state and NPOs. Resettling older ex-offenders is key to evidencing success, which can be leveraged to apply pressure on the state. At the same time, older and disabled ex-offenders prove challenging to support over the long term, whether living alone in the community or in a residential care facility. While NPOs like Mother House positioned themselves as the moral voice challenging an uncaring state, it was not always easy to gauge whether formerly incarcerated older people being supported were fully on board. In this context, direct disagreements and complaints, or more diffuse and inchoate states of agitation, boredom, and restlessness could all be read as ways that older people reasserted agency against being dissolved into the moral projects of others, even if this meant putting oneself at greater risk of carceral entrapment. This chapter looks at the ways resistance and refusal interrupt the process of resettlement in ways that complicate the claims of both state and nonprofit organizations.

"Go Off and Die."

The kind of dramatic confrontation between Igarashi and the civil servant on the phone was a regular occurrence for Mother House and for other NPO workers who tried to close the care gap between rigid state-administered institutional support and the immediate and embodied precariousness of formerly incarcerated older people. Of course, Igarashi needed cash in the first place to get Jī resettled, but the real gap, as he saw it, was not about funding, but a gap in human connection, care, and concern. Several recent incidents confirm that this gap could quickly escalate with dire consequences.

In 2017, for example, sixty-five-year-old Takahashi Kiyoshi returned to Fukushima Prefecture after serving an eight-year sentence for arson.[2] He had saved 12,000 yen from his work in the prison, spending half of it in the first two days out on food and alcohol, and without anywhere to live, he applied for shelter at a rehabilitation facility (*kōsei hogo shisetsu*). His application, however, was rejected on the grounds that the probation office felt he had "no desire to rehabilitate." Takahashi later recalled the rejection, saying "I thought they were telling me to go off and die."

It would take a month to get registered for public assistance, and he could not secure a rental agreement for an apartment without a guarantor. He was soon arrested for attempting to rob a convenience store and sentenced to four more years in prison. After his release, he spent two months at a rehabilitation facility, but again had difficulty finding more permanent housing because of his past conviction for arson. Takahashi bought a knife and went to Fukushima station, where he stabbed two people, resulting in minor injuries. At the age of seventy, he was convicted of attempted murder and sentenced to eleven years in prison. It was later revealed that he had talked to others in prison about "getting the message to the public about his treatment by the probation office."[3] While it may not have been his goal to return to prison, shaba had become so unbearable for Takahashi that only an act of random violence could give him voice.

This incident, and the escalation of violence produced by the failures of the post-custody carceral welfare institutions, has several parallels to an infamous incident that occurred on a cold January night in 2007. Fukuda Kyuemon, a seventy-four-year-old man standing only around 150 cm tall, had been released from Fukuoka Prison in December 2006, but with no family to take him in and very little money, he had been homeless since his discharge. In an attempt to get arrested and return to prison, he shoplifted from a local store and then immediately turned himself over to the police. Rather than detaining him, the police suggested that he apply for public assistance at the local ward office. When Fukuda told the welfare office staff that he had just come out of prison and had no place to live, he was told that without proof of identity or an address, he would be unable to receive benefits. Someone at the office in Kita-Kyushu heard that he was from Kyoto and so they decided he ought to go there instead, handing him a train ticket. But Fukuda didn't understand where he was going, and instead, disembarked at Shimonoseki in the neighboring prefecture of Yamaguchi. By the time Fukuda arrived, it was late, and with no place to go, he planned to spend the night at the station.

At around 1:50am on January 8, 2007, Fukuda lit a small fire in the outdoor trash can of a fast-food restaurant near the train station. It was a windy night, and the fire soon spread to the old wooden roof of the main train-station building. Fed by the wind, the flames reached up to twenty meters high, completely destroying the historic building and a total area of almost 4,000 square meters around it. Fortunately, neither Fukuda nor anyone else was hurt during this fire, but he was quickly discovered and arrested near the scene. This was the eleventh fire that Fukuda had been arrested for; fifty of his fifty-four years of adult life had been spent in Japanese prisons.[4] Prison is hardly an ideal environment for someone who is old and frail, but for Fukuda, it was familiar and secure. He was more accustomed to the order and rhythm of prison life, a place where his intellectual disability had less effect on his everyday life, than he was of the dangerous world outside.

Although numerous judges had noted his intellectual disability in the past, Fukuda had never been offered disability support or care on release. Like Takahashi and most other older offenders, Fukuda was estranged from his family and had no guarantor. He was released after serving the full sentence in prison, so from the perspective of the criminal justice system, they were no longer obliged to look after his welfare. Fukuda was a free man.

It had been more than two years since Fukuda was released from prison when I saw him appear at an event arranged by the Center for Prisoner Rights, a nonprofit organization based in Tokyo. At a screening of a short documentary film about his case, Fukuda was invited to the microphone, the audience of around a hundred people erupted in applause, as if this small, thin man, his hands behind his back, nervously looking around the room, was a celebrity. He was dressed in a brown three-piece suit with an orange tie, his silver hair still dark around his ears. He straightened his posture as the event host placed a microphone in front of him. When the applause subsided, he asked, "How are you feeling?"

He stumbled over his words a little, understandably flustered, but managed to say, "Ev-everything's good." This sparked another shorter round of applause from the audience.

"Fukuda-san," the host continued, "now all these people here can see you in real life, and they can see what I see, that you're not some kind of scary monster or something—you're really quite cute! The audience had a little laugh at this and Fukuda-san nodded, but kept quiet. The host continued, "When you came out of prison and I saw you, I thought, this is great! This ojī-chan is so cute and charming, this will make a great film!"

As Fukuda-san continued standing at the front of the laughing audience, the other speakers, such as the director of the NPO that ended up connecting with him for his post-release transition, told his story. Every now and then they would turn his way for a quick confirmation of a detail.

"Why was it that you lit the fire?" The film director asked at one point.

"Um, I—it—it was cold."

"It was cold? What were you thinking you'd do after lighting it?"
"Uh, well, I don't know."

He laughed a little too, although shaking nervously. The interaction reminded me of the broken, unsettled rhythm of most of my interviews with formerly incarcerated older men.

As the filmmaker and NPO support staff reassembled the narrative of what happened to Fukuda after he was released, they constructed a story that flowed across a clear narrative arc toward this moment of recognition. But I couldn't help but feel uneasy about the spectacle in the face of the obvious fragmentation and brokenness that remained, not only in Fukuda's memory and understanding of the incident, but also in the prison and public institutions that were meant to support him. How many others would also be rejected and rerouted through this maze of carceral welfare that still existed?

The day of the incident, Fukuda had contact with police and civil servants, none of whom gave him food or accompanied him to a safe place off the streets. Prison had trained him to obey commands, to accept what he was told, to fill the gaps with routine. For Fukuda, shaba must have seemed completely shattered and bewildering. But even while the words (and worlds) didn't quite come together in front of the crowd, in the end, he did appear content. Perhaps I just wanted it to be so. Perhaps I was also wanting this brokenness to be repaired.

In each of these cases, it appears that gaps in after-prison "reentry" support precipitated an escalation of criminal activity (from theft to assault and shoplifting to arson, respectively) and potentially avoidable reincarceration. Seen in the wider frame of processes of exclusion and containment, however, the "penal morality play and bureaucratic farce" of reentry lies within the logic of carceral circuitry, rather than outside it.[5] The same kind of "institutional thoughtlessness" around aging seen within prison, is reproduced in the welfare system outside. In David Garland's formulation of the penal-welfare nexus, both prison and welfare cooperated toward rehabilitative aims.[6] As the Japanese criminal justice system and the welfare system have become more punitive, I would argue that this nexus has remained, but its character has changed. Public welfare institutions have become so restrictive and anonymous that they are driving people away, while at the same time, prisons are becoming better equipped to provide care for frail and disabled older people. This new penal-welfare meshwork is a configuration where care and punishment exist together, and where the dominant ideological aim appears to be separation and containment through circulation. This is retribution, not only for a crime, but for being old and alone, the embodiment of "no future," or of a future that must not be recognized.[7]

Unsettleable Age

When Igarashi, Kei, and I arrived at Jī's house, the clothes still swung on hangers hooked over doorways. On the table in front of the TV was a half-empty bottle of tea, a pack of cigarettes, and what looked like envelopes and other papers. Aside from Jī's room, the kitchen and other rooms looked cleaner than I remembered, but Jī still seemed unsettled. His bags were still packed, and his bed was in the same place.

Formerly incarcerated older adults, like Jī, remain unsettled in ways that typical public assistance and welfare services do not always recognize, even several years after release. Once an arrest is made, the person becomes a subject of the criminal justice system, so social welfare agencies step away.[8] It is precisely because these institutions and services are *not* coordinated that complex cases of older adult offenders are never fully understood and evaluated from the kind of holistic and humanist perspective that Igarashi tried to cultivate. It was the institutional *disconnection* that created the older carceral subject as always fragmented, incomplete, and unattached—an *unsettleable* subject. This is not to say that formerly incarcerated older adults living with disabilities were passive in the face of carceral churn, only that the voice and form in which refusal manifested was itself fragmented and disjointed. As Jī tried to recover some sense of agency as his locus of control grew more and more attenuated, his efforts were sometimes met with confusion or hostility.

Jī's housemate greeted us at the door, looking exhausted. When I came in, he told me in a low voice that he had cleaned the room up a few days earlier, when Jī was sick.

> I woke up and came downstairs and something was smelling really awful and then I could see it looked like shit on the kitchen floor. Like there was shit from the bathroom to the bed and the heater was on full blast. He was saying that he was cold, so I guess it was like a fever, and I took his temperature and it was about 37 degrees. So anyway, I cleaned it all up. He had shit on his trousers so I just tossed them. Then had to help cleaning his backside and everything. He was looking really out of it, so we went to the hospital. Man, we had to wait forever. We got there about eight and didn't get seen until almost noon. They just took his temperature and said that they couldn't find anything else

wrong, so he just got something for the fever. Then he was feeling a bit better, asking me if it was ok to go and smoke and stuff.

As I listened to this story, I watched Jī. He still looked a little dazed and unsure about what was going on, but Igarashi didn't seem to pay attention, and greeted him only briefly before telling him to come to the kitchen table. Igarashi cleared off a corner of the small table and opened his laptop. Jī put on a pair of glasses and walked carefully to the table, limping a little with his left leg. He leaned on the back of a chair in front of the laptop as Igarashi started to explain the ledger on the screen detailing the money he had before the arrest, and the debt he owed.

The conversation was straightforward at first. There were rent and cleaning fees, and other damages to the apartment. Jī tried to explain what happened, how it wasn't his fault, but Igarashi dismissed these excuses, and in the end, Jī admitted that he caused the damage. Igarashi let out an exasperated laugh, saying, "You and I have to live in society, right? You can try to fight against this, but you're going to lose. You got to take responsibility for this."

Igarashi turned to the computer again, explaining that Jī was 45,646 yen in the red, but that Mother House would pay the debts for him and take a little from Jī's public assistance money each month to pay the loan back. "Listen, I'm sorry to put it this way," Igarashi told him sternly, "but you got caught and put into detention and went to court. Then your assistance was cut off. If it wasn't for that, none of this would have happened."

Igarashi didn't mention anything about the conversation in the car on the way over, where he passionately defended Jī and admonished the civil servant. His tone and attitude when talking to Jī was tough love. When Jī interrupted again, trying to explain to Igarashi that it was all because of S____ (another ex-offender that Jī met in the rehabilitation center after release) who had defrauded Jī of all his money, Igarashi had had enough. He heard the story already and had no interest in hearing it again. In a sudden temper, Jī stood up in front of Igarashi (rising a full head taller), as if getting ready for a fight, and Igarashi pushed out his chest and stepped in closer, daring him on.

IGARASHI: So all this business about S____ you just have to drop it, okay?
JĪ: But he stole my money!
IGARASHI: But there's no proof of any of that. If he had your bank passbook and signature stamp and did it legally, the police can't do anything about it. The detectives who looked at it said that you went to the bank together and you transferred the money over to him. That's it!

JĪ: Who's the piece of shit that said that?!

IGARASHI: The detective said it! He said it to you!

JĪ: He never said anything like that!

IGARASHI: He did say it! And I was there, and you just don't want to hear it! There's a statement and everything!

JĪ: He didn't—

IGARASHI: What? Listen! We got the police, they looked into it, there was no proof, that's it! Did you remember that? Did they talk to you?!

JĪ: They said something—

IGARASHI: What did they say?!

JĪ: I don't remember.

IGARASHI: You don't fucking remember! You don't remember! The detective told you right then, we can't do anything!

JĪ: They should do something.

IGARASHI: I'm not even a policeman! I'm not a detective, but I'm starting to think I can't believe this whole story of yours. I took everything you said as honest! I asked a lawyer about this, and they said if there's no proof you can't go further with it! That's it!

Igarashi's voice had become so elevated in that small kitchen that it felt like a spike pounding into my ears with each shout. Jī made a surprisingly intimidating show of anger himself, but the effort seemed to sap his strength almost as soon as it came, and as his protests were shouted down, he tottered backward and sat down again muttering to himself.

After a few minutes, the tension in the air relaxed, and as with the phone call earlier, Igarashi switched to his softer, more consoling tone. He told Jī that he could have a regular allowance and if he needed more, he could access his money, but that he also needed to think about how to budget. Igarashi also leveraged shame, reminding Jī of all the people who were trying to help him, including his housemate, who was standing next to me, still pinned to the wall. By the end of this lecture, Ji looked lost and bewildered, slumped at his kitchen table in his white undershirt and green shorts. Igarashi closed and packed up his laptop and Jī shuffled back to his seat in front of the television.

Jī's money was no longer his to control, nor did he have control over where he lived. He couldn't go to the bank or find the former friend who betrayed him and stole his money. Even his body reminded him with every painful step, how his life was no longer his to control. While he was not in prison, it was hard to see what kind of possibilities Ji had for building a new life, even with the support of Mother House. It is hard to know what Jī made of the confrontation with Igarashi that day. Afterward, when I mentioned it, he just told me that Igarashi likes to boss him around, but it didn't bother him too much. In the moment, however, when Jī literally stood up to Igarashi, shouting and threatening revenge, it was all he could do to somehow hold onto his own will, even though in the end, his fatigue and confusion, his age and frailty, left him unsettleable once again.

CHAPTER 7

Warm Heart, Cool Hands

By 2012, six years after the Shimonoseki train station arson, every prefecture in Japan (forty-seven in all) had at least one Community Livelihood Resettlement Support Centre (*chiiki seikatsu teichaku shien senta*). All of these centers are private corporations, commissioned by the prefectural authorities with central funding from the Japanese government.[1] The purpose of the centers was to close the gap in post-custodial welfare support for those with physical, intellectual, or psychological disabilities, or who were over the age of sixty-five, classified as "special adjustments" cases (*tokubetsu chōsei*). These individuals were alone, with no one such as a family member, to act as guarantor, and would therefore have served the entirety of their sentence in prison. A new feature of these Centers was that post-custody arrangements including housing, healthcare and seikatsu hogo (basic welfare allowance for those who are poor and unable to work) would be made in the months prior to release, so ex-offenders would immediately have a place to go and a care plan that would be consistent both with their needs and their preferences. Closing this gap is critical, since about half of the older adults who return to prison after reoffending do so within the first six months after.

As Community Resettlement Centers became more established, the number of cases they handled increased. Still, in 2020, these centers only managed a total of 1,486 cases nationally. This included 595 who were still incarcerated but whose cases were being assessed and 120 who decided to quit the service. Of the remaining 771 individuals, 342 were over sixty-five, or around one in five older ex-offenders released after serving a full sentence that year (1,627).[2] In addition to post-custody support, Community Resettlement Centers were also called on to assist in the introduction of "entry support" (*iriguchi shien*) meant to divert older and disabled offenders from prison before or during trial. This scheme is relatively new and implementation remains uneven across regions, yet numbers receiving this support have been far below the need.[3]

Although working in close coordination with state agencies to support broad government policy objectives, the Community Resettlement Center staff are placed in such a way that they must bridge between the inside and the outside, carefully guiding each client on their own path of resettlement. While the scheme was meant to be a cooperative partnership between prisons, probation offices, and the Ministry of Health Labor and Welfare, the fact that Community Resettlement Centers identified and operated as welfare agencies meant there were gaps where things did not always line up. Like staff at NPOs that focus on homelessness, the Resettlement Center staff did not use the term "recidivism prevention," or see it as their goal. As one member of staff remarked "We're not the Ministry of Justice, so we don't think about recidivism. We're a welfare organization. Our job is to ask 'how can we support this individual to live well?'" That said, the aims and measures of success set by the government are explicitly about preventing re-offense, and Centers are evaluated for results, so we cannot ignore this function entirely.

After weeks of taking in Igarashi's critical perspectives on official responses to ex-offender resettlement, and seeing for myself the conditions of places like San'ya, I initially approached these Centers with a cautious skepticism. At the same time, because of their targeted attention to older and disabled ex-offenders, Community Resettlement Centers seemed to be much more capable of handling complex cases than small, nonspecialist NPOs. While the forms of support offered by NPOs sometimes included linking individuals to more specialized facilities for those living with disabilities, most, like Mother House, did not have that expertise or capacity to handle the complex cases of older people. For some formerly incarcerated older adults then, the Community Resettlement Centers seemed to offer an ideal arrangement: not only did they provide support with housing, basic needs, and the bureaucracy of resettlement, but they could even arrange health and social care services. At the same time, depending on how they operated, the Centers could also be seen as an extension of the carceral, posing little challenge to the operation and ideology of the overall system of criminal justice while expediting the transfer of disabled and older people into other forms of confinement, such as nursing care homes, where poorly supervised conditions and precarious and overburdened staff have created their own conditions of neglect and abandonment.[4] How would Community Resettlement Centers not only provide basic support, but also foster places of dwelling (*ibasho*) where fragmented carceral subjects could encounter another way of being?

I started asking around to see if I could visit one of these Centers to see what they were like, and within a couple of weeks I had managed to find myself sitting in the back seat of a dark gray Toyota sedan, riding along with two staff members of a Resettlement Center, visiting clients. As we drove, we talked about both the practical and ideological operation of Community Resettlement, which one staff member called *"warm heart, cool hands."* In other words, it was good to be friendly toward the client, but when it came to decisions about their care plan, you had to think more pragmatically. If you let the feeling drive you, you end up encouraging the client to be dependent. Instead, keeping their hands cold meant offering just enough support for the client to become independent.

When we came to the topic of establishing trust between case workers and clients, I mentioned to the staff members that I had been working with Mother House and Igarashi, who tried to establish trust as a fellow ex-offender (*tōjisha*). The staff member in the passenger seat, dressed in a dark gray suit groaned, but chose his words carefully. His response exposed the friction produced between NPOs and Community Resettlement Centers despite having similar aims:

> YAMAZAKI: Mother House is, well, [Igarashi] is a *tōjisha*. He got out of [prison], and he thought that he wanted to do something and well, he's trying very hard, and doing fine for himself. But, you know, he's doing things in other people's backyards. He's not someone from these areas, but he thinks he's doing the right thing! [Always saying] "I'm doing the right thing, I know what's right!" But he gets a house and puts several people in the house somewhere and tells everyone to go there, but he hasn't negotiated with the community, so all these people move in and nobody around there understands what's going on! So you've gotta think about that. So maybe what he says is right, but the *relationships* are thin.
>
> JASON: Yes, and there are some in the community who get along with him and some who don't.
>
> YAMAZAKI: Wherever he's put these houses there's always been a big uproar. The welfare office and a lot of other places don't get along with him. I

mean, I don't think that what he's doing is wrong. But he's pushy. Really pushy. And if you're like that, well, people [in the community] start saying that they won't ever let someone [resettle ex-offenders in the community] again. And so at some point in the future, that could make things harder for us. The way we do things is we'll say something to the community members like "Look, it's no problem if these people come to live in your community, right? What's the difference between you and them? If they are given a chance, they do well, it's just that when they were small, they were the victims." When we get the community to understand that, they open up. So places that have provided accommodations once will say "we'll do it again, we're happy to." Then the trust (*chakujitsu*) can spread. But if we don't do that, then when I'm gone, what's going to happen? It can't be about me. It's about the fact that we've established this trust between institutions through our policies, and so whoever is doing this job can continue on the way it is.

JASON: Yes, makes sense for sustainability.

YAMAZAKI: So, to be honest, I wonder how [Mother House] is going to carry on if they keep using the same technique. I worry. If that person (Igarashi) goes away, what happens?

This question about what Yamazaki called "sustainability" makes an important distinction between organizations driven by the charismatic personality of the leadership, and those organized through long-term relationship-building. Both, as Yamazaki mentions, can have similar intentions and can do good, and both have their limits. Mother House's limitations when it came to formerly incarcerated older adults might necessitate different tactics and community partnerships than he had made in the past. Unlike Mother House, the Community Resettlement Centers did not try to create a community or a place of belonging for formerly incarcerated people, nor were they interested at all in spiritual or religious matters, but they did attempt to make different arrangements for individuals based on their preferences, such as where they wanted to live, or what kind of care they wanted. While some individuals might occasionally develop friendships with their case workers, these relationships had clearer boundaries, and clients never visited the office or hung out together as they did at Mother House or NPOs in San'ya.

The director, Suzuki, passed me the client file and talked me through it as we made our way to a residential long-term care home. As I looked over the chart, I could see that the client was seventy years old, and had been in and out of prison numerous times over his life, but it was particularly frequent after the age of sixty. He had an intellectual disability and some chronic physical problems, such as diabetes. Suzuki joked that they went out of their way to find a facility that allowed residents to drink alcohol and smoke, but the client had recently stopped both, so it no longer mattered. He swiveled around in his seat, taking the file back.

"They also took him to the doctor recently and found cancer in his lungs," he continued, "But even though we've tried explaining this to him, we're not totally sure he understands everything. It doesn't seem to be progressing very quickly, and, well, he's up there in age. The thing is if he decides that he doesn't want to do the surgery after all, that's up to him, and we'll support him through that decision. If he talks to the doctor and really understands the situation and decides to get surgery, we'll support that too. The important thing is that *we're* not making the decision about what's best."

This attitude of "warm heart, cool hands" was evident when we went to visit Omuro-san, who was placed in a large for-profit residential care home. The local community association approved of Omuro-san moving into the home and helped to provide financial support.

Omuro: Everyday Is Long

The lobby was clean and spacious with bright alpine landscape paintings hung above the hand rails along the walls. We were met at the entrance by a woman in a tan suit and stylish glasses, who introduced herself as the head of the care home, greeting Suzuki like an old friend before giving her brief report on Omuro and his adjustment to the new environment.

Omuro soon appeared, moving slowly but unaided, and the five of us sat together on rose-colored chairs in a corner of the room. We all smiled and made small talk as if we were ordinary visitors, just coming in for a leisurely friendly chat. Still Omuro, who was released about half a year prior to our meeting, seemed nervous at first and avoided eye contact.

For the Resettlement Support Center staff and the director, this was an opportunity to get a sense of how Omuro had been settling in and if there was any need to make adjustments in his care plan. The care home director and the younger resettlement center staff member both seemed to be trying a little too hard to lighten the mood with jokes and questions and big smiles. Suzuki, on the other hand, listened. There was a quiet intensity to his listening, and when he spoke, he would bring our attention back to a series of phrases used by Omuro, and then ask what was really important.

Even when we were only talking about Omuro's career as a fisherman or his strategies in Pachinko, Suzuki was thinking about how to learn from these hints to integrate more meaning into his care services.

I was most interested in what it felt like for Omuro to adjust from prison to life in the care home. While residents were not locked into the home, those like Omuro, who had no friends or family to visit, had neither the means nor a reason to leave. Compared to life on the inside, the care home was boring:

JASON: Now that you're here, you've got a lot of free time then?
OMURO: Now I'm bored.
JASON: How do you spend your days?
OMURO: Well, what do I do? I watch TV. There's nothing to do. I want to work but . . . [long pause] If you work then the day is short.
JASON: You want to have a job?
OMURO: I want to work. I don't like to just be still. Something to keep my hands busy. Even some little jobs that I could do (*naishoku*). If you have a job, then the day goes quickly.
JASON: Are the days long here?
OMURO: Every day is long.

The home director, Takeda, turned to me with a serious look on her face, clearly not pleased with Omuro's review. "We thought, is he going to gamble or drink or something? We worried, but really there's nothing. He's living such a nice quiet life, aren't you?" Omuro nodded, still gazing down at the table.

She then asked about his family, which seemed odd to me, since she must have known that he had broken off contact with them.

TAKEDA: Do you want to see your wife and children?
OMURO: I'd like to see them, but they won't have anything to do with me, so. Next time they see me will be when I die maybe. I think I'd like to talk with them, but (tearing up)—old age comes before you know it. Just like that! Before you know it.

When he began thinking about his family, Omuro's emotions finally arose through the dull, dry crust of boredom that had settled on him. Although he had given up on seeing his wife and children, as well as his older brother who he used to be close to when he was younger, the thought of them was heartbreaking. He has completely lost contact, he had become *muen*.

The director changed subjects again, instead asking questions about his arrest. Omuro's main problem seemed to be gambling, which drove him into debt and led him to start stealing. He explained that when he had friends, he didn't have problems with the police. He only got into trouble when he was alone.

TAKEDA: Omuro-san, I've never asked you before, but you've been caught by the police lots of times. When you were caught by the police, what sort of thing did you think about? Did you talk to someone about it?
OMURO: I didn't have friends.
TAKEDA: Alone.
OMURO: I was by myself.
TAKEDA: I see.
OMURO: When I was with other people, I had money.
TAKEDA: You had times when you got away with it? So you thought you'd keep on doing it, but your luck run out. But you're not alone right? There are lots of staff around for you.
OMURO: Yeah they are I guess.
JASON: Do you have anyone you can talk to now?
OMURO: No one. I can't make conversation with anyone.
JASON: Can't make a conversation?
SUZUKI: Is it okay if I ask something? We've been having such a nice conversation today about your work on the fishing boat, about pachinko and where you were from and so on, but I never heard you mention anything about friends. Has it always been hard to make friends? Since you were little?
OMURO: Right.

We spoke with Omuro a little longer, and Suzuki suggested to the home director that they could discuss some way to offer a chance to do some work. As he left, Suzuki tried to leave things optimistic, saying "I know it takes time, but perhaps in a year or so, you'll be able to see some of your family again."

Before we left, Suzuki and I took the elevator up to Omuro's room on the third floor. There was a common area with tables and chairs, but none of the other residents appeared to be around. The atmosphere was still and quiet, reminding me of the silence of the Japanese prison. A couple of residents had left their doors ajar, but were nowhere to be seen.

Omuro's room, which measured about three times as large as most *doya*, was spotless. The duvet was spread neatly across the bed, and a pair of white slippers were lined up together on the floor at one end. There were no photographs of family or drawings made by grandchildren as we could see in the other rooms as we passed. The walls were bare. The only decoration, a pink plastic flower, was given to Omuro-san by the staff so that he could be sure that it was his room, and he wasn't lost.

We stood in the doorway, near the sink. Along the broad edge of the sink was a yellow plastic cup, a bar of soap, a disposable razor, a green toothbrush placed bristles-down hanging over the sink rim, and a half-used tube of toothpaste on which he had written his prisoner number and his name. The number had a way of bringing the prison into the room. It seemed to make the complete absence of other expressions of identity or relationships even more painful.

Nakai: "You Can Do It, Dad"

Family, which was such an emotionally painful topic for Omuro, was also important to another client of the Community Resettlement Center, who we visited on another ride-along occasion. Like Igarashi, Suzuki also recognized the ways problems in the family often set the stage for criminal behavior later in life, and conceived of rehabilitation as a process that depends on a motherly approach. He explained,

> It takes time to work with [formerly incarcerated older people], to reassure them. We can't be their mother, but if they don't have someone who will protect them the way a mother does, it won't work out. I think that's the most important thing.

Suzuki continued with reference not to a spiritual or transcendent power of the mother, but rather the developmental psychological importance:

> Psychologists call it attachment disorder. This is really big. They've just never fit in everyday society. Their mother who would never keep their promises, parents who weren't around when they were needed, parents who would punish them if they said anything. They've just figured out how to act in response to that sort of environment. So in some sense we might think they're strong for being able to live homeless and on their own, but in society—they have absolutely no strength to live as a member of society.

Like a "good mother," Suzuki envisioned the role of resettlement first as a matter of accepting the person regardless of their past. This he saw as the difference between the welfare and the penal institutions. Formerly incarcerated older people who received assistance from Resettlement Centers did not have guarantors, but in a few rare case, they did maintain a slender spider's thread of connection with some of their adult children and held onto a hope that these children would take them back some day. While ex-offenders often expressed a deep wish to apologize and make amends to those hurt by their crimes, this was usually impossible and in serious cases, inadvisable. However, when it came to children, apologies could be voiced more freely, and some form of amends could be made.

Our first stop of the day was to visit Nakai, a sixty-eight-year-old man who was recently rehoused with another formerly incarcerated man in a shared three-room apartment outside of Tokyo. I sat in the back seat of the gray Toyota sedan, while two staff members from the Community Resettlement Support Centre rode in the front, talking about different client cases and where to get a good bowl of noodles for lunch. Nakai's "follow-up" visit with Nakai would also involve seeing a doctor and filling a prescription for treatment for alcoholism. Suzuki flipped through the notes in the case file before looking back at me: "People who need hospitals are especially difficult for us." I asked if the hospitals often refused to see ex-offenders, and Suzuki explained,

> These are people who don't have anything. No family, no guarantor. Nothing. So, when that's the case, it's not easy for the hospital to process you. They don't want to take you. There's nowhere to go. One of the guys we are going to visit has some experience as yakuza, but his body is fit and he wants to work. So, we've found a social enterprise farm, and they have a little garden, and he's doing what he can to help out with that.

Despite these arrangements, however, Suzuki was concerned, since the man's housemate was another formerly incarcerated individual who had a problematic past with gambling and alcohol addiction and who was not in recovery. While Nakai has been able to stay clean and sober so far, he has had some tense confrontations with his roommate, and the two have been trying to avoid each other. It hasn't been easy in such a small apartment when neither one has regular work. Nakai opened the heavy brown metal door of the apartment, the last in a row of four on the second floor of an old stucco building that has turned a yellowy beige with time. A clear plastic umbrella hung on its blue hooked handle from the windowsill beside the door. Nakai was dressed in a quilted navy vest over a thick flannel shirt and black track suit trousers. The light gray hair cut close around a pair of pendulous ears, matched the color of his long, wispy eyebrows. Like Chiba (Chapter 1), Nakai's experience of prison started earlier in life, and he spent many years moving in and out. Being a member of the yakuza meant that he had a kind of family to return to, one that would understand and accept (even praise) his history of incarceration. Yet even when he left the yakuza, he continued getting arrested.

> NAKAI: I used to work in restaurants, a lot of jobs handling knives. Then somewhere along the way, not sure how really, I got onto another path. The yakuza path. That was a long one for me. At first, I thought that yakuza were cool, I really looked up to them. All the films with the cars and money and stuff— that was in my head. (How old were you?) When I got into the yakuza? Uh, about twenty-two or twenty-three. I'd been to the prison lots of time. Then I left the yakuza and ended up back in prison. I thought this was the end of it. But I started doing bad things like stealing.
> JASON: What did you do—I mean, what were the types of crime that you were convicted of when you were in the yakuza?
> NAKAI: Mostly, extortion. I never robbed or committed rape or murder. But aside from that, I did it all. (O: Did you use a knife?) When I'd get drunk, I'd get a knife out and wave it around, and even though I didn't attack anyone, it looked like I was threatening people, and I'd get picked up. Even going right up to the police station. All that stupid stuff I did. I was out of control. I'm not like that now.
> SUZUKI: Now you're really pleasant.
> YAMAZAKI: Yes, you seem like you are the nicest person, just really gentle.
> NAKAI: Really?
> YAMAZAKI: Yes, you make me want to be gentler (laughs).
> JASON: Do you feel like you've changed?
> NAKAI: I do! Before, I'd go to a (rehabilitation) facility and it was just another institution. All these people, it was too much and there was no one to look after you. They just order you. But if someone says to me, "go here, go there," I'm going to think, "I'm never going to go there!", right? I'm human, so that's how I think. But now I think, "oh I should go to the hospital but I don't want to"—but I also knew that the [Center staff] would come and pick me up, so that just helps a lot. I'm not really one who likes to talk a lot, but being with all of you and talking like this, makes me feel it's nice to talk (O: It is good now and then)

Nakai's life hasn't been easy, but his disobedience to authority is, at least in part, a consequence of fear and shame. When others had tried to help in the past, he had a habit of running away. But things had eventually caught up with him.

Once we arrived at the clinic, we left it to the Center staff to meet and discuss things with the doctor. Nakai walked to the end of the waiting area, to a room made of plexi-glass walls, and lit a cigarette. I took a seat near Nakai and asked about his family, who, according to the file, lived up north.

> NAKAI: I have a son and daughter. I've a grandchild that's about to be born. My son said to me "If you mess up and go back to prison, we're done." Until now they have looked after me. They'd found a place for me to stay, helped me get the TV and electricity set up. When I went to prison, I lost all that. This time, on the phone with my son. "Dad, this is the last!" and I said "you're my only child that will look out for me." And I really believe that was my last, so that's why I'm here now.
>
> JASON: Before, you never made a promise like that?
>
> NAKAI: No, I just went off to prison like it was no big deal. My children never said anything like that to me either. I never heard them say something like "My dad's a yakuza I want you to stop it." This time they told me "Dad, you have to quit yakuza and you have to quit drinking! If you don't, I don't want to see you again!"

Nakai's voice broke and quivered as tears began to pool in his eyes. Soon they are pouring down his cheeks. I don't know if I started crying because of his story, or because it was so easy to feel Nakai's pain and fragility as he sat, so close. I reached out and put a hand on his shoulder.

> NAKAI: I'm doing my best. I'm coming here, trying to get better.
>
> JASON: When you were in prison, did they come to see you?
>
> NAKAI: They never came, but they did send letters. I wanted them to come, but it was a long way from [where they live] to [the prison]. It costs a lot. The grandchild has school as well, so they sent letters. Getting letters is nice. (Crying again) it makes me so happy! However many times I read them, I still weep! There are people who never get any letters. I read those letters so many times.
>
> JASON: Of course, it's so important to know that someone like family or someone special is out there thinking about you. Do you still have some hope of seeing your son and grandchild?

NAKAI: I'm looking forward to it. As soon as I can quit drinking and get my life back together (crying). I don't know if I can do it.

JASON: It's like you've come to see what's really most important to you?

NAKAI: (crying) I just wish that I could hug them. (Long pause) The biggest thing for me now is my children telling me, "You can do it, Dad!"

JASON: "You can do it, Dad."

NAKAI: It's the hardest thing I've ever done. I'm just so grateful. I can't believe all these tears are falling.

JASON: Do you think about the past?

NAKAI: The past is just so many terrible things, so I just pretend it's not there. The way I treated my family, my friends, all the bad things that happened. This is really the last time for me. If I drink again and go back to prison, I really don't think I'm coming out. That's how I feel. Now I think about my children. I don't want to show them that side of me.

I asked Nakai what he would most want people to know about prison in Japan. "Going back to prison would be easy! If I wanted to, I could go right back there tomorrow" he told me. "Staying out here in society like this, that's the hardest." I asked what he did every day to keep himself busy. He regained his composure and explained why life in shaba was still hard, the monotony, the difficulty connecting with other people, the constant feeling of his past haunting his present, closing off his ability to build a new life.

I go to sleep around 11 or 12, wake up at 8 a.m., make breakfast and watch some TV, make lunch, make dinner— the same thing, like that every day. I'm still only sixty-eight, so I'd like to get a part-time job or something, but with this medication and everything, it's not so easy. And it's hard to be around people. I can't just talk freely like this. If I went around telling people that I had been in the yakuza and all that, they wouldn't want to have anything to do with me.

I could work in the garden, but no one talks to me. It must be because I'm a person with tattoos. So, the conversation ends up being kind of limited. They think, oh, he's a former yakuza, he must be a scary person. But I'm not like that. That's how I feel. So, I get sad about that. Judging me just because I have tattoos. And then I'm older. So, people think who knows when he's going to have problems.

I have enough money for food, but now it's getting colder and I don't have any warm clothes. I've got to get a heater or something. It's going to be freezing in that room. The thing I'm most unhappy with is I want to live on my own. The guy that I live with is a gambler. He gambles, every day. I used to gamble myself, it's a kind of sickness, just like alcohol. So, we don't get along, we're fighting all the time. I asked the landlord, and they just said, "that's how it is," so I just said, I just won't say anything else. If I try to fight, I'm going to lose. If I do that, they'll call the cops and I'll be back in prison. So, I just have to endure. I just don't talk to him if I can avoid it.

After picking up Nakai's medication, we drove to a second-hand clothing shop that Suzuki was familiar with, and the four of us browsed down the aisles for warmer clothes. The shopping trip felt like an ordinary activity, something that one might do along with family. But I couldn't help but feel that the staff lingering around in their suits and ties made Nakai a conspicuous customer.

Formerly incarcerated older adults like Omuro-san experienced loneliness and social disconnection over the life course, but as family relationships and work became out of reach due to age and criminal history, there were no new relationships to take their place. Prison life may have instilled habits of cleanliness and order, but it crippled his sense of self and ability to communicate with others. For those who already struggled with relationships prior to incarceration, or who, like Jī, were living with a disability that made communication difficult, prison hollowed out an already fragile world. Despite the limited successes of Community Resettlement Support Centers, even individuals like Omuro and Nakai struggled with life in care facilities, and particularly the alienation and loneliness caused by the habituation of prison routines and stigma faced by revealing one's past. Suzuki and the Center staff admitted that while the arrangement was not perfect, the care was good, and over time, they would accept this new life style. But while they were settled on paper, they remained unsettled, disconnected, *muen*.

CHAPTER 8

Wounded Kinships

Carceral circuits work by separating individuals not just from public life, but also from any sense of a redeemable past and from any form of livable future, reducing them to the status of deviants, and containing them within cycles of structural violence. For older adults, social isolation was the single most significant factor predicting incarceration, and once they were in the carceral circuit, their isolation deepened. If the first insight I took from the experiences of formerly incarcerated older adults was that carceral circuits operated across the prison-welfare continuum, the second was that carceral isolation was constructed, controlled, and reproduced in parallel and mutually exclusive to constructions of the family. This is not to say that the solution to Japan's aging prison population is a return to "traditional family" values, but rather that the labor of carceral exclusion produces the social imaginary of a traditional family itself.

The closer I looked at the rise in social isolation and incarceration of older people, the more I kept running into the family, or rather, its absence. Whether I was listening to stories of older adults' lives prior to incarceration or after, the absent presences of the family haunted both personal narratives and the bureaucratic architecture of carceral circuits. To rephrase Saidiya Hartman's claim that "slavery is the ghost in the machine of kinship," in Japan, kinship seemed to be the ghost in the machine of the carceral.[1]

The ghost of kinship haunted the dark and silent corridors of San'ya's cheap one-room *doya* accommodations. One afternoon, the staff member I was shadowing led me through the empty lobby of one of the *doya* houses on our way to visit an older client, when my eye was caught by a pink plastic toy cash register sitting on a table next to a black ashtray and a roll of toilet paper. The bright colors were sickly sweet against the backdrop of mismatched browns—the floor, walls and furniture—but even more jarring was the way the toy brought childhood, and by association, the family into a space where both were extremely rare. I asked my guide if he knew of any families in the building, but he told me that he had never seen one. I tried asking the older man we visited, but he did not know of any families either. The abandoned toy, like its absent family, remained a haunting presence. After we left, I asked the staff member how he thought the absence of family impacted formerly incarcerated older people. His reply underlined the complex ways that family and isolation were intertwined across the carceral circuit:

> The reason that the number of older prisoners has risen is because they're all alone (*hitori bochi*). For example, you might have an older person, okay? Living in a nice household with grown up children and maybe grandchildren or something, and they're looking out for the older family members. Now, let's say that grandpa steals some rice wine (*sake*). In that case, they get caught by the policeman but then some of the family would go to the shop owner and the son or daughter go and apologize and talk to them and offer some kind of compensation (*benshō*). But the grandad has already been arrested. Now the policeman has to decide if they are going to take it further or not, and they might see that person has a family and a house to go back to and everything so there's no need to go to a judge after all and they can be released (*fukiso*). So they won't go to jail. Because he had a family supporting him. The reason that older prisoners are increasing is that they go out and steal the wine, but they don't have a family. So then, who is going to apologize or give compensation? Who is going to support that person? There's no one to do that. So, there is nothing they can do but arrest them, charge them, and if they go to court, they'll be found guilty, right? So now that person is going to prison. What is the difference? The person who has family, even if they break the law, won't go to prison. The person who doesn't have family is going to go to prison. The reason there are so many older prisoners now is because they are all alone. Even when they come out, they're still alone, so they do it again, and back again. So then that keeps going on and on. The reason is because older people alone have increased and there is not enough support for them. It's not because there is a huge increase in crime or Japanese people are a bunch of criminals!

While not every family is willing to ask the police and courts to commute a sentence, the staff member's narrative implies that the carceral system is just as much about disciplining families as it is about punishing the isolated. The two functions worked hand in hand, each reinforcing the other. This was a story that other NPO staff knew as well, especially if they were called by the police, as Igarashi was when Jī was arrested, to stand in the role of the family member, taking on responsibility for the care and resettlement of the accused. With the numbers of solitary-dwelling older people in the community climbing rapidly across Japan, the staff member's story demands serious consideration. It implies not only that the family remains deeply embedded within the Japanese penal-welfare system, but that it is the absent presence, the ghost of family, that propels the older carceral subject along the circuitous path from prison to community and back again.

As intergenerational kinship ties have grown thinner and more uncertain, more people spend later life alone. From 1998 to 2018, the number of older Japanese people (65+) living alone tripled to more than six million households (21 percent of older women and 13 percent of older men), with predictions of continued increases to close to nine million by 2024 (about one in four older women and one in five older men).[2] Living alone has become increasingly easier over the years, as many of us realized during Covid-19 lockdown periods, with groceries and everyday items brought to the door by delivery services. The Japanese long-term care insurance (LTCI) system that began in 2000 also promoted home-based care, or "aging in place," as a means of reducing both the need for unpaid family care or residential institutional care. In the LTCI system, benefits were prioritized for older people living alone, meaning that living apart from family members (whether they were involved in caring or not) was actually being incentivized by the government. Similarly, Public Assistance for Livelihood Protection allowances are calculated on the basis of household units (the assumption being that co-residence implies shared resources and mutual care), rather than on the basis of each separate individual's circumstance. Living with family members who were earning an income could bring down the total amount of benefit allowance received by the older person. As neoliberal retrenchment of the welfare state has led to a "post-welfare" society, familialism has returned to an empty home.[3]

Not everyone who lives alone feels lonely or disconnected from others, but for a large proportion of those living alone (especially men), solitude can be profound; weeks may pass without speaking to anyone. The Japanese Cabinet Office Survey of older people's housing and living conditions reported that in 2018, more than 70 percent of solitary dwelling older men felt they had no one they could depend on (with the proportion increasing for those who were unmarried and/or in poor health).[4] Loneliness has become a growing concern in Japan, not only for older people, but across ages and generations as uncertainties and anxieties seep in through the cracks of a life course that has become despairing and fragmented.[5]

The mutually reinforcing links between age, family problems, isolation, incarceration, welfare, poverty, and homelessness that trap individuals in carceral circuits was glaringly obvious to the staff members of NPOs assisting unhoused people. When I asked about the referrals received from Community Resettlement Centers, a staff member at one of the NPOs told me she estimated that for around 90 percent of the cases they see, there is a history of "complicated family problems." She then laid out the pattern of cascading disadvantages and increasing marginalization at each step:

> [Usually] The family was poor, or they were raised by a single parent, there was abuse. Feels like most of them have had it hard. From there, they can't crawl out from under that. For example, they won't go to school, they don't enter society because they're carrying this wound in their *kokoro* (heart), and it just keeps going, you know? Then when they're old, it really eats them up and they're lots living on the streets and stuff like that. For people who were raised in that kind of environment, recovery is really hard.

In this narrative, the "complicated" family returns in old age as a wound that will not heal, perpetually exposed to the world and the "cold winds of shaba." The wound "eats them up," hollowing out the world from the inside, isolating them from the capacity to be with others. Age and a history of incarceration made it even more difficult to "crawl out from under" the weight of disadvantage, cutting them off from both the social field of production (i.e., education and work) as well as the field of reproduction (maintaining a stable family of one's own); they became "ordinary refugees" of Japan's post-welfare society.[6]

This chapter examines the ways non-kin actors such as NPO staff, perform family in ways that go beyond the practical role of mediating between carceral institutions and the ex-offender in times of crisis. Becoming like family meant cultivating mutuality of care and dependence, the relational analog of making a house a "home."[7] Becoming family gave ex-offenders the chance to rewrite their story about what it meant to carry this wound, to create spaces of belonging and mutual care.

Compared to the "warm heart, cool hands" approach of the Community Resettlement Center, becoming a family entailed a deeper sense of responsibility and risk. Another concern was that in acting as a substitute for the family, volunteers and staff of NPOs could be seen as complicit in the very familialist logic that produced the exclusion of older people. It was difficult to challenge a penal-welfare structure based on the idea of family while acting like a family. Instead, organizations like Mother House were attempting to reimagine and embody forth a new incarnation of the family, one that was purged of the carceral logic of hierarchical authority and the enclosure of rights and property within lineages. Instead, they embraced family as an inclusive, multigenerational body situated in local places of belonging, and founded on alternative forms of relationality (*en*) and common identity generated through lived experience of tōjisha and practices of care.

Carceral kinship observed in places like the US and Brazil, or among Indigenous and First Nations communities around the world, where experiences of incarceration are shared across generations have also been viewed as both an inheritance of violence and a foundation for resistance.[8] In contrast, Mother House members had no blood-ties to one another, nor were generational histories of incarceration part of their individual or shared narratives. They did, however, embrace many of the emotional and strategic elements observed in other forms of carceral kinship, such as the combination of both reformist and radical strategies, the use of the symbolic power of the mother, and a "love-politics" rooted in care and mutual vulnerability.[9] In addition, elements of Japanese kinship, such as bonds of *en* and ties to the spirits of the dead mingle with other religious and spiritual practices, situating these carceral kinships in a local cultural space. By reframing Mother House as a place to reimagine the family and generate fugitive worlds of care rather than merely an organization focused on the narrow aim of preventing recidivism, I consider the possibility of escape from ageist carceral circuits.

Ghosts of Kinship

About one month after he had left the detention facility, Mother House moved Jī to a new rented house in a small residential neighborhood surrounded by quiet farms. At a moderate pace, it would take me about twenty minutes to walk from the vicinity of the train station, where most of the shops were located, to Jī's house. Jī couldn't walk that far on his own, and the bus to the station came only once an hour. I usually picked up a bag of food from the supermarket on my way over, selecting a mix of some of his favorite comfort foods like instant noodles along with some fresh fruit and vegetable side dishes that he did not make as often.

As I let myself in through the front door, I could hear the television in the next room, the volume turned up louder than usual. On one side of the entrance were Jī's blue clogs, and in the opposite corner, a collection of umbrellas and Jī's cane. Jī was the only one home, as he was most days since being resettled again. Although Kei had moved in with Jī, he had found part-time work, and between that and his volunteering at Mother House, he was busy most days, sometimes spending nights at Mother House to save on commuting. If he was going to be away, he would ask one of the other tōjisha to stop and check in on Jī.

The kitchen was clean and uncluttered, but that was most likely because it was rarely used. When I opened the refrigerator to put away the things I brought, the only food inside was a bottle of mayonnaise and a large plastic tub of kimchi.

Jī spent his days in the front room of the house, since his leg pain made climbing stairs dangerous. It was the only room in the house designed in a traditional Japanese style, with sliding paper doors and a floor of interlocking tatami mats. The walls were the color of wet sand and rough to the touch, while the support beams were smooth, straight and an unpainted blonde wood-grain. The contrast between the two gave an illusion of depth in the small space.

A large sliding door provided a floor to ceiling window out onto the small garden, which was little more than dirt and rock, hidden behind a cinder block wall. Next to this window was another glass door, the outer shutters drawn closed, so the glass reflected the room. Jī's bed, equipped with remote controlled posture adjustment and grab handles was provided by the social welfare service, and occupied most of the room. The bubblegum pink sheets and blankets softened the intrusive feeling of this oversized contraption in a space otherwise dominated by warm, natural materials and textures.

Jī's room did not bear the impressions and stains of years of habitation. It was a temporary shelter, a site of dis-settlement. No need to clean or to pretend it was a home, no need to make attachments or drink from a real glass, no point in filing papers away, no one was coming over anyway. I wanted to ask if he thought that this might be his last home, but I wanted to be careful about being too direct on the subject of dying. "It's hard to think about what's going to happen as you get older, isn't it?" I started, "You never know how many years you have left." I let him think about this for a moment, hoping he understood where I was going.

"Two years!" he suddenly announced abruptly, like a door shut slamming shut.

"Two years?" I repeated, a little stunned. "You're saying that you figure you have only two years left (to live)?"

"Two years," he said again, this time in a softer voice.

"Well, who knows?" I said, starting to recover, "Maybe we can meet again in two years and see?"

A long pause followed. He didn't offer any additional explanation. I didn't press him. We let the silence pool up again. Two years seemed arbitrary at the time, like he had given himself a sentence to serve, like he was still "doing time," even on the outside. Was it hopeful or pessimistic? What kind of time was "two years"?

Jī sat on the edge of the bed, facing the window at the front. Usually he would face the reflecting side, sitting for long moments staring at himself. Before either turning to his left to watch television, or to his right, where a low table was covered with papers, envelopes, medication packages, a calendar, a half-full tub of pickled plums, a pair of scissors, and a comb. The objects, like his life story, reflected a fragmentation rather than an assemblage. They were all pieces of life that had lost their sense of order or relationship to each other, shuffled around in an arbitrary pile.

In front of Jī was a wooden chair that he used as a table for his meals, often simply white rice mixed with kimchi, plums, or some other garnish, or a bowl of instant ramen. The packaging from his meals was collected in a clear plastic bag underneath the chair. Jī drank cold tea out of an aluminum can that used to contain pineapple chunks, according to the label, the rough edges where the lid was cut off still visible around the rim. A box of Lark cigarettes and a lighter were set next to the can.

Jī did not elaborate on why he thought he only had two years left, instead switching on the television. The quiet of the room was broken sharply by the young and happy actors on the commercials, selling vacations or luxury homes. They were commercials I'd seen many times before, but the bright, enthusiastic images were even stranger than usual when viewed next to Jī. He changed the channel to the sumo tournament, and since we had both been following it closely this year, we talked about who each of us thought was likely to move up in rank and who might be demoted. The slow, steady, ritualistic pace of the tournament fit the atmosphere of the room much better than the manic sensory flood of the commercials. As each wrestler swaggered and squatted, the tension would build up until it would suddenly erupt in a colossal smashing of skin against skin. In seconds, the bout would be over, and the slow pacing of the next pair would resume the rhythm. Watching sumo with Jī was almost hypnotic.

Apart from his commentaries on sumo, however, I continued to struggle to understand Jī's speech. When I asked him to repeat something, he would say it over and over while I repeated what I thought I had heard. Sometimes we would figure it out. Other times I would let him go on, thinking that I would figure it out after he had said a few more words. He could get frustrated if I pushed too far. His tongue seemed thick in his mouth like a ball of cotton wool. His lips never quite constricted enough, the words tumbled out, soft and choppy and wet. After a few sentences, we would just sit in silence and rest. Jī would sometimes put on his glasses and find a piece of paper that had been in the pile on the table next to his bed. It would be a letter from the ward office, or something from his doctor or pharmacist. Jī would hold the paper in his hands, reading it slowly, then put it back on the table. It was part of his routine, his ritual, the way sumo wrestlers would stretch or toss handfuls of salt in the air before settling into position.

Just beyond the table of papers, propped against the wall, was a large color photograph in a simple black frame of a woman who seemed close to Jī's age. Next to the portrait, was a brown glass vase with sakaki branches covered in deep green leaves, and a bundle of incense sticks next to a burner. It was a funeral portrait of his mother, and one of the few personal possessions he kept.

JASON: I see you have a photo of your mother there.
JĪ: I look like her, don't I?
JASON: Will you be buried with her? After you die, have you thought about what will happen to your remains?
JĪ: Nothing.
JASON: You won't be put anywhere?
JĪ: *Muen-botoke* [a disconnected ghost].
JASON: If you become a *muen-botoke*, that will be so lonely!
JĪ: It's fine.
JASON: Really?
JĪ: I don't need any fuss.
JASON: Now, do you feel *muen* already?
JĪ: I've lost contact with my siblings, my daughter. So I'm *muen-botoke*. I don't have a child to take care of me.
JASON: (checking to make sure I understood) A child?

JĪ: A child. A child—I don't have a household. No one to carry on. So I'm *muen-botoke*.

Jī's insistence that he and his mother would become disconnected ghosts on the one hand seemed to foreclose on any hope of resettling in the world, while on the other, it bound his fate even closer to that of his mother's, the two of them connected in their disconnection. Indeed, if Jī was the last of his household lineage left to care for the spirit of his mother, building new forms of kin-like connections with Kei or others at Mother House might feel like abandoning her, his last connection to his life before prison.

For others, the prospect of becoming *muen-botoke* did not pose such fraught decisions. For isolated older people leaving prison, creating bonds of connection (*en*) with others that will continue after death provides both comfort regarding the end of life and the sense of being valued while still living. One of the most moving scenes in the documentary about Fukuda (the man arrested for the Shimonoseki arson described in Chapter 6) was one in which staff were explaining to Fukuda that they had secured a place for his remains in an ossuary (*nōkotsudo*), and would continue to look after them. When Fukuda realized what this meant, he began wiping the stream of tears from his face, overcome with emotion. "I'm not disconnected (*muen*) anymore!" he smiled triumphantly.

Even in places like San'ya, where everyday sociality is marked by precarity, invisibility, and uncertainty, NPOs, clergy, and community members have pooled their efforts to establish ways for the deceased to be reintegrated into the fabric of social memory by establishing new gravesites and rituals.[10] For Jī, being *muen* left him without the security of post-death ceremonies, a ghost in waiting, with little to direct or project back into the present moment. But there was the image, the photograph of his mother. Constant and watchful, a face like his own, mirroring his own fate, the image of his mother was the last thin line of connection to the world and to the just bearable life.[11]

Mother

"Man, look at you all!"

Arisa, Igarashi's wife, was passing through the cafe where I happened to be working on a laptop alongside three other men. "This looks like the front of a yakuza office with all of you in here like this!" she half-joked, setting her bags of groceries on the table.

"Especially you, Tatsu!" she went on, pointing at the assistant manager, who was seated with his feet on his desk, fanning himself. He was an intimidating figure, gruff-voiced, shaved head, with a face usually twisted into a scowl. Arisa pointed at the folding fan. It was white, with the Chinese character meaning "Love" written on one side in black calligraphy.

"Look at your fan, that's just the sort of thing a yakuza boss would wave around, don't you think? They're crazy about calligraphy like 'love,' or 'loyalty' stuff like that."

Tatsu frowned, but Arisa kept on going. She laughed and struck a tough pose as if she was in a Japanese gangster movie. Tatsu finally relented. "Give me a break, will you?" he pleaded, cracking a smile. Relieved, the rest of us all had a laugh at this petite mother of three, her hair tied back in a long ponytail doing a goofy impression of a yakuza tough guy.

While Arisa was not an employee of Mother House, her presence always had a way of keeping the mood a little lighter, and she played an important role as the only one at Mother House who would openly poke fun at Igarashi, relieving some of the stress some members felt when they were tired of deferring to his rules. Often times, she would drop off a child or two in the office, giving a few of the men a chance to work on their babysitting skills. The presence of children in Mother House, at birthday parties for members, or occasional outings, created an atmosphere of family life where ex-offenders could practice caring for others, rather than just receiving care. As a woman and someone without an official status in Mother House, Arisa knew that she could joke at the serious diligence of the men, softening their hard exteriors with a couple of well-placed jabs.

Everyone being supported by Mother House, like Jī and Kei, and all of the Mother House regular staff, were men. While this reflects the demographic make-up of the penal system in Japan (less than 10 percent of incarcerated individuals are female in Japan, nearly a third of whom are over sixty-five), the male dominated space seemed to be obviously at odds with the organization's maternal moniker. From an outside perspective, the idea that the formerly incarcerated men and NPO staff at Mother House were somehow becoming a family might seem to be a stretch.

And yet, under the masthead of each of the Mother House newsletters was the message, "You were born to be loved and to love others. You are needed and important. Mother House is your family." This was sent out every month to around 800 incarcerated individuals and supporters. Making this happen was one of the most labor-intensive jobs for the volunteers, who usually came in for several days over the week before newsletters were mailed. The days I spent preparing the newsletters with volunteers were full of conversations and laughter, each of us keeping our fingers in a steady rhythm with the others, printing, collating, folding, and packing envelopes. On these days, the gender dynamics at Mother House changed dramatically, since the majority of volunteers who helped with the newsletter were women from the Catholic Church, including a couple of nuns. The nuns appeared older than most of the men, stern yet graceful; they were motherly figures who some formerly incarcerated men would approach for private guidance and consultation. Many of the women who volunteered at Mother House were also corresponding with incarcerated men, a project that Igarashi had (somewhat misleadingly) named "Love Letters." While Igarashi meant for the name to express the sentiment "Perfect love casteth out fear" (1 John 4:18), it was not unusual for the incarcerated pen pals or prison staff to mistake it for a Christian match-making service.

The name Mother House, is a direct reference to the charitable work of Mother Teresa of Calcutta, but the recurring figure of the mother in the work of ex-offender rehabilitation drags in other associations of the mother's archetypal nurturance, devotion, and unconditional love. For formerly incarcerated men in particular, finding a sense of connection to this love, which they may not have experienced in their own family, was part of finding self-acceptance and forgiveness. The figure of the mother is understood by many as fundamental to Japanese cultural conceptions of personhood and ethical orientation to the world. In the Buddhist-based psychotherapeutic practice of Naikan, for example, Ozawa-de Silva notes that intense reflection on one's mother is central to the practice of embodying a powerful sense of guilt and indebtedness that moves the client toward healing.[12] While Naikan's philosophy originated in Pure Land Buddhism and is practiced as a kind of spiritual counseling in a variety of contexts today, its technique was first used in the early twentieth-century in Japanese prisons, where it was framed as a secular form of self-reflection.[13] Even prison chaplains who do not use this specific technique do utilize the image of the mother in the practice of spiritual counseling. Lyons, for example, describes a powerful interaction that he observed between a female Buddhist Chaplain (Fukai) and an "elderly man who had been arrested repeatedly for minor offenses":

> She tried first to speak to the man in the language of Buddhism. "Next time, before you do something bad, try to remember the face of the Buddha." His

eyes remained on the floor. He said, "I don't know the face of the Buddha." Fukai nodded once and shifted focus to the family. "Where is your mother? Do you still have contact with her? Why don't you visit her when you get out? I am sure she thinks about you." The man remained impassive. "I don't know."

Fukai pressed. "You have to remember your mother. The next time, before you do something that will send you back here, please try to remember the face of your mother." The man said, "I can't remember." Undaunted, Fukai said, "You have to try. Please do your best."[14]

In this interaction, the image of the mother, substituted for the Buddha, is suggested as a presence that can be conjured as a conscience in moments where self-will falters. She is the place of belonging and care that one can always return to, a face that accepts without judgement, and without the need for explanation. While psychologists and anthropologists have debated the uniqueness of the significance of mothers in Japanese culture (both empirically and theoretically), it is undeniable that like other places in the world, mothers hold tremendous cultural symbolic meaning, especially for those whose trust has been wounded, and who long for security and care.

When Igarashi decided that Mother House should not only have an office, but also a home-like *ibasho*, it converted part of the open garage-like space it rented next to the old office into its "café."[15] Igarashi named the Mother House's *ibasho* the Maria Café, doubling the mother image of Mother Teresa with the even more monumental icon of saintly motherhood. The space itself was much less grandiose. A few mismatched chairs were brought in, and several stuffed animals, including a large Winnie the Pooh, were placed in the front to make it look more inviting. On the grand opening day, a camera crew from one of the news channels was there, and special tables were set up to give it more of a sidewalk café feel (alas, this did not last beyond that day).

As one of the only "customers" at the event, the cameras hovered close by as I played my role. The Mother House men acted as if we had just met, and politely took my money, poured, and served my coffee. The reporters asked what I thought about a café staffed by former prisoners. "When you say it like that, it sounds scary, doesn't it!" I replied in mock surprise, "But everyone is very friendly and the coffee is good. I like it here!"

When the camera turned away, I laughed a little, feeling slightly embarrassed by my awkward act, but Igarashi was very pleased. After all, while *ibasho* might be romanticized as places where one can "be oneself," it might just as well be the case that an *ibasho* is a place to perform different selves for the sake of others you wish to share the space with. After the broadcast, the extra tables were packed away and the café rarely saw customers, despite the open doors. Like other Mother House ventures, Igarashi often moved ahead with his vision without engaging in typical drawn out negotiations with neighborhood community leaders that might have fostered more trust and exchange. While bringing the public into the space was a challenge, the café still functioned as a place of community for Mother House members, especially during the monthly tōjisha meetings. In this sense, even this underdeveloped effort deserves credit for going beyond the care-planning role of the Community Resettlement Support Centers, and did strive to cultivate empathetic encounters (*deai*) and identity amongst the ex-offenders and others, or what Igarashi referred to as "relationality" (*kankeisei*).

When I asked Igarashi about the role of family for formerly incarcerated older people, he replied,

> When we talk about older people's crimes, first of all, their families have fallen apart. The father has been abusive or something. Children are perceptive, right? They're really sensitive. And of course, the wives also respond. What happens with old people then is they reoffend. So then they go to the Community Resettlement Support Center. This is a special thing in Japan for older people and disabled people, but it is run by each of the prefectures it its own way like a contracted corporation, so it's all over the place. So there are some places that do things well and others that don't. If the Community Resettlement Center is handling the case, then first of all there has to be a written agreement. For me, instead of that, these are human beings, so you have to meet them, and attend to the relationality (*kankeisei*) and then to the extent that you don't have any connection to them, to get them to tell you all about themselves, I don't think they're going to tell you everything. That won't work. That's relationally. Pay attention to that.

The growing number of older offenders is due in part to the inability of the family to support and include older members. Could Mother House expand its rehabilitative framework to provide a home for older ex-offenders? I thought about Jī, alone in his room, his only relative, a disconnected ghost like himself. Yet the presence of mothering and kinship remained vital and sustaining. I wondered if an *ibasho* like the Maria Café and the fugitive family formed around it could be the kind of place where he would find a new sense of relationality. What surprised me, however, was that for Jī, kinship emerged not in the dedicated space of the café or during soul-bearing peer support meetings, but rather in the accompaniment through ordinary spaces of the same administrative institutions that I had argued perpetuate carceral churn.

Forgotten Items

Each week, Kei and I took a train across the Sumida River from Mother House into the city for an evening bible study. One evening, on our way back to Mother House to pick up the car, I asked Kei what he thought of the lesson, a section from the book of Mark (10:46), where Jesus healed the blind man Bartimaeus. Kei gave me a confident look, surprised that I was still thinking about it. He got it easily from the start: "If you want to be healed, you have to shout. If you're sick, you'll be healed, if you're a sinner, you'll be forgiven."

When we got off the train, Kei got a phone call from another Mother House member who lived near Kei and Jī. As we walked, Kei's side of the conversation started sounding alarming. "He walked? Is he okay? Uh-huh. Are you kidding? Okay, we're on our way." He put the phone away and shook his head. "It's Jī. Sounds like he tried to go the hospital today."

"He walked all that way?" I asked, trying to picture Jī slowly making his way down the long road to the hospital. Even at a healthy pace, the walk would have taken at least half an hour.

Kei read my thoughts. "It took him four hours because he had to stop a lot to rest because of his leg."

"Is he okay?" I asked.

"Yeah, sounds like he got there and thought he could see a doctor, but he didn't have an appointment or the right paperwork. You know Jī, he got angry and thought they were just kicking him out. It sounds like it almost got serious."

"What happened?"

Kei paused at the car door. He wasn't sure what had happened, but told me, "Somehow they found out where the house was and they took him home. Shall we go?"

We took the highway. Kei kept the windows open so the cold night air blew in, but he was still starting to yawn. When we reached the house, Jī was lying in bed, watching television with the lights out.

Kei shouted over to him. "Jī! We're back! Are you awake?"

jī: I was asleep!
kei: What happened today? I heard you walked.
jī: Eight a.m.
kei: "You left at 8 a.m.? And when did you get back? (Jī holds up three fingers) 3 p.m.? Seven hours? Jī, you can't be doing things like this. If you get caught, you're on suspended sentence right now!

Kei sighed, his voice cooling down into steady tone of concern. "You'd get in real trouble if you did something. I won't even be able to visit you in detention probably."

When Kei told me about Jī walking to the hospital, I had mostly been worried about the pain he must have endured and the danger of him falling or getting hurt on the way. It didn't cross my mind that the perfectly ordinary chore like a frail older man visiting a hospital (with an appointment or not) could end up in an arrest and prison time. But Kei was right. This was a close call, and if he had really had a fight with someone at the hospital while on a suspended sentence, it would be hard to keep him out of prison.

Early the next morning, I came downstairs to see that Jī was already up and dressed, sitting on the edge of the bed. He had on his baseball cap with the words "Believe in Yourself" emblazoned on the front in English. It had been a while since I had seen Jī outside of his lounging clothes, so it was nice to see him dressed in a shirt, a cardigan, and khaki trousers. Kei came down, spotting Jī's new look like I did. "Ready for your big day?" Kei was wearing a black baseball cap, black t-shirt, gray sweatpants, looking much more like an ex-gangster than he might have intended. As we left, he threw on a hooded sweatshirt, covering up his tattoos.

Jī seemed to be in good spirits despite the chaos of the day before and that fact that we were about to take him to a neurologist to screen him for dementia. We fished his identification and insurance paperwork out of the pile of papers by his bed, but we still had to stop at the ward office to file additional papers before we were off to the clinic. When we finally arrived at the clinic, Kei borrowed a wheelchair for Jī and we pushed him into the busy waiting room.

The clinic walls, furniture, and linoleum floors were all in different shades of light gray and cream with few decorations. A small plastic basket with the label "forgotten items" was placed on a shelf by the reception window, as if to remind us of why we were there. Kei and I looked around and immediately noticed a calendar on one of the walls. It was distributed by the National Police Agency (*keisatsu-chō*) and showed a photograph of two uniformed officers smiling as they watched a small child riding his bicycle. Kei pretended to be the voices of the officers, saying things like "Hey kid, you're under arrest for driving without a license!"

We waited a few more minutes in silence before Jī turned to me, smiling and saying clearly "I'm totally senile (*boke*)!" Although he didn't seem worried, I felt like I ought to be comforting him. "The doctors will let us know, so we'll have to wait and see what they say." He shrugged. "It didn't use to be this way. I used to be able to see really well, but I can't see anymore, can't walk."

Soon Jī was called into one of the examination rooms, where two women in pink smocks and stiff nurse caps pushed his wheelchair in front of the physician, a young man in a clean white jacket. Before addressing Jī, the doctor turned to Kei and asked if he was the oldest son of the patient. Kei was surprised for moment, then shook his head "No-no-no-no-no." I also had to take a momentary pause after the doctor's question, as if I was snapping back into a world where it was not normal for a gangster and an anthropologist to take a man to the neurologist. Weren't *we* his family?

Kei tried to explain that they lived together, but were not related, and that Jī was being looked after by a group called Mother House. The physician was not quite sure what to make of the situation, but he continued to address Kei as the screening began, asking him various questions about Jī's behavior. Jī sat quietly, waiting his turn, while Kei stood at his side. The physician still had not even greeted Jī, and as the questions continued, I could feel myself getting more agitated. Finally when the doctor asked Kei if Jī sometimes wets himself I heard myself saying out loud, "Why don't you ask *him*!" Everyone ignored me.

Finally the physician did turn to Jī, and using a much louder voice, ran through a version of the Mini-Mental State Exam (MMSE), asking him questions about the date, what he ate ("the same thing every day?" Kei whispered to me as we watched), who was the prime minister of Japan and who was the president of the USA (Jī answered both correctly), and so on. The physician measured Jī's grip, and then asked him to draw a clock and draw a cube. Kei and I looked over his shoulder, and we both agreed that he did well on these tasks, and better than both of us had expected. Afterward, as Kei pushed Jī into the corridor to await additional tests, I told them that I didn't like the way the doctor never even spoke to Jī, even to explain why he was asking all these strange things. Kei thought that if the doctor did all that, the test results wouldn't come out right, so we would just have to do what they said and wait for results. The anonymity, the waiting, the paperwork, the confinement, the guarded authority— even spaces of healing hold these traces of the carceral.

After several more tests, Jī became quiet. Finally the young doctor called us in for a preliminary diagnosis. We gathered around a printout of the MRI scan, as the doctor quickly explained to Kei that there were no unusual signs of brain deterioration or dementia, and the dark spots they found were probably the result of his stroke. Then, in his loud voice, he told us that Jī's results from the other tests gave him a score just below "passing"; however, there were still concerns that Jī might develop more dementia symptoms soon. Jī remained quiet until we had left the clinic, when I asked what he thought about the results. "I'm totally senile!" he repeated, smiling, "Doesn't matter."

The diagnosis seemed to confirm what Kei has suspected, and he tried to reassure me that the doctor was good as we drove to the next appointment at the orthopedic rehabilitation center. Kei was trying to keep Jī's spirits up, playing like his chauffeur, even when he was pushing Jī in the wheelchair. The waiting room at this clinic was almost empty, and as Kei took the clipboard from the reception desk, putting on a pair of small reading glasses to fill out the intake forms, it felt like all eyes were on us, trying to place our relationships. Kei started filling out the boxes, while Jī and I helped.

KEI: (Reading the form) How long have you had the pain?
JĪ: Um, five years.
KEI: (to me) Five years is how many days?
JASON: Uh, 1,832?
KEI: Okay. (fills in a box and keeps reading) uh, Jī are you allergic to anything?
JĪ: No!
KEI: Are you pregnant?
JĪ: Don't be stupid! (Jī starts to laugh a little, and we hear a few of the other women in the waiting room start to giggle as well).
KEI: (loudly, so everyone can hear) Oh right, you're not pregnant at the *moment*, you must have already given birth! I get it.
JĪ: You idiot! Stop fooling around.

The examination went smoothly, although the news, again, wasn't good. Jī would have to do a regular and painful regime of physical therapy if he wanted to keep his knee from deteriorating further. After the appointment, the three of us stopped at a small noodle shop and ordered piping hot bowls of curry noodles. Kei and Jī sat side by side, and perhaps it was the matching caps or the back and forth of their conversation, or the fact that they ordered the same meal, but they could have easily passed for father and son, as everyone from the ward office to the clinic staff had been assuming all morning long.

The clinic, and its unexpected affordances for both concern and humor, brought Kei and Jī together into a space of "carcerality's kinships," where they became more attuned and open to each other, even as (or maybe because) the circumstance was also one of vulnerability and uncertainty.[16] Although Jī was not interested in joining the other Mother House ex-offenders at places where Igarashi hoped they would find restorative kinship, or "relationality," such as support meetings, mass, or Bible study, the clinic, with its own carceral atmosphere, surprisingly, brought us all into a more kin-like configuration. Rather than being complicit with the structural violence of the family and the clinic as carceral institutions, together, as 'family,' Kei and Jī were able to destabilize the power of these places and deepen their own relationship of care.

Jī was not the only one that seemed to enjoy the company. By taking care of Jī, Kei was also 'encountering' himself, as Igarashi explained—a fundamental step toward recovering from decades of life in and out of prison. In this way, kin-work, while entailing its own ambiguous sense of responsibility, was a move away from the carceral past as well as a way of navigating the carceral logics of institutional bureaucracies that only a day earlier had almost resulted in Jī's reimprisonment. While Omuro and Nakai in the previous chapter, rested their hopes on being reunited with (and forgiven by) family, the kin-like connections of Mother House sought to transcend the narrow boundaries of affiliation and descent that insinuate it within the carceral continuum and to transform the family into an entity of mutual of care.

Conclusion

The last time I saw Jī was at a party held at Mother House just before I left. The wide, open-door room of the Maria Café was decorated with colorful papers chains made by the children, and several tables were pushed together to form one long table down the center of the room. Three huge hot pots in ceramic bowls were set up on portable gas burners along the table, each bubbling and steaming with its own bouquet of aromas. I had never seen so many people at Mother House all at once, but it was seeing Jī there, shoulder to shoulder with the other ex-offenders or quietly, curiously watching the families that humbled me the most. I knew it wasn't easy for him to come out, and I had no idea if I was going to see him again. Even if he didn't speak much, he was at least in the orbit of others, and everyone lent a hand to make sure he had something to eat and was happy.

We filled our bowls from the communal pots and felt the warmth of the feast glow deep in our bellies. Arisa gave me a photo book signed by the Mother House members, who had all pitched in to buy me a custom black t-shirt with the word "Oyaji" written in calligraphic Japanese script. *Oyaji* is typically translated as *father* (usually one's own father), but in prison slang, it referred to the prison officers. Someone joked that I was always around watching what they did, so the shirt fit perfectly. At the same time, it was a term of inclusion, endearment, and even kinship. The best kind—the kind that comes with "inside jokes." That was December 2018.

Almost a year later, in October 2019, Kei posted some photographs of Jī dressed in a blue gown, smiling from a hospital bed. Despite his expression, Kei told me that his health had been deteriorating, and finally he was taken to see a doctor. The details about what happened were vague. Kei suspected that they weren't telling him everything, but he knew it was bad. I messaged Kei as soon as I saw the photos:

> KEI: Jī decided to end his affiliation with Mother House. It's too bad. So now we don't know what's happened to him. I pray that he is alright.
> JASON: Really? That really is a shame. I'm surprised because he seemed to appreciate everything Mother House had done for him. Of course, he's free to do as he pleases, but I wonder how he is going to make it on his own. It's really too bad.
> KEI: Yeah, you're right. But you know, his health got worse and he was hospitalized, then he was forced to enter a care facility. So that's how we lost touch.

Mother House continues to extend resettlement support to older adults who are alone and coming out of prison. Like other NPOs, it has had to reflect on what this means for individuals whose lives have become unsettled by age and unraveled from the social fabric. If you can navigate the bureaucracy of state-provisioned welfare systems you might be able to get the minimum support to survive, a fragile and fragmented safety net that deepens social and existential disconnection. While third-sector organizations, using different approaches, try to close this gap in care, they too have their limits. As I thought about what happened to Jī, how he had been separated from the only people he knew, the only people who would stay with him in that hospital, I wondered how it would have been different if Kei actually was a relative. Would he have been expected to take care of Jī, or, at the very least, have been able to stay in touch? I also wondered how different things might have been if Kei wasn't there at all.

What kind of place and what kind of relationships might foster a lasting sense of belonging and support in ways that repair the wounded worlds of formerly incarcerated older people? A few months after Jī left the hospital, Igarashi shared a story of another man in his late seventies who had been part of the Mother House community since he had been released two-years prior. He had been arrested again, and as with the case of Jī, Igarashi would "lower his head" to the victims, and try to negotiate with the prosecutor to keep him out of prison. "I think he'd been lonely his whole life. I'm heartbroken that we couldn't become an *ibasho* and a family for him," Igarashi wrote. *Ibasho* are places of mutual belonging and kinship—where I belong to others and they belong to me—where our stories pour into each other. Being present to the stories of formerly incarcerated older adults, however, is hard work—their voices and memories are fragmented and haunted in ways that seemed more profound than those of other ex-offenders or lonely older people I had spoken to.

This book has shown how the stories of formerly incarcerated older adults and those who accompany them through the transition to a life after prison call into question more broadly held assumptions about aging and criminal justice in Japan. First, the unit of analysis needs rethinking. While prison and shaba each pose distinct problems for older people, both need to be understood in terms of a wider framework of carceral circuits, where the focus is on the systemic dysfunction and fragmentation that actors deal with through indifference and thoughtlessness. It is within these "dead zones of the imagination," as Graeber calls them, that carceral logics and the rhythmic churn of recidivism are normalized.[1] By encountering and accompanying formerly incarcerated older adults in different sites—churches, soup kitchens, care homes, clinics—I have given a partial map of some of the islands of the carceral archipelago, each with their own temporal rhythm and potential for both movement and containment.

Second, older people will continue using prison as a place of refuge as long as, a) there remains no meaningful encounters (*deai*) to others in shaba and, b) the primary function of prisons is retributive, reproducing disconnected (*muen*) subjects (what I have called the *unsettleable*). While life in prisons is hard, as I detailed in Chapter 2, the voices of formerly incarcerated older adults were insistent that the winds of shaba were colder (Chapter 6). Incarceration of people already unsettled by age dismantles the few relationships and connections the older person might have left. This sense of disconnection in shaba was constant among people like Jī, who drifted restlessly, as if prisoners awaiting orders from the prison officers. Therefore, it is not only crucial to map the institutional structures that constitute and propel individuals through the gero-carceral landscapes, it is just as important to understand their unsettled subjectivities. The stories of formerly incarcerated older people also illustrate the entanglement of prison and welfare, its rhythms and embodied exclusions, as well as its spatial and material environment of enclosure, that reproduces the un-settleable carceral subject. Even the boredom and isolation of people like Jī, Omuro, and Nakai (Chapter 7) revealed the slow, heavy weight of waiting without end, another kind of containment and alienation from the narrow definitions socially acceptable modes of growing older in the context of anti-aging social norms and policies.

Third, the disarticulated stories of formerly incarcerated older adults make it difficult for them to be heard amid the overwhelming calls of alarm about crime and the aging society. Just as the public perceive crime to be a growing problem despite falling crime rates, they are also bombarded by stories of the dangers of longevity, despite the many ways older people can and do make positive contributions. Discourses of an aging crisis map aging bodies onto narratives of cultural and social decline; hence, small acts of theft, for example, are amplified by public anxieties around Protection of Livelihood Assistance benefits and other forms of state support for older people. The retribution that older people like Jī face for stealing just a few yen is more understandable when we can see it as a way of punishing older people, as a historical and cultural category of person, for their undeserved "theft" of public money. Keeping older people in prison has become a way to lock up old age itself, and public acceptance of harsh prison sentences for minor crimes legitimates the fear of a deviant and uncontrollable old age as much as it exposes the everyday ignorance and indifference toward those who find themselves on the wrong side of the law. The impulse to control, contain, and invisibilize old age, however, can only be partial—it must be suppressed again and again each time its excesses reappear in the figure of the recidivist older offender.

The larger target of this book is not the formerly incarcerated older adults themselves, but rather the carceral logics recruited to separate and contain individuals perceived as deviating from the social structures of productive (work) and reproductive (family) life.[2] Within the structure of this logic, older ex-offenders' lives are both too long (depleting public resources) and too short (not worth rehabilitating). The value of their life is tightly constrained and attenuated in ways that fail to recognize the full extent of their capabilities to achieve ways of "being and doing" that they have reason to value as a good life in old age.[3]

Abolitionism and Anti-Ageism: A Common Ground

In recent years many more scholars and activists have become engaged in what Jason Scott has called the development of "an ideological ecosystem for abolition . . . that spans academic, public and militant spaces."[4] This book is a contribution to this ecosystem, by connecting anti-ageists, typically more focused on the ways older adults are disproportionately the victims of crimes, and abolitionists, typically focused on the conditions of racialized and impoverished groups rather than older adults specifically. Angela Davis writes that an abolitionist approach would, "require us to imagine a constellation of alternative strategies and institutions, with the ultimate goal of removing the prison from the social and ideological landscapes of our society."[5] Rodriquez elaborates this approach to abolition as imaginative praxis, stating that it is,

> an analytical method, a present-tense visioning, an infrastructure in the making, a creative project, a performance, a counterwar, an ideological struggle, a pedagogy and curriculum, an alleged impossibility that is furtively present, pulsing, produced in the persistent insurgencies of human being that undermine the totalizing logics of empire, chattel, occupation, heteropatriarchy, racial-colonial genocide and Civilization as a juridicial-narrative epoch.[6]

There is room, and indeed, an urgent necessity to add ageism and ableism to this list of interlinked logics that abolitionism must recognize before it can find creative alternatives to replace incarceration. Questioning the borders between prison and other sites along the carceral archipelago is essential to this approach, as is the necessity to reimagine and create the institutions that might give stability and vitality to society after prisons.[7] As anthropologist Savannah Shange succinctly writes, "The dyad between dismantling and creating is endemic to abolition, which is both a world-making and a world-destroying practice."[8]

The criminal justice system compounds older people's suffering and hastens their deaths. While it is true that some offenders intentionally seek incarceration as an alternative to the difficulties they face in the shaba, and that the care, security, and familiarity of prison may even make it "easier" to imagine it as the last refuge (*ibasho*), this should not be misconstrued as evidence that prisons are acceptable places for older people to spend their lives. Chronic health conditions that are particularly prevalent among the incarcerated older people continue or may be exacerbated after release. It is revealing that "accelerated aging," in the sense of a broad-spectrum long-term decline in health and resilience, is widely seen and accepted as an effect of incarceration, as if prisons are places where surplus older people are not only contained, but also produced.[9] An examination of the lives of formerly incarcerated older people shows that problems are not confineable to the walls of prisons and detention facilities, but continue to accumulate after release.

If Japan continues the current trend toward employing more regular care staff, reforming century-old rules such as forced labor, and providing environments and facilities better suited to older people, the appeal of a prison is all the more understandable. While improving the conditions and access to care within prison for currently incarcerated older people is urgently needed to prevent further physical and psychological harm to those caught in the system today, such reforms do not address the root issues that persist for marginalized older people in the community and that constitute the conditions for their imprisonment and recidivism. Nor do the current social welfare and resettlement programs, including the system of Community Livelihood Resettlement Support Centers and other third-sector NPOs, present adequate solution in their current form. As the stories of formerly incarcerated older people receiving support from these organizations indicate, life after prison, whether living in a *doya* or a care home, can be just as isolating and unsettling as prison, and with even less security. For this reason, even strengthening the system of "entry support" (*iriguchi shien*), or finding diversionary alternatives to prison for some older offenders, may simply result in transferring them to other carceral settings in the same way that deinstitutionalization of long-term nursing home care has led to more isolated and vulnerable older people living with little support in the community. While organizations like Mother House recognize that ex-offenders receiving support are still likely to reoffend unless they are actively involved in rebuilding relationships of mutual care and healing, most have limited experience or resources for supporting older people living with disability or cognitive impairment and need additional specialist staff and resources to be integrated into the broader care system.

Any sustainable response to the disproportionate incarceration of older adults, in Japan as well as in other societies with aging prison populations, must fundamentally rethink the institutional organization of society in order to provide places and social connections for the growing number of impoverished and isolated older adults to find meaningful participation and social inclusion before they resort to crime. This is ambitious, in the sense that it will require cooperation across multiple institutions and organizations (many of which have long been set in opposition with one another), as well as with tōjisha, or the formerly incarcerated older people themselves. It will also entail raising public consciousness around issues of older and disabled people affected by the criminal justice system, telling their stories in ways that disarm and deconstruct stigmatizing and alarmist discourses around crime and old age in ways that foster more openness and connection. This work might be characterized as both anti-ageist as well as abolitionist, in the sense that it aims to create the conditions for social relations such that the exclusion of older people and the use of prisons to punish them are no longer seen as necessary or natural.[10]

As the disjointed worlds and fragmented stories of individuals like Jī are brought into the cultural frames of encounters (*deai*), relations (*en*), and place (*ibasho*), their incompleteness becomes an invitation to care; their gaps, a place for presence; their unsettledness, a site on which to build. These cultural frames ground political theories such as the carceral, anti-ageism and abolition in the meaningful worlds of people working to transform justice and create livable futures in which to grow older.

Incomplete Stories

It is conventional at this point in a book to acknowledge the limitations of the kind of ethnographic snapshot of a particular time and place that I have given here. And there are many. The lives and experiences of older people and their relationship to the carceral generate profound questions about institutional power, the social labor of criminalization, and our fears of growing older alone that extend well beyond this book. My lack of access to older people in prisons meant relying mostly on second-hand accounts rather than direct observations, but the growing literature on aging in prison elsewhere has offered compelling and nuanced accounts that show the value of more direct engagement with detention facilities.[11] My access was also limited when it came to formerly incarcerated older women, but this should not be an indication of their lack of importance—quite the opposite. While fewer in number, older women make up a larger proportion of the total number of women arrested and incarcerated, and this rate has been increasing much more rapidly compared to men.[12] Given the important gendered social inequalities in Japan, it is likely that women have very different post-release experiences of carceral circuits, and that the kinds of mothering and kin-work I discussed (Chapter 8) have different implications and can provide further critical insight.

While the stories of formerly incarcerated older adults reveal a past punctured with disruptions and dislocations that resonate with the sense of marginalization and isolation felt by older people more widely, they also speak of hope and the possibility of change. It might seem strange to think of hope for formerly incarcerated older adults as anything more than the "cruel optimism" of redemptive carceral narratives that seem to perpetually dissolve in the cold winds of shaba.[13] But perhaps this is only because the hope that that people like Chiba or Jī or others hold onto is one that also aches with the dull, bone-deep pain of grief. Within this grief, resides a shade of love unextinguished by the grip of the carceral. I picture Jī's sly smile as he talked about being a "disconnected spirit," or becoming "senile," and I can't help but think this was more than just a little dark humor to make me laugh, but a way of letting me know that he was still there, even as a ghost in the fog, still there. As a caretaker of these images and stories, these fragments and scraps of the human story, I too have encountered and shared in the worlds of others and been changed. And in this change lies the fragile hope that our relationships to others can be reimagined, and that justice can be, and must be transformed.

NOTES

INTRODUCTION

1. David Graeber, "Dead Zones of the Imagination: On Violence, Bureaucracy, and Interpretive Labor. The 2006 Malinowski Memorial Lecture," *HAU: Journal of Ethnographic Theory* 2, no. 2 (December 19, 2012): 105–28.
2. Graeber, "Dead Zones of the Imagination," 112.
3. Ministry of Justice (Japan), "Kyōsei Tōkei Chōsa" (Corrections Statistics Survey) (Tokyo: Ministry of Justice, 2023), https://www.e-stat.go.jp/stat-search/files?stat_infid=000040081386; Ministry of Justice (Japan), "Heisei 29-Nenban Hanzai Hakusho" (2017 Crime White Paper) (Tokyo: Ministry of Justice, 2018), https://hakusyo1.moj.go.jp/jp/64/nfm/n64_2_4_8_2_2.html.
4. Ministry of Justice (Japan), "Heisei 30-Nenban Hanzai Hakusho" (2018 Edition Crime White Paper) (Tokyo: Ministry of Justice, 2018), https://hakusyo1.moj.go.jp/jp/65/nfm/gmokuji.html, table 5-2-3-10.
5. Ministry of Justice (Japan), "Heisei 30-Nenban Hanzai Hakusho No Gaiyō" (Outline of the 2018 Crime White Paper), (Tokyo: Ministry of Justice, 2018), https://www.moj.go.jp/content/001309862.pdf.
6. Aisha Khan, "The Carceral State: An American Story," *Annual Review of Anthropology* 51, no. 1 (2022): 49–66.
7. David Adam, "How Far Will Global Population Rise? Researchers Can't Agree," *Nature* 597, no. 7877 (September 21, 2021): 462–65.
8. World Health Organization, "Ageing and Health: Key Facts," WHO Newsroom, accessed January 27, 2023, https://www.who.int/news-room/fact-sheets/detail/ageing-and-health.
9. Ministry of Internal Affairs and Communications (Japan), "Kōreisha no Jinkō" (Population of Older People), last modified September 15, 2021. https://www.stat.go.jp/data/topics/topi1291.html.
10. Brett Neilson, "Anti-Ageing Cultures, Biopolitics and Globalisation," *Cultural Studies Review* 12, no. 2 (2006): 149–64; Brett Neilson, "Globalization and the

Biopolitics of Aging," *CR: The New Centennial Review* 3, no. 2 (2003): 161–86; Amina Mire, "'Skin Trade': Genealogy of Anti-Ageing 'Whiteness Therapy' in Colonial Medicine," *Medicine Studies* 4, no. 1–4 (2014): 119–29.

11. Sarah Lamb, ed., *Successful Aging?: Global Perspectives on a Contemporary Obsession* (New Brunswick, NJ: Rutgers University Press, 2017); Stephen Katz and Toni Calasanti, "Critical Perspectives on Successful Aging: Does It 'Appeal More than It Illuminates'?," *Gerontologist* 55, no. 1 (Feb. 2015): 26–33; Toni Calasanti, "Combating Ageism: How Successful Is Successful Aging?," *Gerontologist* 56, no. 6 (December 2016): 1,093–101; Marty Martinson and Clara Berridge, "Successful Aging and Its Discontents: A Systematic Review of the Social Gerontology Literature," *Gerontologist* 55, no. 1 (Feb. 2015): 58–69; Robert L. Rubinstein and Kate de Medeiros, "'Successful Aging,' Gerontological Theory and Neoliberalism: A Qualitative Critique," *Gerontologist* 55, no. 1 (Feb. 2015): 34–42.

12. Kristen Bell, "Staging Prevention, Arresting Progress: Chronic Disease Prevention and the Lifestyle Frame," in *Preventing Dementia: Critical Perspectives on a New Paradigm of Preparing for Old Age*, ed. Annette Leibing and Silke Schicktanz (Oxford: Berghahn Books, 2020), 175–91; Mark Schweda and Larissa Pfaller, "Responsibilization of Aging? An Ethical Analysis of the Moral Economy of Prevention," in *Preventing Dementia: Critical Perspectives on a New Paradigm of Preparing for Old Age*, ed. Annette Leibing and Silke Schicktanz (Oxford: Berghahn Books, 2020), 192–213.

13. While the success of the Nordic model has been celebrated internationally, there are also serious discussions about its sustainability. One response meant to ease the care receiver's dependence on professional care has been to rethink care as a process of "reablement" that empowers older individuals to continue living as independently as possible for as long as possible and minimizing direct support. The reablement paradigm has also become widespread in other northern European countries and aligns with local cultural models of the person. For a more extensive discussion, see Amy Clotworthy, *Empowering the Elderly?: How "Help to Self-Help" Health Interventions Shape Ageing and Eldercare in Denmark* (New York: Transcript Publishing, 2020). For more cross-national comparative accounts of LTCI, see J. C. Campbell, N. Ikegami, and M. J. Gibson, "Lessons from Public Long-Term Care Insurance in Germany and Japan," *Health Affairs* 29, no. 1 (January 1, 2010): 87–95; Nanako Tamiya et al., "Population Ageing and Well-Being: Lessons from Japan's Long-Term Care Insurance Policy," *Lancet* 378, no. 9797 (September 2011): 1183–92; Naonori Kodate and Virpi Timonen, "Bringing the Family in through the Back Door: The Stealthy Expansion of Family Care in Asian and

European Long-Term Care Policy," *Journal of Cross-Cultural Gerontology* 32, no. 3 (September 2017): 291–301; Emiko Ochiai, "Unsustainable Societies: The Failure of Familialism in East Asia's Compressed Modernity," *Historical Social Research* 36, no. 2 (2011): 219–45.

14. Shingou Ikeda, "The Necessity of Reduced Working Hours under the Re-Familization of Elderly Care," *Japan Labor Issues* 5, no. 30 (2021): 16–33; Ochiai, "Unsustainable Societies"; Kodate and Timonen, "Bringing the Family."

15. As of 2022, the number of people waiting for a space in residential nursing homes (*tokubetsu yōgo rōjin hōmu*) has decreased to about 270,000 nationally. This is roughly half of the 532,000 waiting for beds in 2013, just before the revision of eligibility threshold according to the Ministry of Health, Labour and Welfare (MHLW) "Tokubetsu yōgorōjin hōmu no nyūsho mōshikomi-sha no jōkyō (reiwa 4-nendo)" (Status of Applicants to Enter Special Nursing Homes) (Tokyo: MHLW, 2022), https://www.mhlw.go.jp/stf/houdou/0000157884_00004.html. Private nursing homes, not covered through LTCI, had grown dramatically in the first part of the century, but in recent years have been in decline. This is mainly due not to the decrease in demand, but because of the lack of experienced care staff.

16. "Dai 8-Ki Kaigo Hoken Jigyō Keikaku Ni Motodzuku Kaigo Shokuin No Hitsuyō-Sū Ni Tsuite" (Report on the Required Number of Nursing Care Staff Based on the 8th Long-Term Care Insurance Business Plan) (Tokyo: Ministry of Health, Labour and Welfare, July 9, 2021), https://www.mhlw.go.jp/stf/houdou/0000207323_00005.html.

17. Lynne Nakano, *Community Volunteers in Japan: Everyday Stories of Social Change* (London: Routledge Curzon, 2005).

18. Ministry of Health, Labour and Welfare, "Graphical Review of Japanese Household," (Tokyo: Ministry of Health, Labour and Welfare, 2018), 8.

19. Japan Industrial Safety and Health Association, "Kōreisha Rōdōsha No Katsuyaku Sokushin No Tame No Anzen Eisei Taisaku" (Safety and Health Measures to Promote Active Participation of Elderly Workers), JISHA, March 2018, https://www.jisha.or.jp/research/report/201703_01.html.

20. Matsumiya Ashita, "Kōrei-Sha No 'kankei-Sei No Hinkon' to 'kodoku-Shi' 'koritsu Shi'" (The Poverty of Social Networks on the Elderly and Dying Alone), *Nihon Toshi Shakai Gakkai Nenpō* (Annual Report of the Japanese Association of Urban Sociology 2012), no. 30 (2013): 15–28; Teppo Kröger, *Care Poverty: When Older People's Needs Remain Unmet* (Cham, Switzerland: Palgrave Macmillan, 2022).

21. Jason Danely, "The Limits of Dwelling and the Unwitnessed Death," *Cultural Anthropology* 34, no. 2 (May 22, 2019): 213–39; Nils Dahl, "Governing through

Kodokushi: Japan's Lonely Deaths and Their Impact on Community Self-Government," *Contemporary Japan* 32, no. 1 (January 2, 2020): 83–102; Anne Allison, "Not-Wanting to Die Badly: Facing the Precarity of Dying Alone in Japan," in *Ethnographies of Waiting: Doubt, Hope and Uncertainty*, ed. Manpreet K. Janeja and Andreas Bandak (London: Bloomsbury Academic, 2018), 181–202; Anne Allison, *Being Dead Otherwise* (Durham, NC: Duke University Press, 2023).

22. Anne Allison, *Precarious Japan* (Durham, NC: Duke University Press, 2013), 85.
23. Jason Danely, *Aging and Loss: Mourning and Maturity in Contemporary Japan* (New Brunswick, NJ: Rutgers University Press, 2014); Casper Bruun Jensen, Miho Ishii, and Philip Swift, "Attuning to the Webs of En: Ontography, Japanese Spirit Worlds, and the 'Tact' of Minakata Kumagusu," *HAU: Journal of Ethnographic Theory* 6, no. 2 (September 1, 2016): 149–72.
24. World Health Organization, "Healthy Life Expectancy (HALE) at Age 60 (Years)," WHO, last modified April 29, 2024, https://www.who.int/data/gho/data/indicators/indicator-details/GHO/gho-ghe-hale-healthy-life-expectancy-at-age-60.
25. Khan, "The Carceral State," 54.
26. John W. Traphagan, "On Being a Good Rōjin: Senility, Power, and Self-Actualization in Japan," in *Thinking about Dementia: Culture, Loss, and the Anthropology of Senility*, ed. Annette Leibing and Lawrence Cohen (New Brunswick, NJ: Rutgers University Press, 2006), 269–87; Katrina Louise Moore, "A Spirit of Adventure in Retirement: Japanese Baby Boomers and the Ethos of Interdependence," *Anthropology & Aging* 38, no. 2 (November 28, 2017): 10–28.
27. Carol Lawson, "Subverting the Prison: The Incarceration of Stigmatised Older Japanese," *International Journal of Law in Context* 17, no. 3 (September 2021): 336–55.
28. Graeber, "Dead Zones of the Imagination," 124.
29. Masahiro Suzuki and Akinori Otani, "Ageing, Institutional Thoughtlessness, and Normalisation in Japan's Prisons," *International Journal of Comparative and Applied Criminal Justice*, published online March 13, 2023, https://doi.org/10.1080/01924036.2023.2188236; Elaine Crawley, "Institutional Thoughtlessness in Prisons and Its Impacts on the Day-to-Day Prison Lives of Elderly Men," *Journal of Contemporary Criminal Justice* 21, no. 4 (November 2005): 350–63; Elaine Crawley and Richard Sparks, "Is There Life after Imprisonment?: How Elderly Men Talk about Imprisonment and Release," *Criminology & Criminal Justice* 6, no. 1 (February 2006): 63–82.

CHAPTER 1

1. See Alison Young, "Japanese Atmospheres of Criminal Justice," *British Journal of Criminology* 59, no. 4 (June 6, 2019): 765–79; and Christopher Aldous

and Frank Leishman, "Police and Community Safety in Japan: Model or Myth?," *Crime Prevention and Community Safety* 1, no. 1 (January 1, 1999): 25–39 for two different yet interesting critical takes on the police outposts in Japan.
2. Jeffrey Todd Ulmer and Darrell J. Steffensmeier, "The Age and Crime Relationship: Social Variation, Social Explanations," *The Nurture Versus Biosocial Debate in Criminology: On the Origins of Criminal Behavior and Criminality*, ed. Kevin M. Beaver, J. C. Barnes, and Brian B. Boutwell, 377–96 (Thousand Oaks, CA: Sage Publications, 2014).
3. Louise Ridley, "No Place for Old Men?: Meeting the Needs of an Ageing Male Prison Population in England and Wales," *Social Policy and Society* 21, no. 4 (October 2022): 597–611; Stephen Ginn, "Elderly Prisoners," *BMJ: British Medical Journal (Online)* 345 (October 20, 2012): 24–27; Irene Marti, *Doing Indefinite Time: An Ethnography of Long-Term Imprisonment in Switzerland*, Palgrave Studies in Prisons and Penology (Cham: Springer International Publishing, 2023), 4.
4. Ronald H. Aday and Jennifer J. Krabill, "Older and Geriatric Offenders: Critical Issues for the Twenty-First Century," *Special Needs Offenders in Correctional Institutions* 1 (2012): 203–33.
5. Tina Maschi, Deborah Viola, and Fei Sun, "The High Cost of the International Aging Prisoner Crisis: Well-Being as the Common Denominator for Action," *Gerontologist* 53, no. 4 (August 1, 2013): 544.
6. Marti, *Doing Indefinite Time*; Jamie Fellner and Patrick Vinck, *Old Behind Bars: The Aging Prison Population in the United States* (New York: Human Rights Watch, 2012); Tina Maschi and Keith Morgen, *Aging Behind Prison Walls: Studies in Trauma and Resilience* (New York: Columbia University Press, 2020); Elaine Crawley and Richard Sparks, "Older Men in Prison: Survival, Coping and Identity," in *The Effects of Imprisonment*, ed. Alison Liebling and Shadd Maruna (Abingdon, Oxon: Routledge, 2011); James B. Waldram, *Hound Pound Narrative: Sexual Offender Habilitation and the Anthropology of Therapeutic Intervention* (Berkeley: University of California Press, 2012); Natalie Mann, "Ageing Child Sex Offenders in Prison: Denial, Manipulation and Community," *Howard Journal of Criminal Justice* 51, no. 4 (2012): 345–58.
7. Lawson, "Subverting the Prison."
8. National Police Agency, "Reiwa 2 nen Hanzai Hakusho Dai 5 hen saihan saihikō" (Crime White Paper, Part 5 Recidivism 2020), 226.
9. For more on Japan's Volunteer Probation Officer System and its relationship to Professional Probation, see Koichi Hamai and Kevin Ellis Ellis's "Criminal Justice in Modern Japan: From Re-Integrative Shaming to Popular Punitivism," *International Journal of the Sociology of Law* 34 no. 3 (1 September 2006): 157–78;

and Andrew Watson, "Probation in Japan: Strengths and Challenges and Likely New Tasks," *European Journal of Probation* 10, no. 2): 160–77.
10. Emma K. Russell, Bree Carlton, and Danielle Tyson, "Carceral Churn: A Sensorial Ethnography of the Bail and Remand Court," *Punishment & Society* 24, no. 2 (2022): 151–69.
11. Dominique Moran, *Carceral Geography: Spaces and Practices of Incarceration* (Abingdon, Oxon: Routledge, 2016), 106.
12. Michel Foucault, *Discipline and Punish: The Birth of the Prison*, trans. Alan Sheridan (New York: Penguin, 1991), 297.
13. Edward Fowler, *San'ya Blues: Laboring Life in Contemporary Tokyo* (Ithaca, NY: Cornell University Press, 1996), 31–34.
14. Nick Gill et al., "Carceral Circuitry: New Directions in Carceral Geography," *Progress in Human Geography* 42, no. 2 (April 1, 2018): 183–204.
15. Emphasis mine. Gill et al., "Carceral Circuitry," 189; this echoes other work that has used carceral geography to demonstrate the ways prisons have enabled the extractive capture of land and wealth from the most impoverished communities. See Brett Story, *Prison Land: Mapping Carceral Power across Neoliberal America* (Minneapolis: University of Minnesota Press, 2019); and Ruth Wilson Gilmore, *Abolition Geography: Essays Towards Liberation*, ed. Brenna Bhandar and Alberto Toscano (London: Verso, 2022).
16. For more on the production of human waste, or the "conditions of disposability" in contemporary capitalism, see Ian G. R. Shaw and Marv Waterstone, *Wageless Life: A Manifesto for a Future beyond Capitalism* (Minneapolis: University of Minnesota Press, 2020), 26–27. Waste surplus populations have been similarly theorized as "lumpen" in the ethnographic work with criminalized drug injectors in the US by Philippe Bourgois and Jeffrey Schonberg, *Righteous Dopefiend* (Berkeley, CA: University of California Press, 2009), and by Joshua Burraway, "Remembering to Forget: Blacking Out in Itchy Park," *Current Anthropology* 59, no. 5 (October 2018): 469–87.
17. For more on the way "shit" in Japan represents the undisciplined, corrosive, or potentially dangerous waste produced by the system, in contrast to other forms of waste that might be brought under control through scientific, rationalized "hygienic" regimes, see Alexander R. Bay, "Disciplining Shit," *Japan Forum* 31, no. 4 (October 2, 2019): 556–82; and Warwick Anderson, "Crap on the Map, or Postcolonial Waste," *Postcolonial Studies* 13, no. 2 (June 2010): 169–78.
18. The 2022 dystopian film *Plan 75*, in which older people are offered the option to be euthanized as part of a national plan to deal with the aging society, makes sense as a plot because the devaluation of later life is already part of the current society. On the other hand, the film might also be read as a

speculative version of the ancient tale of obasuteyama, a repetitive iteration of deeply rooted ambivalence toward old age. See Danely, *Aging and Loss*; and Mayumi Hayashi, *The Care of Older People: England and Japan, A Comparative Study* (London: Routledge, 2015), 39. Interestingly, Tom Gill notes a day labor union leader in Kotobuki (Yokohama) referring to the yoseba (day labor areas) as an example of modern day "ubasute-yama," where "old women would be left to die when they had outlived their economic usefulness." Gill, *Men of Uncertainty: The Social Organization of Day Laborers in Contemporary Japan* (Albany: State University of New York Press, 2001), 148.

19. Avery Gordon, *Ghostly Matters: Haunting and the Sociological Imagination*, 2nd ed. (Minneapolis: University of Minnesota Press, 2008).

20. Taking inspiration from Maroon cultures arising out of transatlantic slavery, scholars and activists have deepened our understanding of enclosure within carceral circuits through notions of "fugitivity" and "evasion," which can act as a generative ground for imagining new forms of sociality that are not bound by binary constructs of incarceration/freedom, criminal/citizen, in/out, see, for example, Damien M. Sojoyner, "Another Life Is Possible: Black Fugitivity and Enclosed Places," *Cultural Anthropology* 32, no. 4 (2017): 514–36; and David C. Thompson, "Evasion: Prison Escapes and the Predicament of Incarceration in Rio de Janeiro," *Cultural Anthropology* 38, no. 1 (2023): 36–59.

21. Ministry of Justice (Japan) Bureau of Corrections, "Ninshishō keikō no aru jukei-sha no gaisū chōsa (hōkoku)" (Rough Survey of Inmates with Dementia Tendencies [Report]), 2019. Other estimates have been closer to 14 percent, though investigators suspect that numbers may be even higher. See Shunsuke Ichimiya, "More than 10 Per Cent of Those Entering Prison Have 'Likely Dementia,'" *Mainichi Shinbun*, July 27, 2020.

22. Reliable data on the health and disability status of Japanese prisoners is difficult to find; estimates are based on surveys of prison populations in the UK, where researchers have estimated between 85 and 90 percent of older prisoners are affected by a physical and/or mental health conditions. Caroline Lee et al., "A Systematic Integrative Review of Programmes Addressing the Social Care Needs of Older Prisoners," *Health & Justice* 7, no. 1 (December 2019): 9; Adrian J. Hayes et al., "The Health and Social Needs of Older Male Prisoners," *International Journal of Geriatric Psychiatry* 27, no. 11 (2012): 1,155–62.

23. George Pro and Miesha Marzell, "Medical Parole and Aging Prisoners: A Qualitative Study," *Journal of Correctional Health Care* 23, no. 2 (April 2017): 162–72; Violet Handtke et al., "The Collision of Care and Punishment: Ageing Prisoners' View on Compassionate Release," *Punishment & Society* 19, no. 1 (January 2017): 5–22.

24. Joji Yamamoto, *Ruihan Shogaisha* (Repeat Offender with a Disability) (Tokyo: Shincho Bunko, 2009); Takao Kimura and Sachie Sawaki, "Kōrei/shōgai hanzaisha no shakai fukki shien shisaku genjō to kadai" (The Current State and Issues of Social Rehabilitation Support Measures for Elderly/Disabled Offenders). *Nihon Fukushi Daigaku Shakai Fukushi Ronshū* 128 (March 2013): 83–113.
25. Lawson, "Subverting the Prison."
26. Lisa Du and Grace Huang, "Japan's Hospitals Turn Thousands of COVID-19 Patients Away," *Japan Times*, August 26, 2021, https://www.japantimes.co.jp/news/2021/08/26/national/japan-hospitals-covid-19.
27. As of 2018, 26,000 to 27,000 of *kodokushi* occurred every year (there is no official definition of "lonely death" so statistics are not reliable), see Kanbara Hiroshi Kodoku-shi, suikei 2. 7 "Man-ri tsukamenu jittai ʻkuni ni teigi naku" (Estimated 27,000 Solitary Deaths, Unable to Grasp Reality), *Asahi Shinbun*, September 18, 2018, https://www.asahi.com/articles/ASL5X55P8L5XTIPE026.html. In 2024, the official annual number of *kodokushi* of people 65+ had risen to 68,000.. Renters I have spoken to are reluctant to move into a property if the last resident was *kodokushi*, and property owners sometimes discount the price to find replacement renters.
28. Joji Yamamoto, *Keimusho Shika Ibasho Ga Nai Hito-Tachi: Gakkōde Wa Oshiete Kurenai, Shōgai to Hanzai No Hanashi* (People Who Have No Place but Prison: The Stories about Disability and Crime That Schools Don't Teach) (Tokyo: Otsuki Shoten, 2018); Linghan Luo, "Welfare Support for Elder People: From the Vantage Point of the Cooperation between Judicial and Social Welfare" (Masters Thesis, Hitotsubashi University, 2016).
29. bell hooks, "Theory as Liberatory Practice," *Yale Journal of Law and Feminism* 4 (1991–1992): 1.
30. With permission, I am not using a pseudonym for Mother House or its director, Igarashi Hiroshi. Mother House is very open about its approach and has appeared in numerous news features, articles, and occasionally academic publications. I have sought to mask the identities of the staff at other organizations in San'ya as well as at the Community Resettlement Support Center where I did fieldwork.
31. Kïyoshi Adachi, "The Development of Social Welfare Services in Japan," in *Caring for the Elderly in Japan and the US*, ed. Susan O. Long, 191–205 (London: Routledge, 2000).
32. Nofit Itzhak, "Signifiers for the Divine," *American Ethnologist* 47, no. 3 (2020): 276–88; Amira Mittermaier, *Giving to God: Islamic Charity in Revolutionary Times* (Berkeley: University of California Press, 2019); Amira Mittermaier,

"Bread, Freedom, Social Justice: The Egyptian Uprising and a Sufi Khidma," *Cultural Anthropology* 29, no. 1 (February 3, 2014): 54–79.

CHAPTER 2

1. Foucault, *Discipline and Punish*.
2. Foucault, *Discipline and Punish*, 201.
3. See the detailed discussion of Foucault's theory of panopticism in Didier Fassin, *Prison Worlds: An Ethnography of the Carceral Condition* (Malden, MA: Polity Press, 2017); see Moran, *Carceral Geography*, 8–9, for how the metaphor of the panopticon has been translated to urban spaces.
4. Foucault, *Discipline and Punish*, 298.
5. Foucault, *Discipline and Punish*, 297, 298.
6. Andrew Coyle, *Prisons of the World* (Bristol: Policy Press, 2021), 111.
7. Mari Yamaguchi, "Japanese Prisons Face Swelling Elderly Population," *Washington Times*, January 6, 2011, www.washingtontimes.com/news/2011/jan/6/japans-prisons-face-swelling-elderly-population.
8. Marti, *Doing Indefinite Time*; Diete Humblet, *The Older Prisoner* (Cham, Switzerland: Palgrave Macmillan, 2021).
9. Aday and Krabill, "Older and Geriatric Offenders"; Crawley and Sparks, "Older Men in Prison"; Crawley, "Institutional Thoughtlessness"; Seena Fazel et al., "Health of Elderly Male Prisoners: Worse than the General Population, Worse than Younger Prisoners," *Age and Ageing* 30, no. 5 (2001): 403–7; Natalie Mann, *Doing Harder Time?: The Experiences of an Ageing Male Prison Population in England and Wales* (Farnham, Surrey: Ashgate Publishing, 2013); Janet M. Parrott et al., "Mental Health and Offending in Older People: Future Directions for Research," *Criminal Behaviour and Mental Health* 29, no. 4 (2019): 218–26; Susan Baidawi et al., "Older Prisoners-A Challenge for Australian Corrections," *Trends and Issues in Crime and Criminal Justice*, no. 426 (2011): 1; Ridley, "No Place for Old Men?"; Philip Snoyman et al., "Ōsutoraria nyūsausuu~ēruzu shū no keiji shisetsu ni okeru korei no keiji shisetsu ni okeru kōrei hanzai-sha" (Elderly Offenders in Penal Institutions in New South Wales, Australia), in *Kōreisha Hanzai No Sōgōteki Kenkyū* (Comprehensive Research on Elderly Crime), ed. Yoko Hosoi and Bunri Tatsuno (Tokyo: Kazama Shobo, 2021), 386–99.
10. Katrina Forsyth et al., "'They Just Throw You Out': Release Planning for Older Prisoners," *Ageing and Society* 35, no. 9 (October 2015): 2,011–25; Crawley and Sparks, "Is There Life after Imprisonment?"; Louise Robinson et al., "Providing Social Care Following Release from Prison: Emerging Practice Arrangements Further to the Introduction of the 2014 Care Act," *British Journal*

of Social Work, May 13, 2021; Elaine Crawley, "Release and Resettlement: The Perspectives of Older Prisoners," Criminal Justice Matters 56, no. 1 (June 1, 2004): 32–33.

11. Young, "Japanese Atmospheres," 776; See also Yvonne Jewkes and Alison Young, "Sensory Reflections on a Japanese Prison," in Sensory Penalities: Exploring the Senses in Spaces of Punishment and Social Control, ed. Kate Herrity, Bethany E. Schmidt, and Jason Warr, 177–93 (Bingley: Emerald Publishing Limited, 2021).

12. Coyle, Prisons of the World, 111.

13. Joanna Weschler, Prison Conditions in Japan (New York: Human Rights Watch, 1995).

14. Yoko Kinomoto and Naomi Ishishita, "Jukeisha dōshi no rōrō kaigo 'kona yarō to omou koto mo aru' [rupo onomichi keimusho] – Middle" (Elderly Care between Older Prisoners: "Sometimes I Think 'What a Bastard'" [Report from Onomichi Prison]), Chugoku Shimbun, August 17, 2022, https://www.chugoku-np.co.jp/articles/-/200493.

15. As I was writing this, the law regarding mandatory work in prison, established by the 1908 Penal Code as the primary method of rehabilitation for offenders, was changed. On March 8, 2022, the Cabinet agreed that this regulation should be revised, particularly because of its impact on frail and disabled prisoners; the new system is due to start in June 2025. This will be the first revision in 115 years of this part of the Penal Code. See Kazuya Ito, "Keimusho no `sagyō', jittai wa rihabiri kōrei-ka taisaku ni `kōkin-kei' shinsetsu" (Prison "Work," Reality Is Rehabilitation New "Detention Sentence" to Counter Aging Population), Asahi Shimbun, March 9, 2022, https://digital.asahi.com/articles/ASQ386K80Q37UTIL028.html.

16. According to official estimates in 2021, the average daily cost for expenses (e.g., food, clothing, hygiene) for each prisoner was 2,208 yen, or 805,920 yen per year (about $6150 USD). National Police Association, "Hanzai tokei shiryo reiwa 4nen 1~8 gatsu bun," (Crime Statistics Information 2022 January – August), 2022, 62. However, Matsuyama calculated the total cost at 3.2 million yen (closer to $24,300 USD). Kanako Matsuyama, "Rōjin hōmuka suru keimusho, 'deru no ga kowakatta' kōreika de iryōhizō mo" (Prisons Turning into Elderly Care Homes, "I Was Scared to Leave" Also the Rising Cost of Seniors), Bloomberg, April 16, 2015, https://www.bloomberg.co.jp/news/articles/2015-04-15/--i8j977ra. Those with disabilities or healthcare needs (the majority of older prisoners) could cost as much as three times this amount. According to the Japanese Ministry of Justice, "All income related to prison work, for which the country has signed work contracts

with private companies and provides the labor of prisoners, belongs to the treasury. Prison work income for FY 2021 was approximately 2.8 billion yen." Ministry of Justice Prison Work (*Keimu sagyo*) https://www.moj.go.jp/kyousei1/kyousei_kyouse10.html.
17. Angela Davis, *Are Prisons Obsolete?* (New York: Seven Stories Press, 2003); Ruth Wilson Gilmore, *Golden Gulag: Prisons, Surplus, Crisis and Opposition in Globalizing California* (Berkeley: University of California Press, 2006); Story, *Prison Land*.
18. Yamamoto, *Keimusho shika ibasho*, 40.
19. Yamamoto, *Keimusho Shika Ibasho*, 41.
20. Hila Avieli, "'A Sense of Purpose': Older Prisoners' Experiences of Successful Ageing behind Bars," *European Journal of Criminology* 19, no. 6 (November 1, 2022): 1660–77; Humblet, *The Older Prisoner*; Maschi and Morgen, *Aging Behind Prison Walls*.
21. Dominique Moran, *Carceral Geography*, 147.
22. Andrea De Antoni, "Down in a Hole: Dark Tourism, Haunted Places as Affective Meshworks, and the Obliteration of Korean Laborers in Contemporary Kyoto," *Japan Review*, no. 33 (2019): 271–98; Kevin Walby and Justin Piché, "The Polysemy of Punishment Memorialization: Dark Tourism and Ontario's Penal History Museums," *Punishment & Society* 13, no. 4 (October 1, 2011): 451–72; Ministry of Justice, "Dai 43-kai Fuchū keimusho bunkamatsuri'~-toshi ni ichido no aki no kansha-sai ~ no kaisai ni tsuite" (About Holding of "The 43rd Fuchu Prison School Festival" - Autumn Thanksgiving Once a Year), accessed January 29, 2023, https://www.moj.go.jp/kyousei1/kyousei05_00038.html.
23. Moran writes that "visits to prison sites may elicit emotional responses and bring to mind questions of morality, and embodied, tactile and material encounters," but that such encounters are always partial and concealed. *Carceral Geography*, 148.
24. Yasuhiro Yamada, "Keimusho, marude kaigo shisetsu ni (tokushu kiji)" (Prisons Have Become Just Like Care Facilities [Special Article]), *NHK Seiji Magazine*, August 21, 2019. https://www.nhk.or.jp/politics/articles/feature/21325.html.
25. Hamai and Ellis, "Crime and Criminal Justice"; N. Komiya, "A Cultural Study of the Low Crime Rate in Japan," *British Journal of Criminology* 39, no. 3 (June 1, 1999): 369–90.
26. Silvia Croydon, *The Politics of Police Detention in Japan: Consensus of Convenience* (New York: Oxford University Press, 2016), 15.
27. John O. Haley, "Apology and Pardon: Learning From Japan," *American Behavioral Scientist* 41, no. 6 (March 1, 1998): 842–67; John O. Haley, "Sheathing

the Sword of Justice in Japan: An Essay on Law without Sanctions," *Journal of Japanese Studies* 8, no. 2 (1982): 265–81; John Braithwaite, "Crime in Asia: Toward a Better Future," *Asian Journal of Criminology* 9, no. 1 (March 1, 2014): 65–75.

28. For a summary and critique of this view, see Misha Bykowski, "Techno-Mediated Safety: Social Atomization and the Growth of Residential Security in Recessionary Japan" (PhD diss., Stanford University, 2020), 14–15; Masahiro Suzuki and Akinori Otani, "Myths of Restorative Features in the Japanese Justice System and Society: The Role of Apology, Compensation and Confession, and Application of Reintegrative Shaming," *Restorative Justice* 5, no. 2 (May 4, 2017): 158–77; Dag Leonardsen, *Crime in Japan: Paradise Lost?* (Basingstoke, Hampshire: Palgrave Macmillan, 2010); and Elmer H. Johnson, *Criminalization and Prisoners In Japan Six Contrary Cohorts* (Carbondale: Southern Illinois University Press, 1997). While situating trends in crime and incarceration within the context of social, economic and political changes, these authors also lean strongly on culturalist explanations for understanding how Japan's criminal justice system responded to changes. Both Leonardsen and Johnson contend that while cultural values of social harmony and orderliness are prominent in Japan's prison system, they also recognize that this can exacerbate susceptibility to the criminalization of groups, including older people, based on moral panics or other perceived threats to social order.

29. Sylvia Croydon, "Making It Their Own: The Development of the Japanese Criminal Justice System," *Electronic Journal of Contemporary Japanese Studies* 18, no. 1 (April 29, 2018).

30. Amnesty International, "Japan: Abusive Punishments in Japanese Prisons," April 22, 1998.

31. Coyle, *Prisons of the World*.

32. Sheldon Garon, *Molding Japanese Minds: The State in Everyday Life* (Princeton, NJ: Princeton University Press, 1997), 35.

33. Adam J. Lyons, *Karma and Punishment: Prison Chaplaincy in Japan* (Cambridge, MA: Harvard University Asia Center, 2021), 71; See also Pia Jolliffe, *Prisons and Forced Labour in Japan: The Colonization of Hokkaido, 1881–1894* (London: Routledge, 2020).

34. Garon, *Molding Japanese Minds,* 41. Joseph Lyons's history of chaplaincy provides in-depth exploration of the development of Japanese penal ideologies. In particular, Lyons points out the contradiction between the vehemently anti-Christian ideology of the Tokugawa-era government and the adoption of a penal ideology rooted in a Western Christian moral narrative of sin, confession, and salvation. Lyons explains how Pure Land Buddhist chaplains

became mediators, adapting their doctrine to this penal model of moral rehabilitation while supporting the spiritual and moral authority of the state. Lyons, *Karma and Punishment*.

35. Takami Kuwayama, "The Discourse of Ie (Family) in Japan's Cultural Identity and Nationalism: A Critique," *Japanese Review of Cultural Anthropology* 2, no. 0 (2001): 3–37.
36. Hayashi, *The Care of Older People*; Carolyn S. Stevens, *Disability in Japan* (London: Routledge, 2013).
37. Garon, *Molding Japanese Minds*, 56–57.
38. Aya Homei, *Science for Governing Japan's Population* (Cambridge: Cambridge University Press, 2022).
39. Stevens, *Disability in Japan*, 39–40.
40. Fassin, *Prison Worlds*, 289.
41. Loïc Wacquant, "Crafting the Neoliberal State: Workfare, Prisonfare, and Social Insecurity," *Sociological Forum* 25, no. 2 (2010): 197–220; David Garland, *Punishment and Welfare: A History of Penal Strategies* (Brookfield, VT: Gower, 1985). Wacquant uses the term "prisonfare" to describe the way penal solutions have taken the place of welfare solutions to conditions of poverty and racialized inequalities, for instance. While some have debated the existence of a penal-welfare nexus, in which neoliberal retrenchment of the welfare state coincides with a punitive turn in penal policy, such a stark equation requires close examination in the case of Japan. One reason is that following neoliberal reforms in the early 2000s, overall crime rates have decreased to their lowest level in decades. This does not necessarily mean that neoliberalization reduced crime and successfully produced good, self-policing citizens. Rather, what I argue is that because prisons and welfare are drawn closer together, individuals who cross these categories will circulate between them, while others will be more likely to exit.
42. This is not only the case in Japan. See Eva Boodman, who has made a similar case in the US context, arguing that the shared genealogy and carceral logic of prisons and nursing homes links abolitionist aims to both institutions. "Nursing Home Abolition: Prisons and the Institutionalization of Older Adult Care," *Journal of Ethical Urban Living* 2, no. 1 (2019): 1–21. Also see Chris Chapman, Allison C. Carey, and Liat Ben-Moshe, "Reconsidering Confinement: Interlocking Locations and Logics of Incarceration," in *Disability Incarcerated: Imprisonment and Disability in the United States and Canada*, ed. Liat Ben-Moshe, Chris Chapman, and Allison C. Carey (New York: Palgrave Macmillan US, 2014), 3–24. This source traces the history of disabled persons' confinement, linking it not only to the production of an

economic underclass, but to the rise of the medical and caring professions. What all of these examples share is the recognition that the conventional borders between prison and welfare (and the ministries and institutions associated with them) obscures the fact that they work and function together and under the same social and political logics.

43. *Hogo* can be translated as *protection*, while *Sara* is an alternate reading for *rehabilitation*. There are several other animal characters representing the probation officer (whale), employer (otter), and Big Brothers Big Sisters (dolphin).
44. Bykowski, "Techno-Mediated Safety."
45. Hamai and Ellis, "Crime and Criminal Justice"; Carl B. Becker, "Report from Japan: Causes and Controls of Crime in Japan," *Journal of Criminal Justice* 16, no. 5 (January 1, 1988): 425–35.
46. Jennifer Turner, Dominique Moran, and Yvonne Jewkes, "'It's in the Air Here': Atmosphere(s) of Incarceration," *Incarceration* 3, no. 3 (November 1, 2022); Moran, *Carceral Geography*; Jewkes and Young, "Sensory Reflections."
47. Peter A. Lutz, "Multivalent Moves in Senior Home Care: From Surveillance to Care-Valence," *Anthropology & Aging* 36, no. 2 (November 19, 2015): 145–63; Matthew Lariviere et al., "Placing Assistive Technology and Telecare in Everyday Practices of People with Dementia and Their Caregivers: Findings from an Embedded Ethnography of a National Dementia Trial," *BMC Geriatrics* 21, no. 1 (February 15, 2021): 121; James Wright, *Robots Won't Save Japan: An Ethnography of Eldercare Automation* (Ithaca, NY: Cornell University Press, 2023).
48. Daniel H. Foote, "The Benevolent Paternalism of Japanese Criminal Justice," *California Law Review* 80, no. 2 (1992): 317–90.
49. Steven H. Lopez, "Culture Change and Shit Work: Empowering and Overpowering the Frail Elderly in Long-Term Care," *American Behavioral Scientist* 58, no. 3 (September 23, 2013): 435–52; Boodman, "Nursing Home Abolition"; Magdalena Zegarra Chiappori, "Remaining, Vital Acts, and Possibility: The Exercise of 'Sustaining Oneself' in a Residential Care Center for the Elderly in Lima, Peru," *Anthropology and Humanism* 47, no. 2 (2022): 297–311.
50. The Japanese Ministry of Health, Labour and Welfare (MHLW) has deemed the use of physical restraints in nursing homes a form of abuse with the exception of cases where the restrained person is hurting themselves or others. However, the enforcement of these guidelines has been minimal, and cases of restraints and other forms of abuse in nursing care homes has risen, with record high numbers of reported incidences in 2021. Since 2018, the MHLW has required that each care facility produces its own guidelines regarding physical restraints. Several care workers I have spoken with since

2013 have described abuse or neglect in the context of staff shortages and precarity: see Jason Danely, "Affect, Infrastructure, and Vulnerability," *Medicine Anthropology Theory* 3, no. 1 (2016): 198–222. For more on comparisons between obasuteyama and care homes, see Jonathan Ferries, "Obasuteyama in Modern Japan: Ageing, Ageism and Government Policy," in *Case Studies on Human Rights in Japan*, ed. Roger Goodman and Ian Neary, 222–44 (Richmond: Japan Library, 1996); Hayashi, *The Care of Older People*, 57–58; Danely, *Aging and Loss*.

51. Giorgio Agamben, *Homo Sacer: Sovereign Power and Bare Life*, trans. Daniel Heller-Roazen (Palo Alto, CA: Stanford University Press, 1998); João Guilherme Biehl, *Vita: Life in a Zone of Social Abandonment* (Berkeley: University of California Press, 2005); Erving Goffman, *Asylums* (London: Penguin UK, 1991).

CHAPTER 3

1. Joseph Hankins, "Yamanote's Promise: Buraku Stigma, Tokyo's Trains, and the Infrastructure of Social Belonging," *Japan Forum* 30, no. 2 (April 3, 2018): 186–204.
2. Mother House was officially established in 2012 as a "Private Nonprofit Group" (*minkan hieiri dantai*), a status that allowed them to begin raising capital and preparing to apply for official NPO Corporation status. Aside from the problem of funding, Mother House also faced the issue of restrictions on who was allowed to establish an NPO. The law restricts formerly incarcerated individuals from applying for an NPO Corporation until at least two years from the completion of their sentence, and several additional restrictions applied to those who have been members of organized crime groups (*bōryokudan*). This was a setback for the founder of Mother House, Hiroshi Igarashi, who had started organizing Mother House only a few months after his release from prison.
3. Igarashi, *Jinsei wo kaeru deai*, 83.
4. Igarashi, *Jinsei wo kaeru deai*, 84.
5. Although Igarashi's story revolves around his conversion and Mother House has built a friendly relationship with the Catholic Church over the years, it is not officially a Catholic Charity, nor does it have any formal connection to Mother Teresa's Calcutta Mission or the affiliated branches in Tokyo. In fact, while Igarashi was consulting with Catholic organizations before setting up his NPO, several were strongly opposed to the name, thinking perhaps that it was a tricky strategy for Igarashi to raise donation money.
6. For more on the concept of tōjisha in activist movements, see Junko Kitanaka, "In the Mind of Dementia: Neurobiological Empathy, Incommensurability,

and the Dementia Tojisha Movement in Japan," *Medical Anthropology Quarterly* 34, no. 1 (2020): 119–35.
7. This was probably a paraphrasing of Victorian prison reformer Elizabeth Fry's famous assertion that British prisons were "schools for crime."
8. Compare with the approach of Buddhist prison chaplains called "doctrinal admonition" (*kyōkai*), which implies both the "teaching practice for purifying the transgressor's heart (*kokoro*)" and the harmonization of that practice with secular state correctional ideology of securing the public good. See Lyons, *Karma and Punishment*, 11–12. Kokoro encompasses not only an individual's thoughts and feelings, but also a connection to others and to the world or "place" (*ba*) shared with others. In this sense, a *kokoro* that is well-cultivated will also result in a self that is capable of intimacy and togetherness with others. See Diana Adis Tahhan, *The Japanese Family: Touch, Intimacy and Feeling* (London: Routledge, 2014), 80–81.
9. Igarashi's use of encounter (*deai*) is inspired by Christian conversion narratives, but it resonates strongly with other notions of spiritual connection, such as "attuning to webs of *en*," or "ties or relations (*enishi*) invisible orders beyond human knowledge, which form webs around all things in the universe" that "may be brought to attention through *unexpected meetings*" (emphasis mine). Jensen, Ishii, and Swift, "Attuning to the Webs of *En*," 160. In a sense, Igarashi is acknowledging both the bad karma and "fate" of the individual that led them to crime, and the agency they have to create new relations to reshape that fate. The notion of *en* also blurs the line between self and other, since both are only possible through the encounter; to meet the other is to meet the self (echoing Buber)

CHAPTER 4

1. Suzuki and Otani, "Myths of Restorative Features."
2. David T. Johnson, "Crime and Punishment in Contemporary Japan," *Crime and Punishment* 36, no. 1 (2007): 371–423; Hitoshi Miyazawa, "Welfare Regime in Japan and Recent Social Security Reform," in *Community-Based Integrated Care and the Inclusive Society: Recent Social Security Reform in Japan*, ed. Hitoshi Miyazawa and Teruo Hatakeyama, 3–17 (Singapore: Springer, 2021); Suzuki and Otani, "Ageing, Institutional Thoughtlessness."
3. Crawley and Sparks, "Is There Life after Imprisonment?"
4. Graeber, "Dead Zones of the Imagination," 123.
5. Maren A. Ehlers, *Give and Take: Poverty and the Status Order in Early Modern Japan* (Cambridge, MA: Harvard University Asia Center, 2018).
6. Garon, *Molding Japanese Minds*; Hayashi, *The Care of Older People*.

7. This cautious approach to approaching the history of carceral institutions has also been voiced in critical responses to accounts of the US police and prison system and its links to slavery. See, for instance, James Forman, "Racial Critiques of Mass Incarceration: Beyond the New Jim Crow," *New York University Law Review* 87, no. 1 (2012): 101–46.
8. Crawley, "Institutional Thoughtlessness."
9. Carolyn Sufrin, *Jailcare: Finding the Safety Net for Women behind Bars* (Berkeley: University of California Press, 2017).
10. Routledge, "Third Space," 399–419.
11. Allison, *Precarious Japan*, 79.

CHAPTER 5

1. See Jieun Kim, "Social Exclusion and Care in Underclass Japan: Attunement as Techniques of Belonging," *Culture, Medicine, and Psychiatry* 45, no. 1 (March 1, 2021): 42–63. Since 1961, Japan has had a basic public pension system for those over the age of sixty-five (*rōrei nenkin*). In 2020, the age of pension eligibility was raised to sixty-eight. Since 2012, eligibility, however, depended on a minimum of ten years of insurance premium payments (typically by an employer). Even if they can meet this threshold, they will only receive an average of about 65,000 yen (approx. $450) per month—far below subsistence. Those who do not meet the twenty-five-year hurdle, such as casual day-laborers, may be left with no pension. In 2018, *Asahi News* reported that 66.8 percent of older people arrested for shoplifting were living on a basic old age pension. Manabu Hiratsuka, "Nenkin seikatsu 'konna shōhin ni okane wa . . .' medatsu manbiki, ōita" (Pension Life: "I Wouldn't Pay for Such a Product . . ." Shoplifters in Oita). *Asahi Shinbun (Digital)*, April 8, 2018.
2. David Graeber, "Dead Zones of the Imagination," 112.
3. Fowler, *San'ya Blues*; Gill, *Men of Uncertainty*, 81–91; Matthew D. Marr, "Gentrification, Machizukuri, and Ontological Insecurity: Bottom-Up Redevelopment and the Cries of Residents in Kamagasaki, Osaka," in *Gentrification around the World*, vol. 1: *Gentrifiers and the Displaced*, ed. Jerome Krase and Judith N. DeSena, 291–313 (Cham: Springer International Publishing, 2020).
4. Ben Crewe, "Depth, Weight, Tightness: Revisiting the Pains of Imprisonment," *Punishment & Society* 13, no. 5 (December 1, 2011): 509–29.
5. Julienne Weegels, Andrew M. Jefferson, and Tomas Max Martin, "Introduction: Confinement Beyond Site: Connecting Urban and Prison Ethnographies," *Cambridge Journal of Anthropology* 38, no. 1 (March 1, 2020): 1–14; Andrew Jefferson, Simon Turner, and Steffen Jensen, "Introduction: On Stuckness

and Sites of Confinement," *Ethnos* 84, no. 1 (January 1, 2019): 1–13; Jennifer Turner, *The Prison Boundary* (London: Palgrave Macmillan UK, 2016).
6. David Garland, "Punishment and Welfare: Social Problems and Social Structures," in *The Oxford Handbook of Criminology*, 6th ed., ed. Alison Liebling, Shadd Maruna, and Lesley McAra, 77–100 (Abingdon: Oxford University Press, 2017); Loïc Wacquant, *Punishing the Poor: The Neoliberal Government of Social Insecurity* (Durham, NC: Duke University Press Books, 2009).
7. Gill, *Men of Uncertainty*, 171–72.
8. Gill, *Men of Uncertainty*, 82.
9. Daniel V. Botsman, *Punishment and Power in the Making of Modern Japan* (Princeton, NJ: Princeton University Press, 2013), 23. The name Kotsukappara means "field of small hills," but also became known as "Kotsu-ga-hara," or "field of bones." As a burial site not only for executed criminals, but for other unclaimed corpses as well, its location marked the outer edge of the city where residents would be safe from the spiritual pollution.
10. Asao Takamori, *Ashita no Jo (Tomorrow's Joe)* (Tokyo: Kodansha, 1983).
11. Tatsuya Shirahase, *Hinkon to Chiiki – Airinchiku Kara Miru Kōrei-Ka to Koritsu Shi* (Poverty and Community – Aging and Solitary Death as Seen from the Airin District) (Tokyo: Chuokoron Shinsha, 2017); Gill, *Men of Uncertainty*; Kim, "Social Exclusion."
12. Hanno Jentzsch, "San'ya 2020: From Building to Hosting the Olympics," in *Japan through the Lens of the Tokyo Olympics*, ed. Barbara Holthus et al. (London: Routledge, 2020), 55.
13. Fowler, *San'ya Blues*, 15.
14. Kim, "Social Exclusion."
15. Anne Allison, *Being Dead Otherwise* (Durham, NC: Duke University Press, 2023), 93.
16. Daisetz Teitaro Suzuki, *Shin Buddhism* (New York: Harper & Row, 1970), 22.
17. Kimura and Sawaki, "Kōrei/shōgai hanzaisha," 106.
18. Ghassan Hage, "Bearable Life," *Suomen Antropologi* 44, no. 2 (2019): 81–83.

CHAPTER 6

1. In Japan, each year, typhoons are identified by number, unlike hurricanes, which get names.
2. Yukiko Sakemoto, "Fukuekichū ni 'hogokansatsujo no sei da' ikiba wo ushinai kasaneta tsumi wa fusegeta no ka" (While Serving Time He Said "It's the Probation Office's Fault": With Nowhere to Go, Could the Additional Crime Have Been Prevented?), *Asahi Shimbun*, July 21, 2022, https://digital.asahi.com/articles/ASQ7N6RZXQ7NUGTB002.html.
3. Sakemoto, "Fukuekichū ni 'hogokansatsujo no sei da.'"

4. Fukuda had been the victim of bullying and abuse as a child, in part because of his disability. After his first arrest for arson, his father committed suicide, and Fukuda-san has said that his guilt was something that made him go back to prison.
5. Michael Hallett, "Reentry to What? Theorizing Prisoner Reentry in the Jobless Future," *Critical Criminology* 20 (2012): 2013–28; Loïc Wacquant, "Prisoner Reentry as Myth and Ceremony," *Dialectical Anthropology* 34, no. 4 (December 1, 2010): 605–620; Weegels, Jefferson, and Martin, "Introduction."
6. David Garland, *The Culture of Control: Crime and Social Order in Contemporary Society*, rev. ed. (Oxford: Oxford University Press, 2002).
7. Kathleen M. Woodward, *Aging and Its Discontents: Freud and Other Fictions* (Bloomington: Indiana University Press, 1991); Fassin, *Prison Worlds*; Allison, *Precarious Japan*.
8. Yamamoto, *Keimusho shika ibasho*, 82.

CHAPTER 7

1. Kimura and Sawaki, "Kōrei/shōgai hanzaisha"; Mizuki Uotani, "Ruihan kōreisha wa naze fue tsudzukete iru no ka: Saihan bōshi ni wa nani ga hitsuyōna no ka" (Why the Number of Elderly Repeat Offenders Continues to Increase: What Is Needed to Prevent Repeat Offenses?), Waseda University Faculty of Culture, Media and Society, Department of Contemporary Human Studies Okabe Seminar Paper Collection, 2013, https://www.f.waseda.jp/k_okabe/semi-theses.
2. Ministry of Health, Labour and Welfare (Japan), *Chiiki seikatsu teichaku shien sentā no shien jōkyō (ryō wa 2-nendo-chū ni shien shita mono)* (Support Status of Community Life Settlement Support Center [Those Who Supported in 2020]) (Tokyo: Ministry of Health, Labour and Welfare, 2020).
3. Ryoko Miki and Taro Asanuma, "Keiji jiken ni kan'yo shita shōgai-sha e no 'iriguchi shien' no genjō to kadai" (The Approach and Issue on Early Stage Support for Disabled Suspects and Defendants Provided by Social Workers Cooperating with Defense Attorneys in Tokyo Model), *Teikyō Kagaku Daigaku Kiyō* 14 (2018): 1–8.
4. Danely, "Affect, Infrastructure, and Vulnerability."

CHAPTER 8

1. Saidiya Hartman quoted in Christina Sharpe, *Ordinary Notes* (London: Daunt Books, 2023), 62.
2. Cabinet Office (Japan), "Reiwa 3 nenban kōrei shakai hakusho" (2021 Annual Aging Society White Paper), (Tokyo: Cabinet Office, 2021), figure 1-1-9. https://www8.cao.go.jp/kourei/whitepaper/w-2021/zenbun/03pdf_index.html.

3. Tetsu Harayama, "Posuto fukushi kokka ni okeru haijo to hōsetsu no kōsatsu" (For Considering Exclusion and Inclusion in Post-Welfare Nation), in *Kōreisha hanzai no sōgōteki kenkyū* (Comprehensive Research on Elderly Crime), ed. Yoko Hosoi and Bunri Tatsuno (Tokyo: Kazama Shobo, 2021), 15–32; Miyazawa, "Welfare Regime in Japan"; Allison, *Precarious Japan*; Danely, "The Limits of Dwelling."
4. Cabinet Office (Japan), "Kodoku/koritsu ni kansuru kakushu chōsa ni tsuite" (About the Various Surveys on Loneliness/Isolation), (Tokyo: Cabinet Office, 2018), table 2-1-11-2. https://www.cao.go.jp/kodoku_koritsu/torikumi/yushikisha/jutenkeikaku/dai5/pdf/siryou2.pdf.
5. Allison, *Precarious Japan*; Chikako Ozawa-de Silva, *The Anatomy of Loneliness: Suicide, Social Connection, and the Search for Relational Meaning in Contemporary Japan* (Berkeley: University of California Press, 2021).
6. Anne Allison, "Ordinary Refugees: Social Precarity and Soul in 21st Century Japan," *Anthropological Quarterly* 85, no. 2 (2012): 345–70.
7. Ozawa-de Silva, *The Anatomy of Loneliness*; Marshall Sahlins, *What Kinship Is—and Is Not* (Chicago, IL: University of Chicago Press, 2013).
8. Ruth Wilson Gilmore, "You Have Dislodged a Boulder: Mothers and Prisoners in the Post Keynesian California Landscape," *Transforming Anthropology* 8, no. 1–2 (1999): 12–38; Khan, "The Carceral State"; Hollis Moore, "Extralegal Agency and the Search for Safety in Northeast Brazil: Moving beyond Carceral Logics," *Cambridge Journal of Anthropology* 38, no. 1 (March 1, 2020): 33–51; Alana Abramson and Muhammad Asadullah, "Decolonizing Restorative Justice," in *The Routledge International Handbook of Decolonizing Justice*, ed. Chris Cunneen et al., 367–79 (London: Routledge, 2023); Angela Garcia, "The Blue Years: An Ethnography of a Prison Archive," *Cultural Anthropology* 31, no. 4 (November 15, 2016): 571–94.
9. Keahnan Washington, "Love-Politics and the Carceral Encounter," *Anthropology News* 60, no. 1 (2019): e65–70.
10. Jieun Kim, "Necrosociality: Isolated Death and Unclaimed Cremains in Japan," *Journal of the Royal Anthropological Institute* 22, no. 4 (September 2016): 843–63; Matthew D. Marr, "The Ohaka (Grave) Project: Post-Secular Social Service Delivery and Resistant Necropolitics in San'ya, Tokyo," *Ethnography* 22, no. 1 (March 1, 2021): 88–110.
11. Hage, "Bearable Life."
12. Chikako Ozawa-de Silva, *Psychotherapy and Religion in Japan: The Japanese Introspection Practice of Naikan* (New York: Routledge, 2006), 130–31. This argument about the importance of the mother is most strongly expressed in Kosawa Heisaku's theory of the Ajase Complex. See Chikako Ozawa-de

Silva, "Demystifying Japanese Therapy: An Analysis of Naikan and the Ajase Complex through Buddhist Thought," *Ethos* 35, no. 4 (2007): 411–46; as well as in the socialization of amae, see Takeo Doi, *The Anatomy of Self: The Individual Versus Society* (Tokyo: Kodansha International, 1986); Takie Sugiyama Lebra, *Japanese Patterns of Behavior* (Honolulu: University of Hawai'i Press, 1976); and "skinship," see Tahhan, *The Japanese Family*. In all of these cases, the mother-child relationship, which is both inter-corporeal and inter-subjective, becomes the prototype for a kind of intimate social relationship with others characterized by the presumption of having one's desires indulged and of understanding and indulging others' desires.

13. Ozawa-de Silva, *Psychotherapy and Religion in Japan*, 7–8; Lyons, *Karma and Punishment*, 212.
14. Lyons, *Karma and Punishment*, 229–30.
15. Allison describes *ibasho* not only as a "place or space when living feels right," but as "Human Time," of "mutual caregiving and open acceptance" full of queer potentiality for social reorganization. *Precarious Japan*, 174–75. While Mother House's *ibasho* was meant to be inclusive, accepting, and diverse, and while it did bring together multiple temporalities (religious, carceral, therapeutic), it was also strongly tied to more normative notions of family and motherhood; Similarly, Ozawa-de Silva, *The Anatomy of Loneliness*, 216–17, does not think of *ibasho* only in spatial terms, but more importantly, as relational, and flexible to other virtual and imaginative spaces; Saito describes a conversation with law professor Yasuda Megum where she describes a dream of creating a "coffee shop" where ex-offenders and those with an interest in them can come together and build relationships. *Rupo Rojin Jukeisha*, 199–200.
16. Klaus Hamberger, "Kinship as Logic of Space," *Current Anthropology* 59, no. 5 (October 2018): 525–48; Khan, "The Carceral State," 58.

CONCLUSION

1. Graeber, "Dead Zones of the Imagination."
2. Nancy Fraser, "Contradictions of Capital and Care," *New Left Review*, no. 100 (August 1, 2016): 99–117.
3. Amartya Sen, "Capability and Well-Being," in *The Quality of Life*, ed. Martha Nussbaum and Amartya Sen (Oxford University Press, 1993). This capability framework was taken up by the WHO in their 2015 "World Report on Aging and Health," in which they approach health in old age as a combination of abilities that allow the older person "to be and to do what they have reason to value." WHO, "World Report on Aging and Health," 28.

4. Jason Scott, "Ethnography at Its Edges: In Defense of How-to Abolitionism: An Anthropological Engagement with Mariame Kaba," *American Ethnologist* 49, no. 3 (2022), 444.
5. Angela Davis, *Are Prisons Obsolete?* (New York: Seven Stories Press, 2003), 107.
6. Dylan Rodríguez, "Abolition as Praxis of Human Being: A Foreword," *Harvard Law Review* 132, no. 6 (2019): 1,578.
7. See, for instance, the work on abolition and place-making in Gilmore, *Abolition Geography*.
8. Savannah Shange, "Abolition in the Clutch: Shifting through the Gears with Anthropology," *Feminist Anthropology* 3, no. 2 (November 2022): 187–97.
9. For an example of the "long tail of incarceration" in the US, as well as a lengthy discussion of the conceptualization and operationalization of chronological age in prison research in Humblet, *The Older Prisoner*, 17–59, see Johanna T. Crane and Kelsey Pascoe, "Becoming Institutionalized: Incarceration as a Chronic Health Condition," *Medical Anthropology Quarterly* 35, no. 3 (2021): 307–26.
10. Story, *Prison Land,* 168–69. While not specifically about ageism, Story's elaboration on the notion of abolition and the carceral resonate strongly with what I have outlined here and extended to the "surplus" population of older adults.
11. Humblet, *The Older Prisoner*; Marti, *Doing Indefinite Time*.
12. Naomi F. Sugie, "When the Elderly Turn to Petty Crime: Increasing Elderly Arrest Rates in an Aging Population," *International Criminal Justice Review* 27, no. 1 (March 2017): 19–39; Lawson, "Subverting the Prison," 336–37.
13. Lauren Berlant, *Cruel Optimism* (Durham, NC: Duke University Press Books, 2011).

BIBLIOGRAPHY

Adachi, Kiyoshi. "The Development of Social Welfare Services in Japan." In *Caring for the Elderly in Japan and the US*, edited by Susan O. Long, 191–205. London: Routledge, 2000.

Adam, David. "How Far Will Global Population Rise? Researchers Can't Agree." *Nature* 597, no. 7877 (September 21, 2021): 462–65. https://doi.org/10.1038/d41586-021-02522-6.

Adams, D. L., and Nirmala Erevelles. "Unexpected Spaces of Confinement: Aversive Technologies, Intellectual Disability, and 'Bare Life.'" *Punishment & Society* 19, no. 3 (July 2017): 348–65. https://doi.org/10.1177/1462474517705147.

Aday, Ronald H., and Jennifer J. Krabill. "Older and Geriatric Offenders: Critical Issues for the 21st Century." *Special Needs Offenders in Correctional Institutions*, no. 1 (2012): 203–33.

Agamben, Giorgio. *Homo Sacer: Sovereign Power and Bare Life*. Translated by Daniel Heller-Roazen. Palo Alto, CA: Stanford University Press, 1998.

Aldous, Christopher, and Frank Leishman. "Police and Community Safety in Japan: Model or Myth?" *Crime Prevention and Community Safety* 1, no. 1 (January 1999): 25–39. https://doi.org/10.1057/palgrave.cpcs.8140003.

Alexander, Michelle. *The New Jim Crow: Mass Incarceration in the Age of Colorblindness*. 10th anniv. ed. New York: New Press, 2020.

Allison, Anne. *Being Dead Otherwise*. Durham, NC: Duke University Press, 2023.

———. "Not-Wanting to Die Badly: Facing the Precarity of Dying Alone in Japan." In *Ethnographies of Waiting: Doubt, Hope and Uncertainty*, edited by Manpreet K. Janeja and Andreas Bandak, 181–202. London: Bloomsbury Academic, 2018.

———. "Ordinary Refugees: Social Precarity and Soul in 21st Century Japan." *Anthropological Quarterly* 85, no. 2 (2012): 345–70. https://doi.org/10.1353/anq.2012.0027.

———. *Precarious Japan*. Durham, NC: Duke University Press, 2013.

Amnesty International. "Japan: Abusive Punishments in Japanese Prisons." April 22, 1998.

Anderson, Warwick. "Crap on the Map, or Postcolonial Waste." *Postcolonial Studies* 13, no. 2 (June 2010): 169–78. https://doi.org/10.1080/13688790.2010.496436.

Ashita, Matsumiya. "Kōrei-sha no 'kankei-sei no hinkon' to 'kodoku-shi' 'koritsu shi'" (The Poverty of Social Networks on the Elderly and Dying Alone). *Nihon Toshi Shakai Gakkai Nenpō*. Annual Report of the Japanese Association of Urban Sociology 2012, no. 30 (2013): 15–28. https://doi.org/10.5637/jpasurban.2012.15.

Avieli, Hila. "'A Sense of Purpose': Older Prisoners' Experiences of Successful Ageing behind Bars." *European Journal of Criminology* 19, no. 6 (November 1, 2022): 1,660–77. https://doi.org/10.1177/1477370821995142.

Baidawi, Susan, Shelley Turner, Christopher Trotter, Colette Browning, Paul Collier, Daniel O'Connor, Rosemary Sheehan, and others. "Older Prisoners: A Challenge for Australian Corrections." *Trends and Issues in Crime and Criminal Justice*, no. 426 (2011): 1.

Bay, Alexander R. "Disciplining Shit." *Japan Forum* 31, no. 4 (October 2, 2019): 556–82. https://doi.org/10.1080/09555803.2019.1594341.

Becker, Carl B. "Report from Japan: Causes and Controls of Crime in Japan." *Journal of Criminal Justice* 16, no. 5 (1 January 1988): 425–35. https://doi.org/10.1016/0047-2352(88)90067-0.

Bell, Kristen. "Staging Prevention, Arresting Progress: Chronic Disease Prevention and the Lifestyle Frame." In *Preventing Dementia: Critical Perspectives on a New Paradigm of Preparing for Old Age*, edited by Annette Leibing and Silke Schicktanz, 175–91. Oxford: Berghahn Books, 2020.

Ben-Moshe, L., C. Chapman, and A. Carey. *Disability Incarcerated: Imprisonment and Disability in the United States and Canada*. New York: Palgrave Macmillan, 2014.

Berlant, Lauren. *Cruel Optimism*. Durham, NC: Duke University Press Books, 2011.

Biehl, João Guilherme. *Vita: Life in a Zone of Social Abandonment*. Berkeley: University of California Press, 2005.

Boodman, Eva. "Nursing Home Abolition: Prisons and the Institutionalization of Older Adult Care." *Journal of Ethical Urban Living* 2, no. 1 (2019): 1–21.

Botsman, Daniel V. *Punishment and Power in the Making of Modern Japan*. Princeton, NJ: Princeton University Press, 2007.

Bourgois, Philippe, and Jeffrey Schonberg. *Righteous Dopefiend*. Berkeley: University of California Press, 2009.

Braithwaite, John. "Crime in Asia: Toward a Better Future." *Asian Journal of Criminology* 9, no. 1 (1 March 2014): 65–75. https://doi.org/10.1007/s11417-013-9176-0.

Burraway, Joshua. "Remembering to Forget: Blacking Out in Itchy Park." *Current Anthropology* 59, no. 5 (October 2018): 469–87. https://doi.org/10.1086/699881.

Bykowski, Misha. "Techno-Mediated Safety: Social Atomization and the Growth of Residential Security in Recessionary Japan." PhD diss., Stanford University, 2020.

Calasanti, Toni. "Combating Ageism: How Successful Is Successful Aging?" *Gerontologist* 56, no. 6 (December 2016): 1,093–101. https://doi.org/10.1093/geront/gnv076.

Campbell, John Creighton, Naoki Ikegami, and Mary Jo Gibson. "Lessons from Public Long-Term Care Insurance in Germany and Japan." *Health Affairs* 29, no. 1 (1 January 2010): 87–95. https://doi.org/10.1377/hlthaff.2009.0548.

Campbell, John Creighton, and Naoki Ikegami. "Long-Term Care Insurance Comes to Japan." *Health Affairs* 19, no. 3 (1 May 2000): 26–39. https://doi.org/10.1377/hlthaff.19.3.26.

Chapman, Chris, Allison C. Carey, and Liat Ben-Moshe. "Reconsidering Confinement: Interlocking Locations and Logics of Incarceration." In *Disability Incarcerated: Imprisonment and Disability in the United States and Canada*, edited by Liat Ben-Moshe, Chris Chapman, and Allison C. Carey, 3–24. New York: Palgrave Macmillan US, 2014. https://doi.org/10.1057/9781137388476_1.

Clotworthy, Amy. *Empowering the Elderly?: How "Help to Self-Help" Health Interventions Shape Ageing and Eldercare in Denmark*. New York: Transcript Publishing, 2020.

Collins, R. D., and R. Bird. "The Penitentiary Visit—a New Role for Geriatricians?" *Age and Ageing* 36, no. 1 (17 November 2006): 11–13. https://doi.org/10.1093/ageing/afl144.

Coyle, Andrew. *Prisons of the World*. Bristol: Policy Press, 2021.

Crane, Johanna T., and Kelsey Pascoe. "Becoming Institutionalized: Incarceration as a Chronic Health Condition." *Medical Anthropology Quarterly* 35, no. 3 (2021): 307–26. https://doi.org/10.1111/maq.12621.

Crawley, Elaine. "Institutional Thoughtlessness in Prisons and Its Impacts on the Day-to-Day Prison Lives of Elderly Men." *Journal of Contemporary Criminal Justice* 21, no. 4 (November 2005): 350–63. https://doi.org/10.1177/1043986205282018.

---. "Release and Resettlement: The Perspectives of Older Prisoners." *Criminal Justice Matters* 56, no. 1 (1 June 2004): 32–33. https://doi.org/10.1080/09627250408552945.

Crawley, Elaine, and Richard Sparks. "Is There Life after Imprisonment?: How Elderly Men Talk about Imprisonment and Release." *Criminology & Criminal Justice* 6, no. 1 (February 2006): 63–82. https://doi.org/10.1177/1748895806060667.

---. "Older Men in Prison: Survival, Coping and Identity." In *The Effects of Imprisonment*, edited by Alison Liebling and Shadd Maruna. Abingdon, Oxon: Routledge, 2011.

Crewe, Ben. "Depth, Weight, Tightness: Revisiting the Pains of Imprisonment." *Punishment & Society* 13, no. 5 (1 December 2011): 509–29. https://doi.org/10.1177/1462474511422172.

Croydon, Silvia. "Social Welfare Reduction: A Shortcut to Prison." History Workshop Online, 17 August 2013. http://www.historyworkshop.org.uk/social-welfare-reduction-a-shortcut-to-prison.

---. *The Politics of Police Detention in Japan: Consensus of Convenience.* New York: Oxford University Press 2016.

---. "Making It Their Own: The Development of the Japanese Criminal Justice System." *Electronic Journal of Contemporary Japanese Studies* 18, no. 1 (29 April 2018).

Cunha, Manuela Ivone P. da. "Closed Circuits: Kinship, Neighborhood and Incarceration in Urban Portugal." *Ethnography* 9, no. 3 (1 September 2008): 325–50. https://doi.org/10.1177/1466138108094974.

Dahl, Nils. "Governing through Kodokushi: Japan's Lonely Deaths and Their Impact on Community Self-Government." *Contemporary Japan* 32, no. 1 (January 2, 2020): 83–102. https://doi.org/10.1080/18692729.2019.1680512.

Danely, Jason. "Affect, Infrastructure, and Vulnerability." *Medicine Anthropology Theory* 3, no. 1 (2016): 198–222. https://doi.org/doi.org/10.17157/mat.3.2.363.

---. *Aging and Loss: Mourning and Maturity in Contemporary Japan.* New Brunswick, NJ: Rutgers University Press, 2014.

---. *Fragile Resonance: Caring for Older Family Members in Japan and England.* Ithaca, NY: Cornell University Press, 2022.

---. "The Limits of Dwelling and the Unwitnessed Death." *Cultural Anthropology* 34, no. 2 (22 May 2019): 213–39. https://doi.org/10.14506/ca34.2.03.

Danely, Jason, Natalie Mann, and Carla Reeves. "Trends in the Aging Prison Population of England and Wales: A Useful Cross-National Comparison with Japan?" In *Comprehensive Study of Elderly Crime: Cross-Cultural Consideration with a View to Social Security, Employment, Family, and Aging*, edited by Yoko Hosoi and Bunri Tatsuo, 501–32. Tokyo: Kazama Shobo, 2021.

Dannefer, Dale. "Cumulative Advantage/Disadvantage and the Life Course: Cross-Fertilizing Age and Social Science Theory." *Journals of Gerontology: Series B* 58, no. 6 (1 November 2003): S327–37. https://doi.org/10.1093/geronb/58.6.S327.

Davis, Angela. *Are Prisons Obsolete?* New York: Seven Stories Press, 2003.

De Antoni, Andrea. "Down in a Hole: Dark Tourism, Haunted Places as Affective Meshworks, and the Obliteration of Korean Laborers in Contemporary Kyoto." *Japan Review*, no. 33 (2019): 271–98.

Doi, Takeo. *The Anatomy of Self: The Individual Versus Society*. Translated by Mark A. Harbison. Tokyo: Kodansha International, 1986.

Drake, Deborah H., Rod Earle, and Jennifer Sloan. "General Introduction: What Ethnography Tells Us about Prisons and What Prisons Tell Us about Ethnography." In *The Palgrave Handbook of Prison Ethnography*, edited by Deborah H. Drake, Rod Earle, and Jennifer Sloan, 1–16. Palgrave Studies in Prisons and Penology. London: Palgrave Macmillan UK, 2015. https://doi.org/10.1057/9781137403889_1.

Du, Lisa, and Grace Huang. "Japan's Hospitals Turn Thousands of COVID-19 Patients Away." *Japan Times*, August 26, 2021, https://www.japantimes.co.jp/news/2021/08/26/national/japan-hospitals-covid-19.

Ehlers, Maren A. *Give and Take: Poverty and the Status Order in Early Modern Japan*. Cambridge, MA: Harvard University Asia Center, 2018.

Ellis, Tom, Julak Lee, and Nick Pamment. "South Korean Probation: Volunteering and Late Onset Crime Control?" *Crime Prevention and Community Safety* 15, no. 4 (November 2013): 292–305. https://doi.org/10.1057/cpcs.2013.11.

Fassin, Didier. *Prison Worlds: An Ethnography of the Carceral Condition*. Malden, MA: Polity Press, 2017.

Fazel, Seena, Tony Hope, Ian O'Donnell, Mary Piper, and Robin Jacoby. "Health of Elderly Male Prisoners: Worse than the General Population, Worse than Younger Prisoners." *Age and Ageing* 30, no. 5 (2001): 403–7.

Fellner, Jamie, and Patrick Vinck. *Old Behind Bars: The Aging Prison Population in the United States*. New York: Human Rights Watch, 2012.

Ferries, Jonathan. "Obasuteyama in Modern Japan: Ageing, Ageism and Government Policy." In *Case Studies on Human Rights in Japan*, edited by Roger Goodman and Ian Neary, 222–44. Richmond, Surrey: Japan Library, 1996.

Foote, Daniel H. "The Benevolent Paternalism of Japanese Criminal Justice." *California Law Review* 80, no. 2 (1992): 317–90. https://doi.org/10.2307/3480769.

Forman, James. "Racial Critiques of Mass Incarceration: Beyond the New Jim Crow." *New York University Law Review* 87, no. 1 (2012): 101–46.

Forsyth, Katrina, Jane Senior, Caroline Stevenson, Kate O'Hara, Adrian Hayes, David Challis, and Jenny Shaw. "'They Just Throw You Out': Release Planning for Older Prisoners." *Ageing and Society* 35, no. 9 (October 2015): 2,011–25. https://doi.org/10.1017/S0144686X14000774.

Foucault, Michel. *Discipline and Punish: The Birth of the Prison*. Translated by Alan Sheridan. New York: Penguin, 1991.

Fowler, Edward. *San'ya Blues: Laboring Life in Contemporary Tokyo*. Ithaca, NY: Cornell University Press, 1996.

Fraser, Nancy. "Contradictions of Capital and Care." *New Left Review*, no. 100 (1 August 2016): 99–117.

Garland, David. *The Culture of Control: Crime and Social Order in Contemporary Society*, rev. ed. Oxford: Oxford University Press, 2002.

———. *Punishment and Welfare: A History of Penal Strategies*. Brookfield, VT: Gower, 1985.

———. "Punishment and Welfare: Social Problems and Social Structures." In *The Oxford Handbook of Criminology*, 6th ed., edited by Alison Liebling, Shadd Maruna, and Lesley McAra, 77–100. Abingdon: Oxford University Press, 2017.

Garon, Sheldon. *Molding Japanese Minds: The State in Everyday Life*. Princeton, NJ: Princeton University Press, 1997.

Gill, Nick, Deirdre Conlon, Dominique Moran, and Andrew Burridge. "Carceral Circuitry: New Directions in Carceral Geography." *Progress in Human Geography* 42, no. 2 (1 April 2018): 183–204. https://doi.org/10.1177/0309132516671823.

Gill, Tom. *Men of Uncertainty: The Social Organization of Day Laborers in Contemporary Japan*. Albany: State University of New York Press, 2001.

Gilmore, Ruth Wilson. *Abolition Geography: Essays towards Liberation*. Edited by Brenna Bhandar and Alberto Toscano. London: Verso, 2022.

———. *Golden Gulag: Prisons, Surplus, Crisis and Opposition in Globalizing California*. Berkeley: University of California Press, 2006.

———. "You Have Dislodged a Boulder: Mothers and Prisoners in the Post Keynesian California Landscape." *Transforming Anthropology* 8, no. 1–2 (1999): 12–38. https://doi.org/10.1525/tran.1999.8.1-2.12.

Ginn, Stephen. "Elderly Prisoners." *BMJ: British Medical Journal (Online)* 345 (October 20, 2012): 24–27.

Goffman, Erving. *Asylums*. London: Penguin UK, 1991.

Goldfarb, Kathryn E., and Caroline E. Schuster. "Introduction: (De)Materializing Kinship—Holding Together Mutuality and Difference." *Social Analysis* 60, no. 2 (1 June 2016): 1–12. https://doi.org/10.3167/sa.2016.600201.

Gordon, Avery. *Ghostly Matters: Haunting and the Sociological Imagination*, 2nd ed. Minneapolis: University of Minnesota Press, 2008. https://www.upress.umn.edu/book-division/books/ghostly-matters.

Graeber, David. "Dead Zones of the Imagination: On Violence, Bureaucracy, and Interpretive Labor. The 2006 Malinowski Memorial Lecture." *HAU: Journal of Ethnographic Theory* 2, no. 2 (December 19, 2012): 105–28. https://doi.org/10.14318/hau2.2.007.

Guenther, Lisa. *Solitary Confinement: Social Death and Its Afterlives*. Minneapolis: University of Minnesota Press, 2013.

Hage, Ghassan. "Bearable Life." *Suomen Antropologi: Journal of the Finnish Anthropological Society* 44, no. 2 (2019): 81–83.

Haley, John O. "Apology and Pardon: Learning from Japan." *American Behavioral Scientist* 41, no. 6 (1 March 1998): 842–67. https://doi.org/10.1177/0002764298041006006.

Haley, John O. "Sheathing the Sword of Justice in Japan: An Essay on Law without Sanctions." *Journal of Japanese Studies* 8, no. 2 (1982): 265–81. https://doi.org/10.2307/132340.

Hallett, Michael. "Reentry to What?: Theorizing Prisoner Reentry in the Jobless Future." *Critical Criminology* 20 (2012): 2,013–228.

Hamai, Koichi, and Thomas Ellis. "Japanese Criminal Justice: Was Reintegrative Shaming a Chimera?" *Punishment & Society* 10, no. 1 (1 January 2008): 25–46. https://doi.org/10.1177/1462474507084196.

Hamai, Koichi, and Thomas Ellis. "Crime and Criminal Justice in Modern Japan: From Re-Integrative Shaming to Popular Punitivism." *International Journal of the Sociology of Law* 34, no. 3 (1 September 2006): 157–78. https://doi.org/10.1016/j.ijsl.2006.08.002.

Hamberger, Klaus. "Kinship as Logic of Space." *Current Anthropology* 59, no. 5 (October 2018): 525–48. https://doi.org/10.1086/699736.

Handtke, Violet, Wiebke Bretschneider, Bernice Elger, and Tenzin Wangmo. "The Collision of Care and Punishment: Ageing Prisoners' View on Compassionate Release." *Punishment & Society* 19, no. 1 (January 2017): 5–22. https://doi.org/10.1177/1462474516644679.

Hankins, Joseph. "Yamanote's Promise: Buraku Stigma, Tokyo's Trains, and the Infrastructure of Social Belonging." *Japan Forum* 30, no. 2 (3 April 2018): 186–204. https://doi.org/10.1080/09555803.2017.1353533.

Harayama, Tetsu. "Posuto fukushi kokka ni okeru haijo to hōsetsu no kōsatsu" (For Considering Exclusion and Inclusion in Post-Welfare Nation). In *Kōreisha Hanzai No Sōgōteki Kenkyū* (Comprehensive Research on Elderly Crime), edited by Yoko Hosoi and Bunri Tatsuno, 15–32. Tokyo: Kazama Shobo, 2021.

Hartman, Saidiya. *Wayward Lives, Beautiful Experiments: Intimate Histories of Riotous Black Girls, Troublesome Women and Queer Radicals*. London: Serpent's Tail, 2019.

Hayashi, Mayumi. *The Care of Older People: England and Japan, A Comparative Study*. London: Routledge, 2015.

———. "The Japanese Voluntary Sector's Responses to the Increasing Unmet Demand for Home Care from an Ageing Population." *Ageing and Society* 36, no. 3 (2016): 508–33. https://doi.org/10.1017/S0144686X14001238.

Hayes, Adrian J., Alistair Burns, Pauline Turnbull, and Jenny J. Shaw. "The Health and Social Needs of Older Male Prisoners." *International Journal of Geriatric Psychiatry* 27, no. 11 (2012): 1,155–62. https://doi.org/10.1002/gps.3761.

Herrity, Kate, Bethany E. Schmidt, and Jason Warr. *Sensory Penalties: Exploring the Senses in Spaces of Punishment and Social Control*. Bingley, UK: Emerald Publishing, 2021.

Hill, Amelia. "Prisons Taking Role of Care Homes and Hospices as Older Population Soars." *Guardian*, June 19, 2017. https://www.theguardian.com/society/2017/jun/20/prisons-taking-role-of-care-homes-and-hospices-as-older-population-soars.

Hiratsuka, Manabu. "Nenkin seikatsu 'konna shōhin ni okane wa . . .' medatsu manbiki, ōita" (Pension Life: "I Wouldn't Pay for Such a Product . . ." Shoplifters in Oita). *Asahi Shinbun (Digital)*, April 8, 2018.

Homei, Aya. *Science for Governing Japan's Population*. Cambridge: Cambridge University Press, 2022.

hooks, bell. "Theory as Liberatory Practice." *Yale Journal of Law and Feminism* 4 (1992 1991): 1.

Hosoi, Yoko. "Kōrei joshi jukeisha no seikatsureki to hanzai keikō" (Life History and Criminal Tendencies of Elderly Female Inmates). In *Kōreisha Hanzai No Sōgo Kenkyū* (Comprehensive Research on Elderly Crime), edited by Yoko Hosoi and Bunri Tatsuno, 239–53. Tokyo: Kazama Shobo, 2021.

Hosoi, Yoko, and Bunri Tatsuno, eds. *Kōreisha Hanzai No Sōgo Kenkyū* (Comprehensive Research on Elderly Crime). Tokyo: Kazama Shobo, 2021.

Humblet, Diete. *The Older Prisoner*. Cham, Switzerland: Palgrave Macmillan, 2021.

Ichimiya, Shunsuke. "Keimusho nyūsho 60-sai ijō no 1 warikyō `ninshishō keikō' kensa sukunaku jittai fumei ruihansha ni utagai rei" (More than 10 percent of Those Over 60 Entering Prison "Likely Have Dementia," Lack of Testing, Actual Condition Unknown, Cases Suspected to be Repeat Offenders). *Mainichi Shinbun*, July 27, 2020. https://mainichi.jp/articles/20200627/koo/oom/040/159000c.

Igarashi, Hiroshi. *Jinsei wo kaeru deai no chikara: yami kara hikari he* (The Power of Encounters to Change a Life: From the Darkness to the Light). Tokyo: Don Bosco Japan, 2016.

Ikeda, Shingou. "The Necessity of Reduced Working Hours under the Re-Familization of Elderly Care." *Japan Labor Issues* 5, no. 30 (2021): 16–33.

Ito, Kazuya. "Keimusho no 'sagyō,' jittai wa rihabiri kōrei-ka taisaku ni ` kōkin-kei shinsetsu" (Prison "Work," Reality Is a New Facility for a "Detention Sentence" to Rehabilitate the Aging Population). *Asahi Shimbun*, March 9, 2022. https://digital.asahi.com/articles/ASQ386K80Q37UTIL028.html.

Itzhak, Nofit. "Signifiers for the Divine." *American Ethnologist* 47, no. 3 (2020): 276–88. https://doi.org/10.1111/amet.12910.

Ivy, Marilyn. *Discourses of the Vanishing: Modernity, Phantasm, Japan*. Chicago: University of Chicago Press, 1995.

Japan Industrial Safety and Health Association. "Kōreisha rōdōsha no katsuyaku sokushin no tame no anzen eisei taisaku" (Safety and Health Measures to Promote Active Participation of Elderly Workers), March 2018. https://www.jisha.or.jp/research/report/201703_01.html.

Jefferson, Andrew M., and Tomas Max Martin. "Connecting and Disconnecting: Exploring Prisoners' Relations with the Outside World in Myanmar." *Cambridge Journal of Anthropology* 38, no. 1 (1 March 2020): 105–22. https://doi.org/10.3167/cja.2020.380108.

Jefferson, Andrew, Simon Turner, and Steffen Jensen. "Introduction: On Stuckness and Sites of Confinement." *Ethnos* 84, no. 1 (1 January 2019): 1–13. https://doi.org/10.1080/00141844.2018.1544917.

Jensen, Casper Bruun, Miho Ishii, and Philip Swift. "Attuning to the Webs of *En*: Ontography, Japanese Spirit Worlds, and the 'Tact' of Minakata Kumagusu." *HAU: Journal of Ethnographic Theory* 6, no. 2 (September 2016): 149–72. https://doi.org/10.14318/hau6.2.012.

Jentzsch, Hanno. "San'ya 2020: From Building to Hosting the Olympics." In *Japan through the Lens of the Tokyo Olympics*, edited by Barbara Holthus, Isaac Gagné, Wolfram Manzenreiter, and Franz Waldenberger, 54–58. London: Routledge, 2020.

Jewkes, Yvonne, and Alison Young. "Sensory Reflections on a Japanese Prison." In *Sensory Penalties: Exploring the Senses in Spaces of Punishment and Social Control*, edited by Kate Herrity, Bethany E. Schmidt, and Jason Warr, 177–93. Bingley, UK: Emerald Publishing, 2021.

Johnson, David T. "Crime and Punishment in Contemporary Japan." *Crime and Punishment* 36, no. 1 (2007): 371–423.

Johnson, Elmer H. *Criminalization and Prisoners in Japan Six Contrary Cohorts*. Carbondale: Southern Illinois University Press, 1997.

Jolliffe, Pia. *Prisons and Forced Labour in Japan: The Colonization of Hokkaido, 1881–1894*. London: Routledge, 2020.

———. "Forced Labour in Imperial Japan's First Colony: Hokkaidō." *Asia-Pacific Journal* 18, no. 20 (October 15, 2020). https://apjjf.org/2020/20/Jolliffe.html.

Kanbara, Hiroshi. "Kodoku-shi, suikei 2. 7 man-ri tsukamenu jittai 'kuni ni teigi naku'" (Estimated 27,000 Solitary Deaths Unable to Grasp Reality "No Definition in the Country"). *Asahi Shimbun*, September 18, 2018.

Katz, Stephen, and Toni Calasanti. "Critical Perspectives on Successful Aging: Does It 'Appeal More Than It Illuminates'?" *Gerontologist* 55, no. 1 (Feb. 2015): 26–33.

Kawai Katsuyoshi. *Rojin ni tsumetai kuni nihon*. Tokyo: Kobunsha, 2015.

Kawakami Mayu. "Waga kuni ni okeru koreisha hanzai no tokuisei ni tsuite." *Daigakuin Kenkyu Nenpo* 47 (2018): 131–49.

Khan, Aisha. "The Carceral State: An American Story." *Annual Review of Anthropology* 51, no. 1 (2022): 49–66. https://doi.org/10.1146/annurev-anthro-041420-013930.

Kim, Jieun. "Necrosociality: Isolated Death and Unclaimed Cremains in Japan." *Journal of the Royal Anthropological Institute* 22, no. 4 (September 2016): 843–63. https://doi.org/10.1111/1467-9655.12491.

———. "Social Exclusion and Care in Underclass Japan: Attunement as Techniques of Belonging." *Culture, Medicine, and Psychiatry* 45, no. 1 (1 March 2021): 42–63. https://doi.org/10.1007/s11013-020-09678-2.

Kimura, Takao, and Sachie Sawaki. "Kōrei/shōgai hanzaisha no shakai fukki shien shisaku genjō to kadai" (The Current State and Issues of Social Rehabilitation Support Measures for Elderly/Disabled Offenders). *Nihon Fukushi Daigaku Shakai Fukushi Ronshū* 128 (March 2013): 83–113.

Kinomoto, Yoko, and Naomi Ishishita. "Jukeisha dōshi no rōrō kaigo 'kona yarō to omou koto mo aru' (rupo onomichi keimusho) – Middle" (Elderly Care between Older Prisoners "Sometimes I Think 'What a Bastard" [Report from Onomichi Prison]). *Chugoku Shimbun*, 17 August 2022. https://www.chugoku-np.co.jp/articles/-/200493.

Kitanaka, Junko. "In the Mind of Dementia: Neurobiological Empathy, Incommensurability, and the Dementia Tojisha Movement in Japan." *Medical Anthropology Quarterly* 34, no. 1 (2020): 119–35. https://doi.org/10.1111/maq.12544.

Knight, Kelly Ray. *addicted.pregnant.poor*. Durham, NC: Duke University Press, 2015.

Kodate, Naonori, and Virpi Timonen. "Bringing the Family in through the Back Door: The Stealthy Expansion of Family Care in Asian and European Long-Term Care Policy." *Journal of Cross-Cultural Gerontology* 32, no. 3 (2017): 291–301. https://doi.org/10.1007/s10823-017-9325-5.

Komiya, Noboru. "A Cultural Study of the Low Crime Rate in Japan." *British Journal of Criminology* 39, no. 3 (1 June 1999): 369–90. https://doi.org/10.1093/bjc/39.3.369.

Kröger, Teppo. *Care Poverty: When Older People's Needs Remain Unmet*. Cham, Switzerland: Palgrave Macmillan, 2022.

Kuwayama, Takami. "The Discourse of Ie (Family) in Japan's Cultural Identity and Nationalism: A Critique." *Japanese Review of Cultural Anthropology* 2 (2001): 3–37. https://doi.org/10.14890/jrca.2.0_3.

Lamb, Sarah, ed. *Successful Aging?: Global Perspectives on a Contemporary Obsession*. New Brunswick, NJ: Rutgers University Press, 2017.

Lariviere, Matthew, Fiona Poland, John Woolham, Stanton Newman, and Chris Fox. "Placing Assistive Technology and Telecare in Everyday Practices of People with Dementia and Their Caregivers: Findings from an Embedded Ethnography of a National Dementia Trial." *BMC Geriatrics* 21, no. 1 (15 February 2021): 121. https://doi.org/10.1186/s12877-020-01896-y.

Lawson, Carol. "Subverting the Prison: The Incarceration of Stigmatised Older Japanese." *International Journal of Law in Context* 17, no. 3 (September 2021): 336–55. https://doi.org/10.1017/S1744552321000422.

Lebra, Takie Sugiyama. *Japanese Patterns of Behavior*. Honolulu: University of Hawai'i Press, 1976.

Lee, Caroline, Samantha Treacy, Anna Haggith, Nuwan Darshana Wickramasinghe, Frances Cater, Isla Kuhn, and Tine Van Bortel. "A Systematic Integrative Review of Programmes Addressing the Social Care Needs of Older Prisoners." *Health & Justice* 7, no. 1 (December 2019): 9. https://doi.org/10.1186/s40352-019-0090-0.

Leeson, George W. "The Growth, Ageing and Urbanisation of Our World." *Journal of Population Ageing* 11, no. 2 (1 June 2018): 107–15. https://doi.org/10.1007/s12062-018-9225-7.

Leonardsen, Dag. *Crime in Japan: Paradise Lost?* Basingstoke, Hampshire: Palgrave Macmillan, 2010.

Levine, Jeffrey M. "Growing Old in Prison." *Journal of the American Geriatrics Society* 69, no. 12 (2021): 3,689. https://doi.org/10.1111/jgs.17456.

Liebling, Alison, and Shadd Maruna. *The Effects of Imprisonment*. London: Routledge, 2013.

Long, Susan Orpett. "Someone's Old, Something's New, Someone's Borrowed, Someone's Blue: Changing Eldercare at the Turn of the Twentieth Century." In *Imagined Families, Lived Families: Culture and Kinship in Contemporary Japan*, edited by John W. Traphagan and Akiko Hashimoto, 137–57. Albany: SUNY Press, 2008.

Lopez, Steven H. "Culture Change and Shit Work: Empowering and Overpowering the Frail Elderly in Long-Term Care." *American Behavioral Scientist* 58 no.3 (2013): 435–52. https://doi.org/10.1177/0002764213503340.

Luo, Linghan. "Welfare Support for Elder People: From the Vantage Point of the Cooperation between Jucial [sic] and Social Welfare." Masters thesis, Hitotsubashi University, 2016.

Lutz, Peter A. "Multivalent Moves in Senior Home Care: From Surveillance to Care-Valence." *Anthropology & Aging* 36 no. 2 (2015): 145–63. https://doi.org/10.5195/aa.2015.105.

Lyons, Adam J. *Karma and Punishment: Prison Chaplaincy in Japan.* Cambridge, MA: Harvard University Asia Center, 2021.

Mann, Natalie. *Doing Harder Time?: The Experiences of an Ageing Male Prison Population in England and Wales.* Farnham, Surrey: Ashgate Publishing, 2013.

Mann, Natalie. "Ageing Child Sex Offenders in Prison: Denial, Manipulation and Community." *Howard Journal of Criminal Justice* 51, no. 4 (2012): 345–58. https://doi.org/10.1111/j.1468-2311.2012.00705.x.

Marr, Matthew D. "Gentrification, Machizukuri, and Ontological Insecurity: Bottom-Up Redevelopment and the Cries of Residents in Kamagasaki, Osaka." In *Gentrification around the World*, vol. 1: *Gentrifiers and the Displaced*, edited by Jerome Krase and Judith N. DeSena, 291–313. Palgrave Studies in Urban Anthropology. Cham: Springer International Publishing, 2020. https://doi.org/10.1007/978-3-030-41337-8_13.

———. "The Ohaka (Grave) Project: Post-Secular Social Service Delivery and Resistant Necropolitics in San'ya, Tokyo." *Ethnography* 22, no. 1 (1 March 2021): 88–110. https://doi.org/10.1177/1466138119845393.

Marti, Irene, Ueli Hostettler, and Marina Richter. "End of Life in High-Security Prisons in Switzerland: Overlapping and Blurring of 'Care' and 'Custody' as Institutional Logics." *Journal of Correctional Health Care* 23, no. 1 (January 2017): 32–42. https://doi.org/10.1177/1078345816684782.

Marti, Irene. *Doing Indefinite Time: An Ethnography of Long-Term Imprisonment in Switzerland.* Cham: Springer International Publishing, 2023. https://doi.org/10.1007/978-3-031-12590-4.

Martin, Liam. "Reentry within the Carceral: Foucault, Race and Prisoner Reentry." *Critical Criminology* 21, no. 4 (1 November 2013): 493–508. https://doi.org/10.1007/s10612-013-9196-1.

Martin, Tomas Max, Andrew M. Jefferson, and Mahuya Bandyopadhyay. "Sensing Prison Climates." *Focaal* 2014, no. 68 (1 March 2014): 3–17. https://doi.org/10.3167/fcl.2014.680101.

Martinson, Marty, and Clara Berridge. "Successful Aging and Its Discontents: A Systematic Review of the Social Gerontology Literature." *Gerontologist* 55, no. 1 (Feb. 2015): 58–69. https://doi.org/10.1093/geront/gnu037.

Maschi, Tina, and Keith Morgen. *Aging behind Prison Walls: Studies in Trauma and Resilience*. New York: Columbia University Press, 2020.

Maschi, Tina, Deborah Viola, and Fei Sun. "The High Cost of the International Aging Prisoner Crisis: Well-Being as the Common Denominator for Action." *Gerontologist* 53, no. 4 (August 1, 2013): 543–54. https://doi.org/10.1093/geront/gns125.

Matsuyama, Kanako. "Rōjin hōmuka suru keimusho, 'deru no ga kowakatta' kōreika de iryōhizō mo" (Prisons Turning into Elderly Care Homes, "I Was Scared to Leave" Also the Rising Cost of Seniors). *Bloomberg*, 16 April 2015.

Miki, Ryoko, and Taro Asanuma. "Keiji jiken ni kan'yo shita shōgai-sha e no 'iriguchi shien' no genjō to kadai" (The Approach and Issue on Early Stage Support for Disabled Suspects and Defendants Provided by Social Workers Cooperating with Defense Attorneys in Tokyo Model). *Teikyō Kagaku Daigaku Kiyō* 14 (2018): 1–8.

Ministry of Health, Labour and Welfare (Japan). *Chiiki seikatsu teichaku shien sentā no shien jōkyō (ryō wa 2-nendo-chū ni shien shita mono)* (Support Status of Community Life Settlement Support Center [Those Who Supported in 2020]). Tokyo: Ministry of Health, Labour and Welfare, 2020.

———. *Dai 8-ki kaigo hoken jigyō keikak ni motodzuku kaigo shokuin no hitsuyō-sū ni tsuite* (Report on the Required Number of Nursing Care Staff Based on the 8th Long-Term Care Insurance Business Plan). Tokyo: Ministry of Health, Labour and Welfare, September 7, 2021. https://www.mhlw.go.jp/stf/houdou/0000207323_00005.html.

———. *Graphical Review of Japanese Household from Comprehensive Survey of Living Conditions 2016*. Tokyo: Ministry of Health, Labour and Welfare, 2018.

———. *Tokubetsu yōgorōjin hōmu no nyūsho mōshikomi-sha no jōkyō (reiwa 4-nendo)'*. (Status of Applicants to Enter Special Nursing Homes). Tokyo: Ministry of Health, Labour and Welfare, 2022. https://www.mhlw.go.jp/stf/houdou/0000157884_00004.html.

Ministry of Internal Affairs and Communications (Japan). "Kōreisha no jinkō" (Population of Older People), September 15, 2021. https://www.stat.go.jp/data/topics/topi1291.html.

Ministry of Justice (Japan). *Heisei 29-nenban hanzai hakusho* (2017 Crime White Paper). Tokyo: Ministry of Justice, 2018. https://hakusyo1.moj.go.jp/jp/64/nfm/n64_2_4_8_2_2.html.

———. *Heisei 30-nenban hanzai hakusho* (2018 Edition Crime White Paper). Tokyo: Ministry of Justice, 2018. https://hakusyo1.moj.go.jp/jp/65/nfm/gmokuji.html.

———. *Heisei 30-nenban hanzai hakusho no gaiyō* (Outline of the 2018 Edition Crime White Paper). Tokyo: Ministry of Justice, 2018. https://www.moj.go.jp/content/001309862.pdf.

———. "'Dai 43-kai fuchū keimusho bunkamatsuri'~-toshi ni ichido no aki no kansha-sai ~ no kaisai ni tsuite" (On Holding The 43rd Fuchu Prison School Festival) – Autumn Thanksgiving Once a Year). Tokyo: Ministry of Justice, 2018. https://www.moj.go.jp/kyousei1/kyousei05_00038.html.

———. *Ninshishō keikō no aru jukei-sha no gaisū chōsa (hōkoku)* (Rough Survey of Inmates with Dementia Tendencies [Report]). Tokyo: Ministry of Justice, 2019.

———. *Reiwa 3-nenban hanzai hakusho* (2021 Annual Crime White Paper). Tokyo: Ministry of Justice, 2021.

———. "Keimu Sagyo" (Prison Work). Tokyo: Ministry of Justice, 2021. https://www.moj.go.jp/kyousei1/kyousei_kyouse10.html.

———. "Kyōsei Tōkei Chōsa" (Corrections Statistics Survey). Tokyo: Ministry of Justice, 2023. https://www.e-stat.go.jp/stat-search/files?stat_infid=000040081386.

Mire, Amina. "'Skin Trade': Genealogy of Anti-Ageing 'Whiteness Therapy' in Colonial Medicine." *Medicine Studies* 4, no. 1–4 (2014): 119–29. https://doi.org/10.1007/s12376-014-0089-8.

———. *Wellness in Whiteness: Biomedicalization and the Promotion of Whiteness and Youth among Women*. London: Routledge, 2019.

Mittermaier, Amira. "Bread, Freedom, Social Justice: The Egyptian Uprising and a Sufi Khidma." *Cultural Anthropology* 29, no. 1 (February 3, 2014): 54–79. https://doi.org/10.14506/ca29.1.05.

———. *Giving to God: Islamic Charity in Revolutionary Times*. Berkeley: University of California Press, 2019.

Miyazawa, Hitoshi. "Welfare Regime in Japan and Recent Social Security Reform." In *Community-Based Integrated Care and the Inclusive Society: Recent Social Security Reform in Japan*, edited by Hitoshi Miyazawa and Teruo Hatakeyama, 3–17. International Perspectives in Geography. Singapore: Springer, 2021. https://doi.org/10.1007/978-981-33-4473-0_1.

Miyazawa, Setsuo. "The Politics of Increasing Punitiveness and the Rising Populism in Japanese Criminal Justice Policy." *Punishment & Society* 10, no. 1 (January 2008): 47–77. https://doi.org/10.1177/1462474507084197.

Moore, Hollis. "Extralegal Agency and the Search for Safety in Northeast Brazil: Moving beyond Carceral Logics." *Cambridge Journal of Anthropology* 38, no. 1 (March 1, 2020): 33–51. https://doi.org/10.3167/cja.2020.380104.

Moore, Katrina Louise. "A Spirit of Adventure in Retirement: Japanese Baby Boomers and the Ethos of Interdependence." *Anthropology & Aging* 38, no. 2 (November 28, 2017): 10–28. https://doi.org/10.5195/AA.2017.159.

Moran, Dominique. *Carceral Geography: Spaces and Practices of Incarceration.* Abingdon, Oxon: Routledge, 2016.

———. "'Doing Time' in Carceral Space: Timespace and Carceral Geography." *Geografiska Annaler Series B: Human Geography* 94, no. 4 (December 2012): 305–16. https://doi.org/10.1111/geob.12000.

———. "Prisoner Reintegration and the Stigma of Prison Time Inscribed on the Body." *Punishment & Society* 14, no. 5 (3 December 2012). https://doi.org/10.1177/1462474512464008.

Nakano, Lynne. *Community Volunteers in Japan: Everyday Stories of Social Change.* London: Routledge Curzon, 2005.

Nakao, Nobumi. "Drastic Increasing of Elders' Crime." *Senshu University Graduate Bulletin of Human Sciences, Sociology* 4, no. 2 (2014): 101–17.

National Police Agency (Japan). *Reiwa 2 nen hanzai hakusho dai 5 hen saihan saihikō* (Crime White Paper, Part 5: Recidivism 2020). Tokyo: NPA, 2020.

———. *Hanzai tokei shiryo reiwa 4-nen 1~8 gatsu bun* (Crime Statistics Information 2022 January–August). Tokyo: NPA, 2022.

Neilson, Brett. "Anti-Ageing Cultures, Biopolitics and Globalisation." *Cultural Studies Review* 12, no. 2 (2006): 149–64.

———. "Globalization and the Biopolitics of Aging." *CR: The New Centennial Review* 3, no. 2 (2003): 161–86. https://doi.org/10.1353/ncr.2003.0025.

Nishida Hiroshi. 2018. "Kōrei jukei-sha de kaigo shisetsu-ka suru keimusho. Sono mirai wa zeikin no tōnyū ka, soretomo shūyō no kaihi ka" (Prisons Are Turning into Aged-Care Homes for Elderly Inmates. Invest Future Taxes or Avoid Detention?). Minnanokaigo, July 5, 2018. https://job.minnanokaigo.com/news/kaigogaku/no509.

Ochiai, Emiko. "Unsustainable Societies: The Failure of Familialism in East Asia's Compressed Modernity." *Historical Social Research* 36, no. 2 (2011): 219–45.

Ozawa-de Silva, Chikako. *The Anatomy of Loneliness: Suicide, Social Connection, and the Search for Relational Meaning in Contemporary Japan.* Berkeley: University of California Press, 2021.

———. "Demystifying Japanese Therapy: An Analysis of Naikan and the Ajase Complex through Buddhist Thought." *Ethos* 35, no. 4 (2007): 411–46.

———. *Psychotherapy and Religion in Japan: The Japanese Introspection Practice of Naikan.* New York: Routledge, 2006.

Parrott, Janet M., Fiona R. Houben, Renske C. Visser, and Douglas L. MacInnes. "Mental Health and Offending in Older People: Future Directions for Research." *Criminal Behaviour and Mental Health* 29, no. 4 (2019): 218–26. https://doi.org/10.1002/cbm.2121.

Plan 75. Chie Hayakawa, dir. Happinet (distributor, Japan), 2022.

Port, Cynthia. "No Future?: Aging, Temporality, History, and Reverse Chronologies." *Occasion*, no. 4 (June 14, 2012). https://shc.stanford.edu/arcade/publications/occasion/aging-old-age-memory-aesthetics.

Pro, George, and Miesha Marzell. "Medical Parole and Aging Prisoners: A Qualitative Study." *Journal of Correctional Health Care* 23, no. 2 (April 2017): 162–72. https://doi.org/10.1177/1078345817699608.

Prost, Stephanie Grace, Adrian J. Archuleta, and Seana Golder. "Older Adults Incarcerated in State Prison: Health and Quality of Life Disparities between Age Cohorts." *Aging and Mental Health* 25, no. 2 (February 2021): 260–68. https://doi.org/10.1080/13607863.2019.1693976.

Rhodes, Lorna A. *Total Confinement: Madness and Reason in the Maximum Security Prison.* Berkeley: University of California Press, 2004.

Ridley, Louise. "No Place for Old Men?: Meeting the Needs of an Ageing Male Prison Population in England and Wales." *Social Policy and Society* 21, no. 4 (October 2022): 597–611. https://doi.org/10.1017/S1474746421000178.

Roberts, Aki. "Explaining Differences in Homicide Clearance Rates between Japan and the United States." *Homicide Studies* 12, no. 1 (1 February 2008): 136–45. https://doi.org/10.1177/1088767907310863.

Robinson, Louise, Sue Tucker, Claire Hargreaves, Amy Roberts, Jennifer Shaw, and David Challis. "Providing Social Care Following Release from Prison: Emerging Practice Arrangements Further to the Introduction of the 2014 Care Act." *British Journal of Social Work* 52, no. 2 (March 2022): 982–1,002. https://doi.org/10.1093/bjsw/bcab082.

Rodríguez, Dylan. "Abolition as Praxis of Human Being: A Foreword." *Harvard Law Review* 132, no. 6 (2019): 1,575–612.

Routledge, Paul. "The Third Space as Critical Engagement." *Antipode* 28 no 4 (1996): 399–419.

Rubinstein, Robert L., and Kate de Medeiros. "'Successful Aging,' Gerontological Theory and Neoliberalism: A Qualitative Critique." *Gerontologist* 55, no. 1 (Feb. 2015): 34–42. https://doi.org/10.1093/geront/gnu080.

Russell, Emma K., Bree Carlton, and Danielle Tyson. "Carceral Churn: A Sensorial Ethnography of the Bail and Remand Court." *Punishment & Society* 24, no. 2 (2022): 151–69. https://doi.org/10.1177/1462474520967566.

Sahlins, Marshall. *What Kinship Is—and Is Not.* Chicago, IL: University of Chicago Press, 2013.

Sakemoto, Yukiko. "Fukuekichū ni 'hogokansatsujo no sei da' ikiba wo ushinai kasaneta tsumi wa fusegeta no ka" (While Serving Time He Said "It's the Probation Office's Fault": With Nowhere to Go, Could the Additional Crime Have Been Prevented?). *Asahi Shimbun*, 21 July 2022. https://digital.asahi.com/articles/ASQ7N6RZXQ7NUGTB002.html.

Saito, Michinori. *Rupo rojin jukeisha* (Report Elderly Prisoners). Tokyo: Chuokoron Shinsha, 2020.

Schweda, Mark, and Larissa Pfaller. "Responsibilization of Aging?: An Ethical Analysis of the Moral Economy of Prevention." In *Preventing Dementia: Critical Perspectives on a New Paradigm of Preparing for Old Age*, edited by Annette Leibing and Silke Schicktanz, 192–213. Oxford: Berghahn Books, 2020.

Scott, Jason. "Ethnography at Its Edges: In Defense of How-to Abolitionism: An Anthropological Engagement with Mariame Kaba." *American Ethnologist* 49, no. 3 (2022): 442–46. https://doi.org/10.1111/amet.13094.

Sen, Amartya. "Capability and Well-Being." In *The Quality of Life*, edited by Martha Nussbaum and Amartya Sen, Online, 30–53. Oxford: Oxford Academic, 1993. https://doi.org/10.1093/0198287976.003.0003.

Shange, Savannah. "Abolition in the Clutch: Shifting through the Gears with Anthropology." *Feminist Anthropology* 3, no. 2 (November 2022): 187–97. https://doi.org/10.1002/fea2.12101.

Sharpe, Christina. *Ordinary Notes*. London: Daunt Books, 2023.

Shaw, Ian G. R., and Marv Waterstone. *Wageless Life: A Manifesto for a Future beyond Capitalism*. Minneapolis: University of Minnesota Press, 2020.

Shirahase, Tatsuya. *Hinkon to chiiki: Airinchiku kara miru kōrei-ka to koritsu shi* (Poverty and Community: Aging and Solitary Death as Seen from the Airin District). Tokyo: Chuokoron Shinsha, 2017.

Snoyman, Philip, Elena Cama, Eileen Baldry, Carla Treloar, and Takashi Furukawa. "Ōsutoraria nyūsausuu~ēruzu shū no keiji shisetsu ni okeru korei no keiji shisetsu ni okeru kōrei hanzai-sha" (Elderly Offenders in Penal Institutions in New South Wales, Australia). In *Kōreisha hanzai no sōgōteki kenkyū* (Comprehensive Research on Elderly Crime), edited by Yoko Hosoi and Bunri Tatsuno, 386–99. Tokyo: Kazama Shobo, 2021.

Sojoyner, Damien M. "Another Life Is Possible: Black Fugitivity and Enclosed Places." *Cultural Anthropology* 32, no. 4 (2017): 514–36. https://doi.org/10.14506/ca32.4.04.

Stevens, Carolyn S. *Disability in Japan*. London: Routledge, 2013.

Story, Brett. *Prison Land: Mapping Carceral Power across Neoliberal America*. Minneapolis: University of Minnesota Press, 2019.

Sufrin, Carolyn. *Jailcare: Finding the Safety Net for Women behind Bars*. Berkeley: University of California Press, 2017.

Sugie, Naomi F. "When the Elderly Turn to Petty Crime: Increasing Elderly Arrest Rates in an Aging Population." *International Criminal Justice Review* 27, no. 1 (March 2017): 19–39. https://doi.org/10.1177/1057567716679232.

Suzuki, Daisetz Teitaro. *Shin Buddhism*. New York: Harper & Row, 1970.

Suzuki, Masahiro, and Akinori Otani. "Ageing, Institutional Thoughtlessness, and Normalisation in Japan's Prisons." *International Journal of Comparative and Applied Criminal Justice*, published online March 13, 2023. https://doi.org/10.1080/01924036.2023.2188236.

———. "Myths of Restorative Features in the Japanese Justice System and Society: The Role of Apology, Compensation and Confession, and Application of Reintegrative Shaming." *Restorative Justice* 5, no. 2 (May 4, 2017): 158–77. https://doi.org/10.1080/20504721.2017.1339955.

Tahhan, Diana Adis. *The Japanese Family: Touch, Intimacy and Feeling*. London: Routledge, 2014.

Takamori, Asao. *Ashita no Jo (Tomorrow's Joe)*. Tokyo: Kodansha, 1983.

Tamiya, Nanako, Haruko Noguchi, Akihiro Nishi, Michael R. Reich, Naoki Ikegami, Hideki Hashimoto, Kenji Shibuya, Ichiro Kawachi, and John Creighton Campbell. "Population Ageing and Well-Being: Lessons from Japan's Long-Term Care Insurance Policy." *Lancet* 378, no. 9797 (September 2011): 1,183–92. https://doi.org/10.1016/S0140-6736(11)61176-8.

Thompson, David C. "Evasion: Prison Escapes and the Predicament of Incarceration in Rio de Janeiro." *Cultural Anthropology* 38, no. 1 (2023): 36–59. https://doi.org/10.14506/ca38.1.03.

Traphagan, John W. "On Being a Good Rōjin: Senility, Power, and Self-Actualization in Japan." In *Thinking about Dementia: Culture, Loss, and the Anthropology of Senility*, edited by Annette Leibing and Lawrence Cohen, 269–87. New Brunswick, NJ: Rutgers University Press, 2006.

Tsudome Masatoshi 2022. "Kaigo rishoku zero: Tokki jidō zero: yōho mushōka" (Zero Care Redundancies: Zero Childcare Waiting Lists: Free Preschool). Asahi News Digital, September 5, 2022. https://digital.asahi.com/articles/DA3S15406677.html.

Turner, Jennifer. *The Prison Boundary*. London: Palgrave Macmillan UK, 2016.

Turner, Jennifer, Dominique Moran, and Yvonne Jewkes. "'It's in the Air Here': Atmosphere(s) of Incarceration." *Incarceration* 3, no. 3 (November 1, 2022). https://doi.org/10.1177/26326663221110788.

Ulmer, Jeffrey Todd, and Darrell J. Steffensmeier. "The Age and Crime Relationship: Social Variation, Social Explanations." In *The Nurture versus Biosocial Debate in Criminology: On the Origins of Criminal Behavior and Criminality*, edited by Kevin M. Beaver, J. C. Barnes, and Brian B. Boutwell, 377–96. Thousand Oaks, CA: Sage Publications, 2014.

Umegaki-Costantini, H., and G. Roberts. "Corporate Policy, Male Breadwinners, and Their Family Care in Aging Japan." *Innovation in Aging* 5, Suppl. 1 (2021): 492.

Uotani, Mizuki. "Ruihan kōrei-sha wa naze fue tsudzukete iru no ka: Saihan bōshi ni wa nani ga hitsuyōna no ka" (Why the Number of Elderly Repeat Offenders Continues to Increase: What Is Needed to Prevent Repeat Offenses?). Waseda University Faculty of Culture, Media and Society, Department of Contemporary Human Studies, Okabe Seminar Paper Collection, 2013.

Wacquant, Loïc. "Crafting the Neoliberal State: Workfare, Prisonfare, and Social Insecurity." *Sociological Forum* 25, no. 2 (2010): 197–220. https://doi.org/10.1111/j.1573-7861.2010.01173.x.

———. "Deadly Symbiosis: When Ghetto and Prison Meet and Mesh." *Punishment & Society* 3, no. 1 (January 2001): 95–133. https://doi.org/10.1177/14624740122228276.

———. "The Great Penal Leap Backward: Incarceration in America from Nixon to Clinton." In *The New Punitiveness: Trends, Theories, Perspectives*, edited by John Pratt, David Brown, Mark Brown, Simon Hallsworth, and Wayne Morrison. Cullompton, Devon: Willan, 2005.

———. "The Penalisation of Poverty and the Rise of Neo-Liberalism Criminal Justice and Social Policy." *European Journal on Criminal Policy and Research* 9, no. 4 (2001): 401–12.

———. "The Place of the Prison in the New Government of Poverty." Center on Institutions and Governance Working Paper, no. 34 (2006).

———. "Prisoner Reentry as Myth and Ceremony." *Dialectical Anthropology* 34, no. 4 (December 1, 2010): 605–20. https://doi.org/10.1007/s10624-010-9215-5.

———. *Punishing the Poor: The Neoliberal Government of Social Insecurity*. Durham, NC: Duke University Press, 2009.

Walby, Kevin, and Justin Piché. "The Polysemy of Punishment Memorialization: Dark Tourism and Ontario's Penal History Museums." *Punishment & Society* 13, no. 4 (October 1, 2011): 451–72. https://doi.org/10.1177/1462474511414784.

Waldram, James B. *Hound Pound Narrative: Sexual Offender Habilitation and the Anthropology of Therapeutic Intervention*. Berkeley: University of California Press, 2012.

Washington, Keahnan. "Love-Politics and the Carceral Encounter." *Anthropology News* 60, no. 1 (2019): e65–70. https://doi.org/10.1111/AN.1074.

Watson, Andrew. "Probation in Japan: Strengths and Challenges and Likely New Tasks." *European Journal of Probation* 10, no. 2 (August 2018): 160–77. https://doi.org/10.1177/2066220318794370.

Weegels, Julienne, Andrew M. Jefferson, and Tomas Max Martin. "Introduction: Confinement beyond Site: Connecting Urban and Prison Ethnographies." *Cambridge Journal of Anthropology* 38, no. 1 (March 1, 2020): 1–14. https://doi.org/10.3167/cja.2020.380102.

Weschler, Joanna. *Prison Conditions in Japan*. New York: Human Rights Watch, 1995.

Woodward, Kathleen M. *Aging and Its Discontents: Freud and Other Fictions*. Bloomington: Indiana University Press, 1991.

World Health Organization (WHO). "Ageing and Health: Key Facts," WHO Newsroom, January 27, 2023. https://www.who.int/news-room/fact-sheets/detail/ageing-and-health.

———. "Healthy Life Expectancy (HALE) at Age 60 (Years)." WHO, last modified April 29, 2024. https://www.who.int/data/gho/data/indicators/indicator-details/GHO/gho-ghe-hale-healthy-life-expectancy-at-age-60

Wright, James. *Robots Won't Save Japan: An Ethnography of Eldercare Automation*. Ithaca, NY: Cornell University Press, 2023.

Yamaguchi, Mari. "Japanese Prisons Face Swelling Elderly Population." *Washington Times*, January 6, 2011.

Yamada, Yasuhiro. "Keimusho, marude kaigo shisetsu ni." *NHK Seiji Magajin*, August 21, 2019. https://www.nhk.or.jp/politics/articles/feature/21325.html.

Yamamoto, Joji. *Gokusōki* (Prison Chronicle). Tokyo: Popurasha, 2003.

———. *Keimusho shika ibasho ga nai hito-tachi: Gakkōde wa oshiete kurenai, shōgai to hanzai no hanashi* (People Who Have No Place but Prison: The Stories about Disability and Crime That Schools Don't Teach). Tokyo: Otsuki Shoten, 2018.

———. *Ruihan shogaisha* (Repeat Offender with a Disability). Tokyo: Shincho Bunko, 2009.

Young, Alison. "Architecture as Affective Law Enforcement: Theorising the Japanese Koban." *Crime, Media, Culture* 18, no. 2 (1 June 2022): 183–202. https://doi.org/10.1177/1741659021993527.

———. "Japanese Atmospheres of Criminal Justice." *British Journal of Criminology* 59, no. 4 (6 June 2019): 765–79. https://doi.org/10.1093/bjc/azy073.

Zegarra Chiappori, Magdalena. "Remaining, Vital Acts, and Possibility: The Exercise of 'Sustaining Oneself' in a Residential Care Center for the Elderly in Lima, Peru." *Anthropology and Humanism* 47, no. 2 (2022): 297–311. https://doi.org/10.1111/anhu.12385.

INDEX

abolition, 33, 52, 54, 118–21
ageism, 119, 144
   anti-ageism, 118, 120–21
   in Japan, 9
aging society, 5–6, 117, 128n18
   low fertility, 37
   and prison population, 12, 22, 29, 120
   uncertainties around, 9
Ajase Complex, 142–43n12
alcohol, 68, 76
   addiction, 92, 96
Alcoholics Anonymous, 14
alienation, 9, 96, 117
Allison, Anne, 8
alms-houses, 38
anti-aging, 5–6, 8–9, 18, 117. *See also* ageism
atmosphere, 41, 90, 103
   of care, 106
   neighborhood festival, 27, 33, 39
   prison, 28, 30–31, 114

Beheading Bodhisattva Jizo, 67
benevolent paternalism, 40
Bentham, Jeremy, 28
boke (being out of it), 112

Buddhism, 61, 107–8
   Pure Land, 69, 107, 134n34

carceral, 9, 121
   borders, 15–16, 24, 27, 36
   and care, 5, 59, 85, 113
   condition, 4–5, 53, 55
   continuum, 16–17, 38, 47, 114
   ethnography, 22, 29, 31
   logics, 5, 8, 16, 55, 101, 135n42
   temporality, 18, 66, 117, 143n15
carceral churn, 9, 15, 17, 80, 110, 128n
carceral circuits, 5, 18, 24, 97–98, 117, 121
   as enclosure, 16, 18–19, 36, 66, 70, 129n20
   as return, 18–19, 79
   welfare as, 62, 97
carceral subjects, 18, 31, 36
   fragmented, 86
   older, 80, 99
   un-settleable, 117
care
   social, 9, 16, 46, 129
   unpaid family, 6–7, 99

care homes, 19, 21, 88–89, 117, 120, 137n50
care poverty, 8
Center for Prisoner Rights (*Kangoku Jinken Sentā*), 78
charity organizations, 15, 36, 42, 63
child socialization, 143
Community Resettlement Support Centers (*chiiki teichaku shien sentā*), 23, 84–87, 91–92, 96, 100–101, 109
connections, 67, 109, 117, 120, 138n9
  to family, 92, 105
  global, 45–46
  ineffable (*en*), 1, 5, 8, 25, 105
  kin-like, 105, 107, 114
  See also disconnection; kinship
Coyle, Andrew, 29–30
Crawley, Elaine, 9
crime
  Japan, 9
  minor, 2, 8, 17, 20, 107, 118
  public concerns, 9, 39–40
  rates, 4, 12, 35–36, 118, 135n41
criminal justice system, 22, 24, 59
  and disability, 61, 78, 120
  restorative approaches, 52
  and social welfare, 80
cruel optimism, 121

Davis, Angela, 33, 118
death, 6, 105, 119
  ceremonies, 105
  lonely, 8, 130
deaths, work-related, 7
dementia, 29, 31, 38, 40, 111, 113, 129n21
  Alzheimer's type, 20
deservingness, 57, 59, 66

disconnection (*muen*) 8, 68–69, 80, 89, 96, 104–5, 116–17
  spirit (*muen-botoke*), 104–5, 109, 121
  See also connections; isolation; loneliness
doya (flophouse), 70, 90, 97–98, 120

embodiment, 3, 14, 16, 28, 76, 117
enclosure, 39, 101
  surveillance and, 28, 40
  See also carceral circuits, as enclosure
encounter (*deai*), 45, 47–52, 59–60, 109, 117, 120, 133n23, 138n9
Entry Support (*iriguchi shien*), 85, 120

Fassin, Didier, 38
Foote, Daniel H., 40
forgiveness, 46, 48, 52, 61, 107
Foucault, Michel, 17, 27–28, 36, 40
  Discipline and Punish, 27–28
Fry, Elizabeth, 138
Fuchu Prison Culture Festival, 27–28, 34–36
fugitivity, 129n20
Fukuda Kyuemon, 77–79, 105, 141n4

gambling, 14, 20, 65, 68, 90, 92
Garland, David, 38, 79
ghost, disconnected. *See* disconnection (*muen*), spirit (*muen-botoke*)
Gill, Tom, 66, 129n18
Gilmore, Ruth Wilson, 33
Graeber, David, 2, 9, 54, 62, 117
guarantor (*hoshōnin*), 2, 19–20, 64, 70, 77–78, 84, 92

habits, 45, 96. *See also* embodiment
heart
  kokoro, 3, 47, 61, 100

warm, 84, 86, 88, 101
home, 44, 61, 100, 109
   as dis-settlement, 68, 102
   long-term care, 21, 88–89, 120
   prison as, 16, 43–44, 91
home care, 7, 21, 99
homelessness, 19, 44, 67, 85, 91, 100
hospital, 80, 93, 110–11, 116
   as carceral institution, 17, 38
   difficulties for ex-offenders, 92
   first modern Japanese, 37
household, 98
   care responsibility of, 37
   elder-only, 7, 99
   inheritance, 68
   lineage, 105
   modern destabilization, 6
housing, 2, 21, 98–99
   and community, 59
   discrimination, 59, 77, 86
   issues for older people, 20
   multigenerational, 7
   support for, 23, 44, 46, 68, 84–86

ibasho, 5, 108, 116, 119, 121, 143n15
   Mother House as, 50, 60–61, 108–9, 116
   See also home
Independence Support Center (*jiritsu shien senta*), 2
institutional thoughtlessness, 9, 54, 59, 61, 79, 117
isolation, 8, 56, 97–98, 100, 117, 121

Japan
   criminal justice system in, 35–36, 40, 79, 134n28
   cultural conceptions of personhood, 107
   gendered social inequalities, 121
   government, 6, 23, 84
   household system (*ie*), 37, 54
   population aging in, 5–6, 9

Khan, Aisha, 4
kinship, 101, 109, 115–16
   carceral, 37, 44, 97, 101
   Japanese, 5, 101
   terms, 53
kōban, 11
kodokushi, 20, 130n27. *See also* death, lonely
Kotsukappara execution grounds, 67, 140n9

Lawson, Carol, 20
life expectancy, 6
loneliness, 44, 46, 69, 96, 100, 142–43n12 *See also* alienation; disconnection; isolation
Long-Term Care Insurance (*Kaigo Hoken*), 6–7, 55, 59, 99, 124–25n13
love, 46–48, 50, 61, 69, 81, 106–7
love-politics, 101
LTCI. *See* Long-Term Care Insurance (*Kaigo Hoken*)
Lyons, Adam J., 107, 134

Ministry of Health, Labour and Welfare (MHLW; *Kōsei Rōdō Sho*), 23, 68, 75, 85, 125n15, 136n50
Ministry of Justice (*Hōmusho*), 22–23, 29, 35–36, 43, 85
Misha Bykowski, 39
MMSE (Mini-Mental State Exam), 112
Moran, Dominique, 15, 133n23
mother, 56, 60, 109
   as archetype in Japan, 91–92, 101,

mother (continued),
  105, 107–8, 142n12
  connection to deceased, 104–5
  See also kinship
Mother House (NPO), 1, 5, 41–53, 102,
  116, 130n30
  challenges supporting older people,
    59, 83, 85, 87, 109, 120
  conflict with state, 46, 76
  criticism of, 86–87
  establishment as NPO, 44, 137n2
  as family, 101, 105–6, 112, 114–15,
    143n15
  gender dynamics, 106–7
  Maria Café, 108–9, 115
  spiritual approach, 44–45, 47, 60, 67,
    138n9
  ties to Catholic Church, 43, 45, 61,
    107, 137n5
Mother Teresa, 42, 44, 46, 50, 60, 107–8

Naikan (Buddhist-based
  psychotherapy), 107
nonprofit organization. See NPOs
normal life, 19–20
NPOs (nonprofit organizations), 12, 22–
  23, 42, 78, 85, 100
  frictions between, 46
  ideologies, 76
  restrictions on establishing, 137n2
  in San'ya, 66, 68, 87, 105
  as substitute for family care, 101

obasuteyama, 40, 129n18, 136–37n50
Otani, Akinori, 9
outcaste groups (hinin), 67
Ozawa-de Silva, Chikako, 107, 143n12

Panopticon, 28, 37, 39, 131n3
parole (kari-shakuhō), 2, 15

Penal Code (Kangoku Hō 1908), 36–37,
  132n15
pension, 7, 19, 62, 65, 139n1
Plan 75 (Chie Hayakawa), 128–29n18
police, 53, 57, 77, 79, 81–82, 90, 99
  USA, 139
population aging
  in Japan, 4–6, 9
  world, 5
post-welfare society, 39, 100
poverty, 7, 59, 100
  older people's, 7–8
  relief, 36–37
poverty business (hinkon bijinesu), 65
precarity, 66
  of care workers, 137
  social, 21, 105
  of welfare dependence, 65
prison, 27, 70, 79, 96, 117–21, 135–
  36n42
  aging in, 4, 12, 14–15, 54, 118, 121
  buildings, 27, 33, 35–36, 38–39
  care in, 2, 16, 20, 31, 49–50
  conditions, 30, 34
  cooperation with third-sector, 23, 85
  easy, 11, 16, 19, 71
  in Europe, 29
  food in, 30–32
  Fuchu (Tokyo), 29, 35
  gender demographics, 106
  invisibility, 25, 40
  in Japan, 28–31, 36–38, 54, 107,
    134n28
  Kyoto, 31
  lack of rehabilitation in, 29, 45,
    47, 62
  life after, 12, 14–15, 21, 44, 82, 89
  nursing home as, 135n42
  Onomichi (Hiroshima), 29
  power in, 27–28

and precarity, 14, 63–64, 66
public image of, 27, 35
release after full sentence (*manki-shussho*), 2, 14–15, 78, 84
release from, 2, 9, 12, 47, 77, 116
religion in, 43, 49, 60–61
return to, 12–13, 15, 69, 71, 77, 94–96
social isolation leading to, 98–99, 105
Sugamo (Tokyo), 35
as tourist attraction, 34
in UK and Australia, 29
and violence, 9, 16, 36, 40
visitation, 44, 94
work in, 32–34, 76, 132n15
prisonfare, 135n41
prison industrial complex, 33
prison pen pal service, 61, 107
prison population, Japan, 35
prison-welfare nexus, 38, 62, 79, 135n41
Japan, 36, 97, 99
probation, 15, 42
mascots, 39–40, 136n43
office, 77, 85
Volunteer Probation Officer System, 127–28n9
Public Assistance for Livelihood Protection (*seikatsu hogo*), 53, 57, 62–66, 69, 74, 77, 80
assistance with, 43, 58
calculation of, 99
older adults' use of, 7–8, 37, 59, 63
public assistance officer (*hogoshi*), 65, 74
punishment, 35–37, 54
karmic, 69
linked to care, 16, 79
for prisoners in Japan, 36
public acceptance of, 27
as spectacle, 34
surveillance and, 27–28

quangos, 23

reablement, 124n13
recidivism, 22, 62, 120
cycle, 17–18, 47, 117
prevention, 50, 74–75, 85, 101
rate, 4, 12, 30
Recidivism Prevention Promotion Act, 58, 73
re-familialization, 6–7
rehabilitation, 50, 59–60, 91, 107
mascot, 136n43
moral (*kaizen kōsei*), 33, 135n34
older ex-offender, 22
work as primary method of, 33, 132n15
rehabilitation center (*kōsei hogo shisetsu*), 23, 76–77, 81, 93
relationality, 101, 109, 114
reoffending, 15, 18, 20, 53, 120
as older adult, 13, 49, 84, 109
See also recidivism
resettlement, 18, 116
anxiety around, 29
assistance, 23, 40, 85, 99
barriers to, 3
community-based, 15
resistance to, 76
role of, 92
ryōnai kōjō (prison care facility), 34

safety net, 8, 19
San'ya, 63, 69–71, 97, 105
history, 66–68
Scott, Jason, 118
security, residential, 39
seikatsu hogo. *See* Public Assistance for Livelihood Protection
shaba, 62–72, 77, 79, 95, 117, 119, 121
as bearable life, 70

shaba (continued),
   Buddhist meaning, 69–70
   hardships in, 16, 70–71, 77, 79, 95, 119
   prison slang, 69
Shange, Savannah, 119
SHAT (*Seikatsu Hogo Akubokumetsu suru Team*), 65
Shimonoseki train station arson, 77, 84, 105
shitamachi, 41–42
shoplifting (*manbiki*), 8, 20, 71, 79, 139n1
silence, 21–22, 63, 103–4, 112
   in prison, 22, 30–31, 90
sin, 37, 44, 47, 134
stigma, 8–9, 16, 19–20, 96
structural violence, 3–5, 9, 34, 46, 54, 62
Sufrin, Carolyn, 59
surveillance, 28, 37, 40, 54, 64, 66
Suzuki, Daisetz Teitaro, 69
Suzuki, Masahiro, 9

third-sector organizations, 5–6, 23, 25, 40, 46, 116, 120. See also NPOs
tōjisha, 23, 46, 50, 52, 86, 101
   as activists, 45, 120, 137n6
   meetings, 45, 109
   relationships between, 59, 102
Tokyo, 23, 26, 33, 41–43, 55–56, 62–63, 68
   earthquake, 35
   Olympics, 67

"Tomorrow's Joe" (Asao Takamori), 67
total institution, 40
transformative justice, 52, 121

unsettleable subject, 80, 117
unsettledness, 4, 8–9, 18, 22, 30, 121

Wacquant, Loïc, 135n41
waste, 18, 34, 128nn16, 17
welfare, 9, 36, 62–63, 68, 92, 100
   disability benefits, 13, 44
   Japanese history, 37
   punitivity of, 5, 16, 47, 79
   social, 5–6, 15–18, 38, 47, 71, 79–80
   state, 8, 36, 58, 99, 135n41
   town, 68
women
   life-expectancy in Japan, 6
   living alone, 99
   older incarcerated, 121
   volunteers, 107

yakuza, 17, 69, 92–95, 106
Yamamoto, Joji, 34
yoseba (day-labor areas), 63, 66, 68, 129n18
Young, Alison, 30–31

zones of abandonment, 15, 40

Milton Keynes UK
Ingram Content Group UK Ltd.
UKHW041305300924
1920UKWH00001B/2